# TERRITORIAL GOVERNANCE AND ENVIRONMENTAL PROTECTION

## VOLUME 2: WRITINGS ON URBAN AND ENVIRONMENTAL ISSUES

### RUŞEN KELEŞ

CAPPADOCIA
UNIVERSITY

2023

Cappadocia University Press: 61
Politics Book Series: 14
ISBN: 978-605-4448-52-4


© February 2023

**Territorial Governance and Environmental Protection**
Volume 2: Writings On Urban and Environmental Issues
**Ruşen Keleş**

Series Editor: Halil Burak Sakal
Book Editors: Hikmet Kuran & Berk İlke Dündar
Preparation: Sümeyra Demiralp
Cover Design: Nazile Arda Çakır
Page Design: *ademşenel.com*
Printing and Binding: Bizim Buro (Certificate No: 42488)

---

Keleş, R. (2023). *Territorial Governance and Environmental Protection Volume 2: Writings on Urban and Environmental Issues.* Eds. Hikmet Kuran and Berk İlke Dündar. Nevşehir: Cappadocia University Press.
386 p, 13,5 x 21 cm.
ISBN: 978-605-4448-52-4
Keywords: 1. Environmental politics, 2. Urbanization, 3. Governance, 4. Urban sprawl, 5.Turkey.

---

## CAPPADOCIA
### U N I V E R S I T Y

50420 Mustafapaşa, Ürgüp, Nevşehir
yayinevi@kapadokya.edu.tr
kapadokyayayinlari.kapadokya.edu.tr
0(384) 353 5009
www.kapadokya.edu.tr

# TERRITORIAL GOVERNANCE AND ENVIRONMENTAL PROTECTION

## VOLUME 2: WRITINGS ON URBAN AND ENVIRONMENTAL ISSUES

### RUŞEN KELEŞ

CAPPADOCIA
UNIVERSITY

2023

# Contents

**ECOLOGICAL CONCERNS AND
SUSTAINABLE DEVELOPMENT** ....................................................... 7

European Approaches to Sustainable Development ................ 9

Urban Planning and Sustainable Land
Management in Turkish Municipalities ......................................... 24

Globalization and Local utonomy ................................................ 32

**European Union and Turkey** .............................................................. 59

Turkey and the European Union ................................................... 61

**Urban Transformation** ......................................................................... 77

The Urban Transformation Project of Northern Ankara ......... 79

**Disaster Management** ........................................................................... 95

Disaster Policy and Management in Turkey ............................... 97

The Administrative Structure of Government in
Turkey (Central and Local) From the Perspective
of Disaster Management* .................................................................. 116

**Smart Cities**

Smart Cities in Emerging Economies:
Reflections from Turkey ..................................................................... 137

**Cooperative Law** ...................................................... 161

Laws On Cooperatives ............................................. 163

**Protection Of Cultural Values** ............................... 221

Protection of Historical and Cultural Tissue in Ankara:
A Case Study on Urban Transformation in Hacıbayram ...... 223

**Istanbul** ................................................................ 237

Implications of Urbanisation for Turkey.
The Case of Istanbul ................................................ 229

**Coastal Management** ............................................ 267

Thoughts on Coastal Zone Management in Turkey ............. 269

**Ethical Duties** ...................................................... 287

Our Ethical Duties Towards Future
Generations in a Globalising World ............................ 289
The Political, Legal and
Ethical Issues in Urban Planning .............................. 299
Local Governance and Democracy ............................ 317
Territorial Governance in Turkey in the
Light of the European Model .................................... 339
Legal Opinion Regarding the Case of Mr. Philippe Mettens,
The Mayor of Flobecq, And The President of The Federal
Public Service in Charge of The Scientific Policy .............. 371
Administrative Culture in Turkey .............................. 376

# ECOLOGICAL CONCERNS AND SUSTAINABLE DEVELOPMENT

# European Approaches to
# Sustainable Development[1]

(I)

I would like to congratulate both the Black Sea Technical University and INTEN- Synergy for their success to organize this important Conference, and I welcome all the distinguished participants. But especially, I would like to extend
my warmest feelings to our esteemed colleagues from Greece
with whom I have a couple of links which might worth to
mention briefly.

First of all, I am a member of the Board of Trustees of the
Biopolitics International Organization (B.I.O.), that is based in
Athens, Greece. It aims to protect the habitats of living crea-
tures. I had the honour to share, some years ago, the Abdi
İpekçi Peace Prize with its distinguished President, Professor Dr.Agni Vlavianos-Arvanitis, for having been regarded
as contributed modestly to the furtherance of Greek-Turk-
ish Friendship.

Secondly, I welcome my Greek friends, in my capacity
of the newly elected President of the World Society for Ekistics, in other words, the World Society of Human Settlements, which is also based in Athens. This well-known institution was created by the initiative of the Doxiadis Center

---

1    Ankara University, Faculty of Political Sciences 4th International Conference
     on Ecological Protection of the Planet Earth: Maritime Policies, Environ-
     ment, and Energy Issues in the Black Sea June 12-15, 2008, Black Sea Techni-
     cal University.

in the early 1960's by late Constantinis Doxiadis to assist the upgrading of human settlements in developing countries.

(II)

Sustainable development and long-term orientation have become recently the guiding principles of a rational spatial development strategy and democratic governance at all levels of authority. The needs for future generations are more increasingly taken into consideration in formulating current policies of urban development, thanks to the contributions of certain international institutions such as the UN, the European Union and the Council of Europe. Particularly, the European institutions are making considerable and constant efforts to internalize all costs, and not to transfer problems and tensions into the shoulders of future generations.

The very definition of sustainable development made by the Brundtland Commission on Environment and Development had put an emphasis on meeting the needs of the present generation without compromising the ability of the future generations to meet their own needs. I believe that these ideas will have far reaching consequences for the protection of natural resources and cultural assets of the countries surrounding the Black Sea. Common environmental problems facing the Black Sea Region include energy, pollution caused by watercourses, problems of coastal cities, industrial development and location of industry, problems of touristic development, architectural identity of the region, unhealthy and unplanned urbanization and disorderly building activities in urban, semi urban and rural areas.

International Environmental Law provides us several guiding principles of high relevance for the analysis of these issues. They are reflected in international legal instruments as the Stockholm Declaration, legal principles proposed by the

Brundtland Commission, and the Rio Declaration. Therefore, it would be appropriate here to remember the meaning of the concepts such as common heritage of mankind, national interests, environmental security, common responsibility, the rights of future generations, and international cooperation.

(a)

Undoubtedly, it is wrong to assume that most of the urban and environmental values are adversely affected by world-wide globalization could be regarded as being in the monopoly of the States owning them. It is widely accepted now that the whole humanity is the real owner of all the assets that fall down within the concept of the common heritage of mankind. In fact, all humanity possesses a right to benefit from them. This signifies at the same time, that nowadays, the concept of national interest (intéret général) has no longer a restrictive meaning confining it to the monopolistic use of the nation-states.

As rightly pointed out by Edith Brown Weiss, writing on global environmental problems, "we are trying to redefine the concept of national interest. Traditionally, this term was used to represent the interests of the nation, as different from or even contrary to that of another nation. However, we gradually begin to understand that global environment represents something that has to be shared by all the nations on Earth. Ozone depletion does not concern differently the interests of the USA than those of Germany or the United Kingdom. It is in the interests all the nations to control the phenomenon of ozone depletion. The same can be said also about dumping into and transporting toxic and hazardous materials in the seas.

In brief, the traditional understanding that is based upon the assumption that the interests of one nation necessarily contradict those of the others has been abandoned.[2] In the light of this analysis, we must admit that all Black Sea countries have a common responsibility to cooperate for the protection of their environment.

### (b)

Environmental security is the next concept of International Environmental Law that can be used in this context. Global environmental problems facing the Earth create at the same time serious security problems. If left unresolved, they may acquire such immense dimensions as to threaten the economic and social stability in the region. We should not allow environmental stresses to cause the emergence of armed conflicts. We should neither allow ecological imbalances to destroy life processes[2].

### (c)

Thirdly, the common responsibility of mankind is another important principle adopted during the Rio Summit in 1992. It has both spatial, temporal and socio-cultural dimensions. All nations are required to be fully respectful for the right to environment and the rights on the natural resources of their neighbors. No nation is permitted to use its natural resources at the expense of other nations All have the obligation to ensure that activities within their jurisdiction or control do not damage the environment of other States or of areas beyond the limits of national jurisdiction.

The principle 7 of the Rio Declaration emphasized that States shall cooperate in good faith for integrity of the Earth's ecosystem. In view of the different contributions to global

2    Edith Brown Weiss, "The Introductory Framework", in E.Brown-Weiss (ed.), Global Environmental Change and International Law, UN University, Tokyo, 1992, p.14

environmental degradation, States have "common but differentiated responsibilities". The term of common responsibility is closely related with the concept of the "common heritage of mankind". This issue has remained in the agenda since the 1940's, in connection with the practices of common responsibility concerning the protection of the space, moon and the fisheries.

(d)

The rights of future generations is the next concept to deal with. The idea that future generations should have certain rights to ecosystems is not new. The Convention on Whales (1946), the Convention on World Heritage (1972) are two examples. These are followed by more recent international legal instruments concerning flora and fauna, oceans, renewable natural resources, environment in general, natural heritage, natural resources, including water, biological diversity, and climate change.

In fact, intergenerational equity concept was mentioned as early as in the Stockholm Declaration in 1972, as a condition of the concept of sustainable development. According to the First Principle of the Stockholm Declaration, "Mankind has an obligation to protect and develop the environment for present and future generations. Similarly, the Fourth Principle of the Rio Declaration considers this Principle as a component of the right to development and emphasizes that "in order to achieve sustainable development, environmental protection shall constitute an integral part of the development process and cannot be considered in isolation from it." The International Court of Justice had expressed in 1996 in an advisory opinion, that if any hesitation arises in connection to the standing to sue of the parties of a conflict, the concept of the rights of the future generations could be an appropriate point of departure".

(e)

As I have pointed out above, the concept of common responsibility requires close cooperation among nations. This need originates from the fact that the right to environment is not simply an individual but also a collective right. The Article 74 of the UN Charter is the expression of good neighborly relations. This principle which was originally confined to social, economic and trade issues, has been expanded later as to include international cooperation in environmental matters and applied to bilateral and regional environmental conventions.

The Principle 27 of the Rio Declaration is a complementary guide which maintains that "States and people shall cooperate in good faith and in a spirit of partnership in the fulfillment of the principles embodied in this Declaration and in the further development of International Law in the field of sustainable development. This principle of international cooperation can be found in almost all documents of International Environmental Law[3].

Philippe Sands emphasizes upon these different and important functions of the concept of sustainable development which might have numerous implications for achieving the goals of international environmental cooperation[4]. One of the reasons for the protection of natural resources is the needs of future generations.

This is the principle of inter-generational equity. The second is the need to use natural resources by paying due regard

---

3    Philippe Sands, Principles of International Environmental Law, Cambridge
      University Press, .2nd ed. 2001, p.250.
4    Ibid,p.253.

to the needs of other States. This is the principle of intra-generational equity. Finally, comes the need to take into account economic considerations in the achievement of the goals of environmental protection, and he integration of environmental considerations with development plans, programmes and projects. This may be called as the principle of integration.

The Black Sea countries have numerous obligations as well as opportunities stemming from other legal instruments belonging to other international organizations than the United Nations. Some of the countries surrounding the Black Sea are members of the European Union (Bulgaria), some others are candidates for the EU membership (Turkey). All are the members of the Council of Europe. As such, they are required to act in accordance with the established norms and regulations of these organizations in the fields of environment, spatial development, urban culture and identity, ecological security, and the like. Such obligations exist legally (de jure) when the state concerned is a party to the conventions in these fields; and ethically when they are not ratified by them.

The CEMAT Guiding Principles for Sustainable Spatial Development adopted by the Ministers responsible for Regional Development in Hannover in 2000 are a collection of recommendations for the adoption of policies to reduce environmental hazards, to protect and develop natural resources and natural heritage, and to ratify such European conventions as the one concerning Natural Habitats (1970), and the European Strategy of Biological and Landscape Diversity.

Similarly, numerous other international legal instruments like the following possess provisions bringing about considerable obligations with regard to the quality of the environment, identity of cities, environmental and natural elements in urban design, protection of the architectural heritage and the like:

1) Framework Convention on Transboundary Cooperation (Madrid 1980)

2) Convention for the Protection of European Architectural Heritage (Granada 1985)

3) European Convention for the Protection of Archeological Heritage (Valetta 1992)

4) European Charter of Local Self-Government (Strasbourg 1985)

5) European Landscape Convention (Lisbon 2000)

6) European Urban Charter (Strasbourg 1992, 2004)

7) Convention on the Access to Information, Participation in Decision- Making Processes and the Recourse to Judiciary in Environmental Matters (Aarhus 1998)

The Ministers of the Member States of the EU responsible for Regional Development in their meeting taken place in Postdam in 1999 adopted the European Spatial Development Perspective (ESDP), according to which three basic principles will guide spatial development throughout Europe: a) The protection of natural resources, b) The protection of cultural heritage and c) the good governance.[5]

The provisions of this document address the risks facing biological diversity, natural resources, water resources, increasing pressures upon cultural landscape and cultural heritage from the point of view of the protection of ecosystem.

(b)

To the list of international legal instruments concerning the environment, spatial planning, cities and urban identities must be added the Aalborg Charter of 1994, revised in 2004. The role of local authorities toward sustainable development,

---

5     European Commission, ESDP, European Spatial Development Perspective: Towards Balanced and Sustainaable Development of the Territory of he European Union, 1999.

natural common goods, choices regarding the living and consumption patterns, planning and design, sustainable local economy, social balance and equity are the main issues addressed in the Aalborg Charter.

(c)

Furthermore, European Ministers responsible for Regional Development have adopted a new Charter in 2007, in Leipzig, called Spatial Agenda of the European Union, set their main goals as the upgrading of physical environment, ensuring the sustainability of natural and cultural values.[6]

(d)

Finally, The Territorial Agenda of the European Union Towards more Competitive and Sustainable Europe of Diverse Regions[7], enumerated the major new territorial challenges as

a) Those regionally diverse impacts of climate change with regard to sustainable development,

b) Rising energy prices, energy inefficiency and different territorial opportunities for the new forms of energy supply,

c) Overexploitation of the ecological and cultural resources and loss of biodiversity among them.

On the basis of these observations, it has been suggested that every region and city, may, through their engagement, contribute to saving energy, to its decentralized supply and to mitigating climate change by supporting the development of low or zero emissions settlement, developing potential new renewable resources of energy supply and promoting energy efficiency. Within this context, territorial priorities of

6   Mimarlar Odası (Chamber of Architects), "Sürdürülebilir Avrupa Kentleri için Leipzig Şartı", Mimarlar Odası, Belgeler, 10 Aralık 2007,pp.12-19.

7   Leipzig, 24-25 May 2007, Meeting on Urban Development and Territorial Cohesion.

the European Union are based on a) development of a balanced and polycentric urban system and a new urban-rural partnership, b) securing parity of access to infrastructure and knowledge, and finally, c) sustainable development, prudent management and protection of nature and cultural heritage.

There is no doubt that the achievement of all these aims requires strengthening of ecological structures and cultural resources as the added value for development. The Black Sea Region as a whole possesses irreplaceable values of ecological structures and cultural and natural heritage, especially cultural and natural landscapes, and the quality of design and process on architecture as well as the built environment.

These values should constitute the foundation of environmentally and culturally oriented development which offers development perspectives, while safeguarding diverse cultural identities. It is therefore advisable to develop networks of valuable nature areas and cultural landscapes in order to create an integrated and sustainable Trans-European green structure with adequate corridors and zones linking protected sites.

(e)

The EU's Sixth Environmental Action Programme called the Commission to develop a new Thematic Strategy on the Urban Environment to help promote a more integrated approach and support action at local level. The measures offered under his Thematic Strategy aim to contribute to a better implementation of existing EU environment policies and legislation at the local level by supporting and encouraging local authorities to adopt a more integrated approach to urban management.

Integrated management of the urban environment should foster sustainable land-use policies which avoid urban sprawl and reduce soil-sealing, include promotion of urban bio-diversity, and perhaps more importantly, raise awareness for urban citizens. The Strategy also includes actions with regard to promoting dialogue between European coastal stakeholders, and promoting integrated coastal zone management (ICZM) programmes within the member States and at the "Regional Seas" level.

(IV)

Black Sea countries are faced, for many years, with rapidly increasing diversified environmental stresses. The sensitivity of these countries towards safeguarding ecological assets is not new. This is more than a legal issue. It has ethical and moral dimensions, too. Both the States and the NGO's make great efforts to accomplish the requirements of these legal and ethical obligations. [8]

The Black Sea has the most polluted waters in the world. Pollution stems from the watercourses, urban settlements, industrial wastes[9], and the ships. Fishery is terribly affected by land-based pollutants and transferred into the marine environment. Pollution created by Chernobyl accident in the middle of the 1980's also affected the Black Sea through Dnieper River. The amount of oil dumped into the sea annually is 110 thousand tons.

Pollution in the Black Sea tends to create considerable social costs in terms of public health, internal and external migration, and unemployment. [10] Therefore, a pressing

8     Ö.Faruk Gençkaya, "States and Non-State Actors in Envvironmental Policy-Making: An Overview of the GEF- BSEP NGO Forum", Stacy D.VanDeveer and Geoffrey D.Dabelko (eds.), Protecting Regional Seas: Developing Capacity and Fostering Environmental Cooperation in Europe, The Woodrow Wilson International Center for Scholars, Washington D.C., 1999, pp.84-88.

9     Oktay Sönmez, "Ölen Bir Deniz", Cumhuriyet,

10    Ömer Faruk Gençkaya, op.cit., pp.84-85.

need arises to create a system of cooperation for the protection of the region.

The most serious problems threatening the environment in and around the Black Sea are the pollution of the Sea, by domestic, agriculture and industrial wastes, toxic materials, discharging of the wastes of the sewerage networks into the Sea, thus creating a remarkable micro- biological pollution as well.

An opportunity was created in the early 1990's within the framework of the Convention of the Black Sea Economic Cooperation. 12 States that have decided to unite their efforts within this endeavor were Albania, Armenia, Azerbaijan, Georgia, Bulgaria, Greece, Moldova, Romania, Russian federation, Turkey, Ukraine, and Serbia.[11]

(a)

Within this framework, six Black Sea countries have signed the Bucharest Convention in April 1992 in order to be able to take necessary measures against pollution. In the first Article of the Convention, environmental pollution is defined very broadly, to include all types of pollution affecting the Black Sea. Three additional protocols have been adopted later on with a view 1) to protect the marine environment against land-based pollution, 2) to cooperate in emergency situations to take measure against pollution through petroleum and other harmful substances, and 3) to prevent pollution from dumping wastes into the marine environment.

(b)

The institutional mechanism in charge of carrying out of the principles of the Convention consists of the Secretariat,

---

11    Martina Petkova, "The Impact of Organization of the Black Sea Economic Cooperation and the North Atlantic Treaty Organization", R.Detrez and B. Segaert (eds.), Europe and Historical Legacies in the Balkans

advisory entities and the periodic thematic and scientific meetings. A Coordinating Commission is located in İstanbul in order to ensure necessary coordination between the activities of the decentralized entities in the State parties.

(c)

A Strategic Action Plan adopted by the Organization in 1996 focused its work on the control of the pollution, the protection of marine and coastal ecosystem, or to restore them in case they are being damaged, and to find out the ways in which they can be put in the service of future generations.

(d)

Bucharest Convention possesses detailed provisions concerning the prevention, reduction and control of the pollution (Art.17-18), the definition of the types of pollution (Arts.6-14), scientific and technical cooperation and monitoring (Arts.5, 15 and 16). Besides, the concerned Ministers of State Parties in a meeting in Odessa in 1993, have adopted the Odessa Declaration, specifying concretely the goals the protection of the marine environment and the kinds of effective measures to be taken.

(e)

In order to complete the picture, I have to add that Regional Activity Centers have been established in each of the cooperating countries, each assuming the responsibility for conducting activities of different nature. Their division of labor and locations are shown below:

1. Sea transportation, environment and environmental security affairs are in the jurisdiction of the Activity Center in Varna, Bulgaria,

2. Land based pollution (Istanbul Turkey),

3. Monitoring and Assessment of Pollution (Odessa, Ukraine),

4. Protection of Biological Diversity (Batumi, Georgia),

5. Methodologies for Integrated Coastal Zone Management (Novorossik, Russian federation),

6. Fisheries and other Marine Resources (Kostence, Romania).

## Concluding Remarks

1) I would like to congratulate the Black Sea University and all of the organizers of this Conference, and I repeat my sincere thanks especially to Professor Şinasi Aydemir, my distinguished colleague and the Dean of the Faculty of Architecture.

2) I hope that this meeting will contribute further to the intensification of the efforts of the academia and national and international bureaucracy in the cooperating countries.

3) It is also hoped that the principles of the International Environmental Law will be put into force more effectively and within an integrated and holistic approach, combining law and morality on one hand, the needs and opportunities of various sectors of the economy on the other.

4) Since the Bucharest Convention was prepared before the adoption of the Rio Declaration and the Agenda 21, efforts must be made to integrate the Rio principles such as the participation, the role of the NGO's, polluter pays, precautionary and the like, with it.

5) Another suggestion is to meet the need to incorporate the Danube River countries into the process of the protection of the Black Sea Marine environment taking into consideration of the polluting activities of the 80 million inhabitants

of the riparian States. Because, nearly 75 percent of the land-based pollution originate from those countries.[12]

6) A final point is to underline the need to provide necessary links with the system of the protection of the Black Sea with other relevant international instruments such as MARPOL (1972-1978), CITES (1973),RAMSAR (1972-1996), BASEL (1989).

## Short Bibliography

- European Commission, European Spatial Development Perspective: Towards Balanced and Sustainable Development of the Territory of the European Union, (ESDP), Potsdam, May, 1999.

- Gençkaya, Ömer Faruk, "States and Non-States Actors in Environmental Policy- Making: An Overview of the GEF-BSEP NGO Forum", Stacey D.Van Deveer and Geoffrey Dabelko (eds.), Protecting Regional Seas: Developing Capacity and Fostering Environmental Cooperation in Europe, The Woodrow Wilson International Center for Scholars, Washington D.C., 1999.

- Güneş, Şule ,"Karadeniz'de Çevresel İşbirliği: 1992 Bükreş Sözleşmesi", (Environmental Cooperation in the Black Sea) ODTÜ Gelişme Dergisi (METU Development Journal), Vol.28, No:3-4, 2001, pp.311-337.

- Mimarlar Odası (Chamber of Architects), "Sürdürülebilir Avrupa Kentleri İçin Leipzig Şartı", Mimarlar Odası, Belegeler, 2007.

- Petkova, Martina, "The Impact of Organization of the Black Sea Economic Cooperation and the North Atlantic Treaty Organization", Raymond Detrez and Barbara Segaert (eds.), Europe and the Historical Legacies in the Balkans, PIE Peter Lang, Brussels, pp.171-181.

- Sands, Philippe, Principles of International Environmental Law, Cambridge University Press, Cambridge 2003 (2nd ed.).

- Weiss, Edith-Brown (ed.) Global Environmental Change and International Law, United Nations University, Tokyo, 1992.

---

12  Şule Güneş, "Karadeniz'de Çevresel İşbirliği, 1992 Bükreş Sözleşmesi", ODTÜ Gelişme Dergisi, Vol. 28, No:3-4, 2001, pp.311-337.

# Urban Planning and Sustainable Land Management in Turkish Municipalities*

*With a population of nearly 80 million and a territory of about 780.000 square kilometers is one of the largest states in Europe and in the Middle East. Turkey is one of the highly urbanizing countries. The share of urban population increased from 18.5 in 1950 to 65 percent in 2000 and to 76 percent in 2010, mainly as a result of rural-urban migration caused by social and economic conditions prevailing in rural areas. Main reasons behind the accelerated urbanization are uneven distribution of ownership of the agricultural land among peasant families, low per capita incomes resulting from obsolete farming techniques, considerable dependence of productivity on climate conditions, pressure of rapidly increasing population upon land and other natural resources, mechanization of agriculture following the Second World War and the expansion of the national highway network made possible by the American assistance called Marshall Plan.*

\*     Prof. Dr. Ruşen Keleş, Prof. (Emeritus) of Local Goverment, Environmental Policy and Urban Development, Ankara University; member of the Group of Independent Experts on the European Charter for Local Self Government; former president of the World Society for Ekistics (science of human settlements), Ankara (TR)
Local Land and Soil News, Zurich, No:44/45, 1/13, 2013.

## The manner of urbanization

Urbanization is not only rapid, but also an imbalanced population movement. It is unbalanced in the sense that is causes striking discrepancies among geographical regions. The degrees and the pace of urbanization of different city-size categories also vary widely from one group to another. The large cities that attract the great majority of urban population increase grow much faster than the cities in smaller size categories. A third type of imbalance is urbanization patterns is clearly observed in the increasing number of squatter dwellings that began to cover extensive areas of the largest metropolises. A final configuration of the imbalances of urbanization lies in the employment structure of major cities where the great majority of migrants are either idle or employed outside the manufacturing sector.

*The Article 35 of the Turkish Constitution stipulates that the right to property shall not be used in contravention of the public interest.* This provision which reflects a modern idea of the need for engaging the holder of the right to ownership in a sense of social responsibility is not implemented appropriately. Land speculation is regarded almost a natural right for developers and speculators who invest enormous amount of financial resources to buy land in and around the cities, touristic and coastal regions with the expectation of unlimited profits in the future. Under these conditions, city master plans are frequently modified in order to replace open spaces and green areas by high-rise residential buildings and other more profitable uses. Frequent modifications in the plans are the main instruments to make the control over land use almost ineffective.

Members of the municipal councils are influenced by the pressures exerted by land speculators. Land use regulations are not implemented in a sustainable manner. Households and businesses are often allowed to settle in environmentally sensitive areas such as steep slopes, wetlands and earthquake prone territories, leaving the considerations of sustainability just on the paper.

## Tasks of municipalities

To guide urban developments through master plan is a public function of local nature, that has to be carried out by local authorities, namely municipalities. Although the city master plans adopted by city councils do not need to be approved by the central government, exceptional provision in the *City Planning Law of 1985* (articles 1 and 9) empowers various ministries, including the *Ministry of Environment and Urban Development*, to play an impressive role in the preparation, approval and implementation stages of the planning process. Excessive centralization of the system does not allow local authorities to carry out their own creative ideas in the urban development process. On the other hand, the central government often intervenes in the process for the protection of biotic and non-biotic components of the ecosystem. In neither case, the concern for sustainable urban management is adequately integrated with master planning activities. Such centralist interventions are also incompatible with the principle of subsidiarity guaranteed by the EU Acquis and the European Charter of Local Self-Government with which is ratified by Turkey.

Land transactions takes place within the framework of the free play of the market forces. National and local politicians did not hesitate, in the past, to cooperate, occasionally, with the major actors who had vital interests in land speculation. Under these conditions, provisions concerning the protection of natural resources, such as land, forestry, historical, cultural and architectural assets could not be implemented appropriately. Briefly, the concern for maximizing the private gains rather than the public interest in using the urban land dominated generally the practice of urban planning.

*Yet, one of the most important constitutional provisions (Art.56), stipulates that everyone has the right to live in a healthy and balanced environment and it is the duty of the State and the citizens to improve the natural environment and to prevent environmental pollution.* The Constitution also provides legal guarantees for the protection of natural and man-made environmental values. *Prevention of the loss of agricultural land is also the duty of the State (Art.44).* It prohibits the depletion of forest and other land and underground resources even for the purpose of providing land to farmers with insufficient land.

## International agreements on sustainability

In addition to the internal legal provisions, Turkey has certain international legal provisions, Turkey has certain international obligations for environmental protection. It had ratified more than thirty international treaties and conventions, which aim at the protection of the environment. *All of these legal documents are binding national and local authorities to protect the environmental rights not only of present, but also of future generations.* The Convention of Granada on the Protection of the European Architectural Heritage (1985), Bern Convention on the Protection of European Wildlife and Living Habitats (1979), Ramsar Convention on Wetland of International Importance (1971), Vienna Convention for the Protection of Ozone Layer (1985), Basel Convention on Hazardous Waste Traffic (1989) are few of them. These and other international agreements together with Bergen Declaration, Paris Charter, Rio and Frankfurt Declarations and the Kyoto Protocol enlarge the scope of the international legal as well as ethical responsibilities of each member states and the international community.

There are nearly 300 associations actively working in the fields of the protection of flora and fauna, other natural assets and historical buildings. Citizens sensitive to environmental issues have the right to apply to the courts for the annulment of the administrative decisions unfriendly to environment, although an actual, personal and legitimate interest in the issue at stake is a precondition for seeking the annulment of an administrative act or decision. Certain concrete steps have been taken recently by such organizations to avoid harmful effects of hydroelectric power plants and similar establishments on natural environment. *Public awareness and consciousness seem to be the real and ultimate guarantees for ensuring the sustainability at national and local levels.* This is also highly important to counterbalance the adverse effects of increasing emphasis on consumerism and anti-planning tendencies enhanced by globalization.

## Short Bibliography

- Keleş, Ruşen:"Urban Development and Sustainable Management for the Mediterranean Towns (Turkey)"; Paper Presented to the Working Group for Urban Management, Mediterranean Commission for Sustainable Development, Priority Action Programme, Regional Activitiy Center, Split, Croatia, April 26-27, 1999.
- Keleş, Ruşen:"International Cooperation for Sustainable Urban Development in the Mediterranean Region"; Paper presented to the Workshop on Urban Management and Sustainable Development in the Mediterranean, Barcelona, Spain, 5-7 July, 2001.
- Keleş, Ruşen: "National Protection: The Case of Protected Areas in Turkey"; Naturopa, Council of Europe, No:85, 1997, pp. 23-24.
- Keleş, Ruşen: "General Legal Framework for Sustainable Land Use and Management Designed by International Environmental Law";

Paper presented to the 36th International Symposium of the European Faculty of Land Use and Development: Core Problems of Sustainable Land Management, Zurich, 25-27 September, 2008.

- Keleş, Ruşen: "Sustainable Urban Development under Unsustainable Conditions" , i Derya Oktay (ed), Inquire into Urban Environment, Eastern Mediterranean University Press, Gazimagusa, 2006, pp. 27-38.

- Keleş, Ruşen and Yılmaz, Meltem: "Sustainable Urban Development and the Patterns of the Right to Ownership: With Special Reference to Architecture and Urban Planning"; in Erwin Hepperle and Hans Lenk (eds), Land Development Strategies: Patterns, Risks and Responsibilities, European Faculty of Land Use and Development, VDF, Zurich, 2009.

- Keleş, Ruşen: "Kentleşme Politikası (Urbanization Policy)"; İmge Pub., Ankara, 2013 (13th edition).

- Keleş, Ruşen, Hamamcı, Can and Coban, Aykut: "Çevre Politikası (Environmental Policy)"; İmge Pub., Ankara, 2012 (7th edition).

# Globalization and Local Autonomy*

## Tendencies Towards Globalization

The World has been undergoing a profound transformation during the last several decades. Particularly three phenomena, namely the government deregulation, the spread of the new information technologies and the globalization of the financial markets characterize the worldwide globalization. The term of globalization is used to refer to both multilateralism in international economic and political relations and also it is viewed as a micro-economic phenomenon. Both foster global trading system, multilateral trade liberalization, changing dynamics of global competition and international competitiveness. (1)

Furthermore, globalization may be regarded as the growth of economic activity spanning politically defined national and regional boundaries of goods and services, through trade and investment, and of people by migratory movements. Finance, banks and population acting as the major actors of the globalization tendencies make it a centrifugal process. As a result, the economic distance among countries and regions is greatly reduced. Another consequence is to reduce the effective sovereignty of national governments. However, both factors contribute to an association between globalization and increased international interdependence. (2)

It can also be assumed that globalization tends to generate a movement among the parts, in order to make up for the ensuing uncertainty and instability, to integrate among themselves. This centripetal effect gives rise to the formation of regional or federal structures and institutions.

Globalization is a label that is used to account for peoples, activities, norms, ideas, goods, services and currencies that are decreasingly confined to a particular geographic space and its local and established practices. (3) It is something that is changing humankind's preoccupation with territoriality and the traditional arrangements of the interstate system. As indicated by Rosenau, any technological, psychological, social, economic and political developments that foster the expansion of interests and practices beyond established boundaries are both sources and expressions of the processes of globalization, just as any developments in these realms that limit or reduce interests are both sources and expressions of localizing processes.

Globalization is rendering boundaries and identity with land less salient while localization is highlighting borders and intensifying the deep attachments to land that can dominate emotion and reasoning. It is often emphasized that these two processes are not necessarily conflictual and mutually exclusive. They are neither static. And neither set of dynamics is fully independent. Therefore, some authors suggested to speak in such terms as "the global institutionalization of the life world and the localization of globality" in order to clarify further the close interrelatedness of the two concepts.

As a result, one can safely assume that globalization and localization, as two centrifugal and centripetal processes are mutually reinforcing patterns of change. On the other hand, there has been a marked change in the structure of the societies during the second half of the 20th century, from the guardian (or regulatory), which required the existence of a centralized institutional structure where local authorities had limited competencies, to the functional state where from the state to the citizens and enterprises go not only authoritative decisions, but the public services as well. In the latter, the relationship between the central and local authorities is losing gradually its hierarchical character.

One of the most striking forces reshaping local authorities was certainly the change in the economic and technological conditions from a parochial to global nature. The impact of the modern means of transportation and communications are of utmost importance in this respect. They make possible to move physical materials quickly and safely through large distances and to transmit information instantaneously to remote places. These developments widen and open up the borders of local and once closed communities. It is now recognized generally that we live in a "global village".(4) This has been possible largely by the fact that personal and institutional contacts intensively increased by the technological progress enlarged the scope in space and in time of human interactions.

Under changing conditions, it can be argued that central coordination of governmental services is no longer possible and we need other self-coordinating and decentralized mechanisms. It has also been maintained that central governments may no longer confine themselves to making decisions in areas of their own choice and according to their own standards (5). As rightly noted by Rupnik, "Governments of nation-states are too small for big problems, and too big for small problems".(6)

While the economic logic requires globalization, interdependence and regional integration; the political logic causes national fragmentation and disintegration. It is a well-known fact that regionalization, decentralization and federalism have been regarded for a long time as an instrument for strengthening the territorial integrity and national unity. However, at present, they are considered, by some nations, as a threat to unity and a first step towards separatism. Certainly, such perceptions may not be correct under all conditions.

The fact that globalization and localization are closely interrelated is clearly observed in the existence and growth of the world (or global) cities. If capital is global, and if its spatial organization is hierarchical, then the situation of the cities of the world in which control functions of capital are located and which house the labor force providing producers' services, will also reflect that hierarchy as rightly observed by Keyder and Öncü.(7) There is no doubt that global economy materializes in particular places. Although the role of national governments in a global economy is reduced dramatically, that does not mean that global economy reduces the centrality of cities. Global markets are located in cities themselves.

The impact of globalization upon cities has tremendous consequences: Greater globalization seems to be the recipe for accumulation. Accumulation brings with it an increase and employment polarization. Under globalizing forces, managing the city becomes an art of balancing between them rudimentary services required by the new immigrants and investing for the purposes of acquiring a certain status in the globalizing world economy.(8)

The formation of the world city, changing power relations between the public and private sectors, concentration of control and command functions in central parts of a few global cities, increasing social and economic polarization and the emergence of dual city, the emergence of postmodern urban landscapes, new modes of urban culture and consumption

and postmodern urmajor consequences of the forces working for the globalization of ban architecture are some of the
world system.

The question whether these profound changes make it
necessary to have more decentralized administrative and political systems depends on the historical, political, socio-cultural and economic conditions of the countries concerned.
However, for better management of territorial entities and
for an effective democratic participation, relying on autonomous and powerful local authorities is becoming widely accepted. National and international efforts are being intensified in order to achieve this end.

## Efforts at the International Level

Globalization has been one of the most frequently used words
during the last two decades in social and administrative sciences. There is no doubt that the Earth, as a world, is closely
connected with the word "globe" in geometry, and consequently with "globalization". However, as indicated above, by
globalization is meant today the tendency towards integration and approaching each other of different localities, peoples, ideologies and economic systems in the world. Within
this context, the unification of Europe has a particular place.
Reorganization of Europe within a new political mechanism,
namely the ideal of European integration has a long history
going back to the prewar years. Recent socio-economic and
political changes facing the world in general and the countries of Europe in particular have given momentum to the
goal of ever broadening integrated Europe by further participation of central and eastern European nations.

Formerly the Common Market, European Economic
Community (EEC), European Community (EC), and finally
the European Union (EU) increased its membership to 15 in

three decades, and it aims to expand further. The number of the member states of the Council of Europe, too, increased from 25 in the early 1950's to 39 at present. Fall of the Berlin Wall and the withering away of the communist regimes, ratification of the Maastricht Treaty and the resurgence of nationalist and separatist movements all over the central and eastern Europe have all contributed to giving the way for a revision in the goals and instituset-up of international, national and sub-national political institutions in Europe.

What is problematic under present circumstances was to answer the question how to harmonize the need of global unity, namely the necessary degree of economic, political and functional integration with local diversities in various fields. One can assume that it is possible for the world system to exist and develop along the process of further globalization and thus harmonize the integration of the whole with the autonomous existence of the constituting parts. (9) This is not impossible. Interdependence of independent states, and the integration of territorial units seem to be the guiding principle of the future restructuring that has a chance of combining unity and diversity. (10)

Enlargement of the integrated Europe as a political institution and various manifestations of globalization in many aspects of life do not exclude the necessity of the existence of powerful and autonomous local and regional entities at the same time. Not only from the point of view of economics, which assumes that development clearly shows spatial (local, regional, national, international) dimension, but also to political scientists all politics may be perceived as having an important local dimension. That is the reason why the autonomy of local authorities is generally considered as a basic value of liberal democracy to be constantly defended against encroachments of the central governments.

On the other hand, ethnic and regional movements tend to strengthen the principle of territoriality. Although ethnicity is usually considered as rather a biological and cultural than a territorial phenomenon, it creates tremendous political consequences for the nation-states. Regions and localities, in this context, are areas which are sensibly different and claim sometimes some degree of administrative and political autonomy.

Finally, unlike the connection of ecological considerations with regard to globalization, ecological consciousness is at the same time an important force towards localism. People more easily unite at sub-national levels to defend the common environmental values of their towns, cities and regions against the polluting forces.

## Europe and the Territoriality

Since the end of the Second World War, two movements of contradictory nature, as touched upon above briefly, went hand in hand: One was the advance of economic and political integration and the other was the resurgence of territorial identities, within a number of states. Following the collapse of the communist regimes in central and eastern Europe, a marked speeding up of these trends has caused some of the nationalities, territories, ethnic groups, new democracies to demand the renewal of their identities and integration into a larger Europe."(11)

On the other hand, a public opinion poll carried out all over Europe revealed that the strongest attachments of all Europeans (85-87%) is with local towns and regions, while a much smaller segment of Europeans expressed that their primary identity perception coincided with the ideal of European citizenship.(12) This means that political and cultural identities of the inhabitants of Europe are mainly embedded in towns, cities and regions, and therefore, the most convenient environment for the realization of European unification can be provided by freely elected representatives of sub-national entities.

Of course, territorial autonomy and integration respond to different kinds of logic. The ambition of the first is to bring power closer to citizens, people itself; while integration tends to transfer the power to new power centers at higher levels, like Brussels. In such a case, the influence of each citizen in the final decision would certainly be much weaker. This can not be reconciled with the principle of autonomy. Because, as indicated by Alexis de Tocqueville, decentralization is one of the vital counterweights for pressures towards global centralizing tendencies, uniformity and individualism.

## Achievements of the European Union

The signature of the Maastricht Treaty on European Union in 1992 can be regarded as preparing the way for the functions of the regions within the process of European unification. Particularly, the inclusion of the principle of subsidiarity in the Treaty as a binding norm and the establishment of the Committee of the Regions can be viewed as a response to the widespread debate on the need for territorial entities to be better represented in the European decision-making processes.

At the beginning, there were fears that a powerful and united Europe would mean the total disappearance of any form of local autonomy, and the creation of a centralized system which would have no allowance whatsoever for the existence of a European territorial dimension. In order to avoid such consequences, the following principal requirements were accepted:

a) a federal structure, having European, national and sub-national units.

b) a clear definition of powers in accordance with the principle of subsidiarity.

c) the rights for the regions to initiate and to participate in action at European level. (13)

In 1988, the European Parliament approved the Community (Union) Regionalization Charter, according to which, from a geographical standpoint, regions are distinct units of self-contained structures and where population share certain common characteristics.(14) The article 14 of this Charter suggests that the regions occupy a position between the state and the municipality, and be largely responsible for implementing the measures which come within the jurisdiction of the member states, while they should also make the most extensive possible delegation of power to the municipal authorities.

The representation of the European regions in the organs of the Union is unsatisfactory at present. It is confined to German Lands, Italian regions and Belgian regions and communities. A 42 member Advisory Council for Regional and Local Authorities, set up in 1988, operates only in an advisory capacity. Lobbying on behalf of the regions is also carried out by the AER (Assembly of the European Regions), 235 regions in Europe have joined together in an independent parliament called AER, to realize the goal of building a four-tier Europe, in which decisions are taken as close as possible to the citizen.

The Treaty on European Union provided for the creation of a Committee of the Regions, Consisting of representatives of regional and local bodies (Ard. 196/a) to act in an advisory capacity. The Maastricht Treaty stipulated that this Committee of the Regions be consulted by the Council or by the

Commission where the Treaty so provides, and in all other cases in which one of these two institutions considers it appropriate. There are certain fields that the Committee must be consulted on.

## The Principle of Subsidiarity

Since the beginning, the incorporation of the principle of subsidiarity into the Maastricht Treaty as a binding legal norm represents an attempt to dissipate the fears of a continuing increase in European centralization. It was thought that territorial units are historically developed form of local autonomy in Europe and they are particularly worthy of reinforcement, as building blocks of a united Europe.

Jacques Delors approves the concentration of powers at the Union level, and he is inclined to regard local solutions as exceptional. On the other hand, Gérard Marcou does not see the principle of subsidiarity compatible with French legal tradition. (15) Finally, it has been pointed out that this principle was not compatible with the supremacy of the Parliament in the British system.

This principle assigns priority, in any action, to the respective lower-level administration rather than the higher one, provided that the former's powers are sufficient. It means that the territorial units would be assigned all those duties necessary for dealing with the matter at that level. In fact, the rule embedded in the second paragraph of the article A of the Treaty stating that 'the decisions shall be taken at level as close as possible to the citizens' is an indicator of the importance given to territorialization within the Union.

The principle of subsidiarity as a guarantee for democracy in general, as well as regional and local democracy, is formulated by the article 3/B of the Maastricht Treaty as the following: "In the area which do not form part of its exclusive competence, the community shall only act, in accordance with the principle of subsidiarity, in so far as the purposes of the measures under consideration can not be adequately achieved at the member-state level, and hence, because of their scope or effect, can be better achieved by the Community."

The principle of subsidiarity ensures the respect for the autonomy of local self-government, not only through "positive obligations" (granting sufficient resources), but also through "negative obligations", in other words, through non-intervention by the central authorities. It provides an appropriate criterion for a vertical allocation of powers from national or regional level right down to local authorities and citizens.(16)

The Socialist International Conference of Mayors that was convened in Bologna recently defined the subsidiarity as decentralization of power and of the functions and the availability of financial resources to put the principle into practice.(17)

## Contributions of the Council of Europe

Standing conference of Local and Regional Authorities of Europe (CLRAE), recently named as the Congress of Local and Regional Authorities of Europe, has acted as a consultative organ representing both local and regional authorities for the last five decades. The Congress tries to ensure the participation of local and regional authorities in the realization of the ideal of an integrated Europe, as well as their representation and active involvement in the work of the Council of Europe. To promote local and regional autonomy and to lead support to local democracy which is gradually being restored in the countries of central and eastern Europe are among the goals of the Council.

Trends towards further decentralization and more local autonomy in no way imply the evaporation of sovereign state, even though its role will continue to diminish and will considerably change in character. The council of Europe, while aspiring for the unity of Europe and for the relaxation of borders as obstacles to the free movement of capital, people, goods and information vigorously opposed to the resurgence of intolerance and xenophobia at any level whatsoever.

There is no contradiction inherent in a movement towards centralization in some policy areas and towards decentralization in some other. The two phenomena complement each other and form two sides of the same process of European integration that is both democratic and respectful of diversity. However, it is certain that broader Europe will base itself as much on the sovereign states themselves as on their territorial sub-units.

The basic philosophy of the Council of Europe regarding local authorities is that "the state of local and regional democracy in a given state is an integral part of the evolution of the domestic reforms achieved in that country, as well as a crucial yardstick to monitor that applicant states or member states actually comply with Council of Europe's prerequisites in line with its fundamental values". (18)

## European Charter of Local Self Government

As stated above, territorial authorities have an important role to play an achieving a greater unity among European states. The right of the citizens to participate in the conduct of public affairs at local level is one of the important democratic values constituting the common heritage. Therefore, the reconstruction and broadening of Europe based on the principles of democracy and decentralization of powers require the safeguarding and reinforcement of local autonomy in different European countries.

In order to achieve this end, the Council of Europe adopted in 1985, the European Charter of Local Self-Government. Its aim is "to offset the lack of joint European standards to protect and further develop the rights and fundamental freedoms of local authorities, which represent the level closest to the citizens, enabling them to participate effectively in taking the decisions which affect their everyday environment". (19)

According to this important international legal instrument, the essential elements of local autonomy are based on the following principles:

## The scope of the Autonomy

- Local authorities will have the right and ability to regulate and manage a substantial share of public affairs under their own responsibility and in the interests of local population (art.3)
- These powers shall be exercised through the local councils to be elected by the people.
- They shall have full discretion to exercise their initiatives with regard to any matter which is not excluded from their competence nor assigned to any other authority (the rule of general competence).
- Public responsibilities shall generally be exercised, in preference, by those authorities which are closest to the citizen (the principle of subsidiarity).
- They shall be consulted insofar as possible for all matters which concern them directly.

## Control over Local Authorities

Any administrative supervision of their activities shall aim only at ensuring compliance with the law and constitutional principles (control of legality). Expediency control is unacceptable. The intervention of the supervising authority shall be kept in proportion to the importance of the interests which is intended to protect (art.5). The Charter is not clear whether the central supervision be a kind of control of a priori or a posteriori nature.

## Financial Autonomy

Another important element of local autonomy as underlined by the Charter concern financial resources. According to this principle, local authorities shall be entitled adequate financial resources of their own of which they will be able to fix the rate, and the provision of grants from the center will not remove the basic freedom of local authorities to exercise policy discretion within their jurisdictions (art.9).

## Cooperation

Autonomous local authorities shall freely cooperate with each other, form consortia with other local authorities to carry out tasks of common interest. To cooperate with their counterparts in other states and to belong to an international association of local authorities constitute another element of local autonomy as understood by the Charter (art.10). According to this important international legal instrument, the essential elements of local autonomy are based on the following principles:

## The scope of the Autonomy

Local authorities will have the right and ability to regulate and manage a substantial share of public affairs under their own responsibility and in the interests of local population (art.3) These powers shall be exercised through the local councils to be elected by the people. They shall have full discretion to exercise their initiatives with regard to any matter which is not excluded from their competence nor assigned to any other authority (the rule of general competence). Public responsibilities shall generally be exercised, in preference, by those authorities which are closest to the citizen (the principle of subsidiarity). They shall be consulted insofar as possible for all matters which concern them directly.

## Control over Local Authorities

Any administrative supervision of their activities shall aim only at ensuring compliance with the law and constitutional principles (control of legality). Expediency control is unacceptable. The intervention of the supervising authority shall be kept in proportion to the importance of the interests which is intended to protect (art.5). The Charter is not clear whether the central supervision be a kind of control of a priori or a posteriori nature.

## Financial Autonomy

Another important element of local autonomy as underlined by the Charter concern financial resources. According to this principle, local authorities shall be entitled adequate financial resources of their own of which they will be able to fix the rate, and the provision of grants from the center will not remove the basic freedom of local authorities to exercise policy discretion within their jurisdictions (art.9).

## Cooperation

Autonomous local authorities shall freely cooperate with each other, form consortia with other local authorities to carry out tasks of common interest. To cooperate with their counterparts in other states and to belong to an international association of local authorities constitute another element of local autonomy as understood by the Charter (art.10).

## Legal Protection

Finally comes the legal protection of local self-government, according to which they shall have the right to a judicial remedy in order to secure free exercise of their powers. Out of 39 member states, 21 have so far ratified the Charter and 7 states have simply signed and the remaining 10 states have not yet signed. Major European powers like France, United Kingdom, Switzerland and Belgium have their own domestic constitutional and political reasons for not to have sign or ratify the Charter of Local Self-Government, although in most of these countries, freedoms and rights of local authorities are respected properly.

The Charter does not provide for an institutional system for the implementation of its provisions. Monitoring is carried out by means of the separate but complementary supervisory systems: 1) Ex-officio supervision by a working group of the Congress, Council's advisory organ, and 2) Supervision on request.

## The Concept of Local Autonomy

The concept of local autonomy does not have any clear definition. Rather there are descriptions of the elements constituting its substance. For instance, the Constitution of Japan is one of the few constitutions using the concept of local autonomy in its article 92. The Constitution requires that regulations concerning local authorities by fixed by law "in accordance with the principle of local autonomy" a) An assembly and a chief executive to be elected by the residents, b) the right to manage property, affairs and administration, and c) to enact their own regulations within the law are regarded as the main components of the concept of local autonomy. Similarly, the Socialist International during its Conference of Mayors that was convened in Bologna in 1995, summarized the basic principles of local autonomy as the followings:

a) "The right to political innovation above the strict uniformity of state legislation.

b) The recognition of the ability to co-ordinate different administrations and public enterprises to enable them to apply policies in the city which integrate and unite.

c) The possibility to assume responsibilities and functions in sectors which are traditionally non local but are fundamental today (economic promotion and employment, justice and security, international participation).

d) The right to demand from the state the necessary legislation and financial means to be able to provide the social services demanded of local governments in areas such as health, education, environment, the fight against poverty, housing and public transport.

e) The recognition of the principle of financial autonomy as an essential element of local autonomy". (20)


## International Union of Local Authorities (IULA)

Almost the same principles of the European Charter of Local Self-Government have been adopted as a base of a World-wide Declaration of Self-Government by 27 the World Congress of the IULA, in its meeting in Rio de Janeiro, in September 1985, just a few months after its approval in June 1985 by the Committee of the Ministers. The Declaration of the IULA referred to the article 21 of the Universal Declaration of Human Rights, stating that "the will of the people is the basis of the authority of the government".

## Regionalization

Steps towards greater decentralization continues to be taken in western European countries, exemplified as the regionalization of the state structures, either in administrative or in political terms. France, Italy and Spain are the examples of the countries which have succeeded to restructure their systems during the last two decades to have elected regional councils having more or less autonomy in the administration of their own affairs. None of these countries opted for the change of their system from a unitary to a federal one, although it was stated that "French system was the most federalist of the unitary systems, and the Spanish the most unitary of the federal systems."

Only Belgium joined the family of the federal states like Germany and Switzerland. In view of the increasing interest in regionalization, the Congress of Local and Regional Authorities of the Council of Europe adopted a resolution in its Third Session in July 1996, to charge the Special Working Group to finalize in 1996-1997 the text of a European Charter of Regional Autonomy on the same lines as the text of the Charter of Local self-government. According to the preliminary draft which was approved by the Congress, regional Authorities are considered as integral components of the states, as witnesses of the diversity of Europe contributing to the enrichment of its culture.

The Charter does not aim to realize the goals which are incompatible with the principles of local autonomy embedded in the Charter of Local self-government. The Draft Charter is particularly insisting that the recognition of regional phenomenon could not constitute for the regions an occasion to threaten the loyalty towards the state or to harm its sovereignty and territorial integrity.(21)

Regional autonomy is defined there as the right and the effective ability of the largest territorial communities in each state, having elected organs, situated between the state and local authorities and possessing either the concessions of self-government (administrative), or the concessions of a state (political) and to be in charge, under their own responsibility and in the interest of their population, with an important share of the public affairs, primarily in order to ensure regional sustainable development.

The Charter is not imposing a choice for a federal system. But it leaves that open to the discretion of each state, emphasizing that the scope of regional autonomy shall be determined by the internal legislation of the states.

On the occasion of the 50th. anniversary of the United Nations, the Swiss Peace Foundation organized an international conference in Basel, Switzerland in September 1995, which ended up with a Charter of Basel. This Charter advocates for federalist solutions to growing number of armed conflicts which threaten more than a fourth of all states in the world. Particularly, the articles 4,5,6 and 7 are of special importance for the relations of the globalization and territorial autonomy:

a) Both the granting and the refusal of self-determination can endanger a state. Therefore new forms of conflict-settling must be found, if both aims are to be brought to agreement.

b) The protection of human rights and of minorities as well as the people's right of self-determination can no longer be regarded as an internal affair of states.

c) That realization of self-determination does not result per se in the creation of a state. Forms of local and regional autonomy must be realized which are compatible with the cultural, linguistic or religious identity of minorities and which allow the realization of self-determination that does not require the creation of new states.

d) The scope of the international law must be further developed in order to comprehend peoples' right to implement democratic principles and the rule of law, including internationally guar- anteed rights to autonomy, participation and subsidiarity.

## Habitat Meetings

The Istanbul Declaration of Habitat II on Human Settlements, that was adopted in June 14, 1996 in Istanbul, recognized local authorities as the closest and essential partners in the decentralization through democratic local authorities. The position of local authorities has to be promoted and works to strengthen their financial and institutional capacities have to be increased, ensuring at the same time their transparency, accountability and responsiveness. Although there was no clear reference to the concept of local autonomy in the text, emphasis on decentralization can be regarded as one of its indicators.

On the other hand, the Habitat Agenda, appeals to governments 'to review and revise legislation to increase local autonomy, and participation in decision-making, implementation, and resource mobilization'. It emphasizes at the same time, the importance of increasing global competitiveness that metropolitan areas should possess. (22) It is not surprising to underline that neither the Vancouver Declaration on Human Settlements (1976), nor the Vancouver Action Plan had any reference to local autonomy and the role of local authorities.

## Concluding Remarks

European countries have realized outstanding achievements in local democracy. The nations joined the competition much later have a chance to examine the successes and the factors underlying the successes of these countries and not to repeat their mistakes. There are important lessons to be taken from the experiences that were witnessed by the western European countries in the field of local democracy during recent years. It is useful to touch upon several of them:

1) Almost all, except few, are determined to reduce the number of their communes. They try to encourage smaller units to unite among themselves in order to form larger units (Council of Europe, The Size of Municipalities, Efficiency and Citizen Participation, Local and Regional Authorities in Europe, No:56, Strasbourg 1995). In Germany, for instance, the number of municipalities has been reduced from 24386 in 1966 to 8501 in 1980. In Japan, similarly, this number decreased from 10000 to 3500, during the last several decades. Although it is assumed that the process of formation of municipalities itself contributes to the progress of participatory democracy, this is not, certainly an automatic and spontaneous phenomenon.

2) The principle of subsidiarity is being largely accepted and put into practice. Thus, central authorities are becoming more relaxed, as they transfer some of their responsibilities to lower-level units. (23)

3) Although there are shortcomings in providing local authorities with resources in proportion to their functions, the number of taxes which local authorities can use independently and fix their rate themselves increases gradually. To have more or fewer independent resources is regarded as a symbol of local autonomy.

4) Central government is gradually abandoning its functional position as a higher-level authority to exercise tutelage control over local authorities, but it is becoming more a co-operating institution guiding and encouraging them.

5) Supervisory (tutelage) powers of the central government are being transformed to a kind of control which consists of checking the conformity of the action or decision with the law, far from being a control of the goals of the action in question or from the conformity with the public interest (expediency control). Ex post supervision is gradually replacing ex ante control and supervision. All kinds of supervision are left to judiciary to decide, upon.

6) In some countries with traditionally centralized systems, governors are no longer the chief executive of the provincial local authorities. This position is held by the President of the General Council (President du Conseil Général) elected from among its members.

7) In order to prevent local autonomy being transformed into a kind of irresponsibility and corruption, principles like auto-control, responsiveness, transparency and accountability are being put into force in an effective and democratic way.

8) New status is being given to some regions, varying between administrative decentralization and political decentralization, taking into account the characteristics of socio-cultural and economic structures, and on the condition of providing some sort of guarantee by the constitutions for national unity and territorial integrity. Especially Spain, Italy and France constitute the example of countries having these experiences. (24) These developments are also an indication of the narrowing down of the difference between the administrative and political decentralization.

9) In order to make the local people benefit fully from the public services, administrative mechanisms aimed at

coordinating the services of the state at local and regional levels, are being developed. Deconcentration in the performance of the state functions is used extensively together with decentralization. In other words, the administration of the territories is realized through a combination of these two styles of governance in varying degrees.

10) Participation channels are becoming widespread in order to enable the people to take part more effectively and more intensively in decision-making at the local level.

11) Finally, as a result of global transformation, local governments attempt to privatize most of their traditional public services and enterprises to private firms and other organizations. (25)

## Notes

1. Charles Oman, Globalization and Regionalisation: The Challenge for Developing Countries,

OECD, Development Center Studies, Paris, 1994, 27.

2.Oman, op. cit, 33.

3. James, N. Rosenau, "The Dynamics of Globalization: Toward an Operational Formulation", paper presented to the Annual Meeting of the International Studies Association, San Diego, April 18, 1996.

4. Massimo Balducci, "Local Self-Government in Europe: The Charter as a Democratic Mecha-

nism to Promote Subsidiarity", Copenhagen Conference on the Occasion of the Tenth Anni-

versary of the European Charter of Local Self-Government, Council of Europe, 17-18 April

1996, Copenhagen.

5. M.Balducci, op. cit., 16.

6. Jacques Rupnik (ed.), Le déchirement des Nations, ed. Seuil, Paris, 1993, 17.

7. Çağlar Keyder and Ayşe Öncü, İstanbul and the Concept of World Cities, Friedrich Ebert

Stiftung, Istanbul, 1993, 11.

8. Keyder and Öncü, op. cit. 37 Raimondo Strassoldo, "Globalism and Localism: Theoratical Reflections and Some Evidence" in Zdravko Mlinar (ed.), Globalization and Territorial Identities, Avebury, Aldershot, 1992, 35-39.

10. Bruce Stokes, Helping Ourselves: Local Solutions to Global Problems, Norton, N.Y. 1981

11. Rénaud Dehousse, "Regional Autonomy and European Integration: The Lessons of Maastricht", Régions d'Europe, 6/1982, 333-338

12. European Parliament, Working Party I: European Union and Local Autonomy, Report by Pasqual Managall, First European Parliament-EC Local Authorities Conference, 1 March 1994, Brussels.

13. European Parliament, Directorate General for Research, The Powers of Local and Regional

Authorities and their Role in the European Union, Regional Policy Services W4,1993.

14. Jean Labasse, L'Europe des Régions, Flammarion, Paris, 1991.

15. Gérard Marcou, "Principe de Subsidiarité, Constitution Française et Décentralisation", Jean-

Décentralisation, Datar, Ed. DeClaude Némery et Serge Wachter (eds.), Entre l'Europe et

l'Aube, Paris, 1993, 88.

16. Lucien Vandelli, "The Effects of Regionalization of Local Autonomy and the Principle of

Subsidiarity", Council of Europe, Regionalization in Europe: Evaluation and Perspectives,

Strasbourg, 1994, 159-168.

17. Socialist International, The Urban Face of Socialism, Socialist International Conference of

Mayors, 28-29 January 1995, Bologna, Italy, 71.

18. Alexander Tchernoff, Report to the Congress, 11 June 1996, G(3)2,5.

19. Council of Europe, Memorandum on the European Charter of Local Self-Government and its System of Implementation, Strasbourg, 4 September 1996, CG/GT/CEAL (31)1

20. Socialist International, The Urban Face of Socialism, Socialist International Conference of

Mayors, 28-29 January 1995, Bologna, Italy, 72-73.

21. Council of Europe, Projet de Résolution sur la Charte Européenne de l'Autonomie Régionale, Troisiéme Session, Strasbourg. 2-4 Jule 1996, CPP(3)3, Résolution, le 20 Mai 1996

22. UNCHS, the Habitat Agenda: Goals and Principles, Commitments and Global Plan of Ac-

tion,3 July 1996.

23. Alain Delcamp, "Principe de Subsidiarité et Décentralisation", Revue Française de Droit

Constitutionnel, Vol.23, 1995, 609-624

24. Antoni Kuklinsi, "Towards a New Spatial Order in Europe", European Spatial Policy, 1/1,

1994, 73-75

25. Robert J. Bennett(ed.), Local Government and Market Decentralisation, United Nations University, Tokyo, 1994; and Robert J. Bennett (ed.), Local Government in the New Europe, Belhaven Press, London, 1993

## Bibliograpy

- Alain Delcamp, "Principe de Subsidiarité et Décentralisation", Revue Française de Droit Constitutionnel, Vol.23, 1995, 609-624.

- Alexander Tchernoff, Report to the Congress, 11 June 1996, G(3)2,5)

- Antoni Kuklinski, "Towards a New Spatial Order in Europe", European Spatial Policy, 1/1, 1994, 73-75.

- Aslanoğlu, Rana, "Globallesme ve Dünya Kenti", Toplum ve Bilim ,69 Bahar, 1996 108-126.

- Barrie, Axford., The Global System: Economies Politics and Culture, Polity, London, 1995.

- Brottehie, J. et al. (eds.) Cities in Competition: Productive and Sustainable Cities for the 21st

- Century, Logman, London, 1995.

- Bruce Stokes, Helping Ourselves:Local Solutions to Global Problems, Norton, N.Y.1981.

- Charles Oman, "Globalization and Regionalisation: The Challenge for Developing Countries",

- OECD, Development Center Studies, Paris, 1994, 27.

- Council of Europe, Memorandum on the European Charter of Local Self-Government and its System of Implementation, Strasbourg, 4 September 1996, CG/GT/CEAL (31)1.

- Council of Europe, Projet de Résolution sur la Charte Européenne de l'Autonomie Régionale, Troisiéme Session, Strasbourg. 2-4 Jule 1996, CPP(3)3, Résolution, le 20 Mai 1996.

- Çağlar Keyder and Ayşe Öncü, İstanbul and the Concept of World Cities, Friedrich Ebert Stiftung, Istanbul, 1993, 11.

- European Parliament, Working Party I:" European Union and Local Autonomy", Report by Pasqual Maragall, First European Parliament-EC Local Authorities Conference, 1 March 1994, Brussels European Parliament, Directorate General for Research, "The Powers of Local and Regional Authorities and their Role in the European Union", Regional Policy Services W4,1993

- Featherstone, M, S.Lash and R.Robertson (eds.), Global Modernities, Sage, London, 1995 Gérard Marcou, "Principe de Subsidiarité,

Constitution Française et Décentralisation", Jean-Claude Némery et Serge Wachter (eds.), Entre l'Europe et la Décentralisation, Datar, Ed. De l'Aube, Paris, 1993,88.

- Jacques Rupnik (ed.), Le déchirement des Nations, ed. Seuil, Paris, 1993, 17.

- James, N. Rosenau, "The Dynamics of Globalization: Toward an Operational Formulation", paper presented to the Annual Meeting of the International Studies Association, San Diego, April 18, 1996.

- Jean Labasse, L'Europe des Régions, Flammarion, Paris, 1991.

- Johnston, R.J, P. Taylor and M. Watts (eds.), Geographies of Global Change: Re-mapping the World in the Late Twentieth Century, Basic Blackwell, Oxford, 1995.

- Lucien Vandelli, "The Effects of Regionalization of Local Autonomy and the Principle of Subsidiarity", Council of Europe, Regionalization in Europe: Evaluation and Perspectives, Strasbourg, 1994, 159-168.

- Massimo Balducci, "Local Self-Government in Europe: The Charter as a Democratic Mechanism to Promote Subsidiarity", Copenhagen Conference on the Occasion of the Tenth Anniversary of the European Charter of Local Self-Government, Council of Europe, 17-18 April 1996, Copenhagen.

- O'Brian, R., Global Financial Interdependence; The End of Geography, Pinter, London, 1992.

- Raimondo Strassoldo, "Globalism and Localism: Theoratical Reflections and Some Evidence" in Zdravko Mlinar (ed.), Globalization and Territorial Identities, Avebury, Aldershot, 1992,35- 39.

- Rénaud Dehousse, "Regional Autonomy and European Integration: The Lessons of Maastricht",Régions d'Europe, 6/1982, 333- 338.

- Robert J. Bennett (ed.), Local Government and Market Decentralisation, United Nations University, Tokyo, 1994.

- Robert J. Bennett (ed.), Local Government in the New Europe, Belhaven Press, London, 1993.

- Slater, Robert O., Barry M.Schutz, and Steven R.Dorr (eds.), Global Transformation and the Third World, Lyenne Rienner Pub., Boolder, 1993.
- Socialist International, The Urban Face of Socialism,Socialist International Conference of Mayors, 28-29 January 1995, Bologna, Italy.
- UNCHS, the Habitat Agenda: Goals and Principles, Commitments and Global Plan of Action, 3 July 1996.

# EUROPEAN UNION AND TURKEY

# Turkey and the European Union*

## Introduction: On the State, Society and Constitutional Setting

Turkish Republic has been proclaimed in 1923. Turkey, according to its Constitution is a democratic, secular and social state governed by the rule of law, respectful for human rights. With its territory and nation, the State is an indivisible entity. Its capital is Ankara. In its flag appears a white crescent and star on a red background. The first three articles expressed above, can not be amended; even their amendment can not be proposed. The total population is about 76 million and 76 percent of the population, in other words, more than three fourths live in urban centers.

Territorially, it is divided into 81 provinces, on the basis of the geographical conditions and the requirements of public services. There are still striking social and economic disparities among geographical regions, particularly between the regions in the West and those in the East.

The legislative body is the Turkish Grand National Assembly (TBMM) which is composed of 550 members of the Parliament. National elections take place every five years, on the basis of proportional representation system, and under the supervision of a Supreme Election Council, composed of

*   Uğur Ömür Gönülşen and Uğur Sadioğlu (eds.), *Workshop on Local Governance and Democracy in Europe and Turkey*, 21-22 March 2013, Hacettepe University, Türkiye Belediyeler Birliği, Ankara, 2015, pp.15-31.

the judges. Enactment of laws is under the exclusive competence of the National Parliament. However, for the sake of acceleration of decisions of executive character, the Parliament may authorize the Council of Ministers to enact decrees having force of law.

International conventions or treaties are ratified by the Parliament with a law. In case there is a contradiction between the rules of a convention and a national law, the first will have the priority, provided that the issue at stake is concerned with fundamental human rights and freedoms.

Means of control available to the Parliament to exercise over the Executive are interpellation and parliamentary investigations. President of the Republic used to be elected by the Parliament up to recently from among its members. After the referendum taken place in 2010 regarding constitutional amendments, presidential elections will be effectuated directly by the voters from now on. Executive power is exercised by the President of the Republic and the Council of Ministers. Administration, in other words, the executive branch functions in accordance with the principles of centralization and decentralization. All acts and actions of the Administration are subject to judicial review. The territory of the country is divided into the provinces on the basis of geographical conditions and the requirements of the public services. The field administration of the State is organized in accordance with the principle of deconcentration. On the other hand, the Constitutional Court, the High Court of Appeals, the Council of State and the Military High Court of Appeals are basic components of the judicial machinery in addition to lower level courts.

Local authorities which are established to function in restricted local communities and which are in charge of limited competences are legal entities of local democracy. There are three types of local authorities in Turkey: a) Municipalities (2950), b) Provincial Local Governments (81), c) and the Village Administrations (36.000). Turkish local authorities are units of administrative decentralization, but not those of political decentralization. The principle of subsidiarity is not mentioned in the Constitution. However, the fact that the Article 127 of the Constitution stipulates that the relationships between the State and local authorities will be arranged in accordance with the principle of decentralization, may mean that the principle of subsidiarity is indirectly adopted there.

The State exercises an administrative control and supervision over local authorities, as distinct from hierarchical control, under the following conditions: a) in order to ensure the performing public services, b) securing uniform public services, c) meeting local needs in an appropriate manner, and finally, d) safeguarding the public interest. The last sentence gives the impression that the State may exercise a control of expediency over local authorities, in addition to legality control.

The Minister of the Interior has the power to suspend the elected organs of local authorities, pending judgment, in case an investigation or a prosecution is initiated against them in connection to their duties. Metropolitan municipalities can be established in large urban centers. All local authorities are entitled to get financial resources commensurate with the importance of their duties.

Local authorities at the regional level do not exist in Turkey. However, there are regional deconcentrated agencies established with a view to perform public services of regional character efficiently. There are also de facto geographical regions with no powers of decision-making. Regional development agencies are established in accordance with the rules of the European Union in order to reduce regional disparities with a competitive vision. Finally, local authorities are empowered to form region-wide unions to carry out their duties more efficiently.

## A Brief History of the Relationships between Turkey and the EU

The Relations between Turkey and the European Union date back to 1959. Turkey first applied for Associate Membership to the European Economic Community. The EEC, as response to Turkey's application, suggested the establishment of an association until Turkey's circumstances permit its accession. The negotiations resulted in the signature of the Ankara Agreement creating an Association between the Republic of Turkey and the European Economic Community on 12 September 1963. The Ankara Agreement is still the strongest legal basis of Turkey-EU relations.

The Additional Protocol of 13 November 1970 set out how the Customs Union should be established. It provided that the EEC would abolish tariff and quantitative barriers to its imports from Turkey upon the entry into force of the Protocol, whereas Turkey would do the same in accordance with a timetable containing two calendars set for 12 and 20 years.

Turkey applied for full membership in 1987. In the Commission's Opinion of Turkey's application for full membership, it was basically underlined that Turkey was eligible for membership. It was also mentioned that Turkey's accession was prevented equally by the EC's own situation on the eve of the Single Market's Completion which prevented the consideration of further enlargement. It went on to underpin the need for a comprehensive cooperation programme aiming at facilitating the integration of the two sides and added that the Customs Union should be completed in 1995 as envisaged.

Association Council adopted its decision on the completion of the Customs Union between Turkey and the EU in industrial and processed agricultural goods. The Association Council decision on the finalization of the Customs Union between Turkey and the European Union lays down the functioning rules of Custom's Union, which has been in force since 1996.

The Customs Union envisaged in the above-mentioned decision is not only a simple abolishment of customs duties and the duties having equivalent effect and adaptation to the Common Customs Tariff of the EU. It also entails abolishment of all disruptive mechanisms that may cause unfair advantage over the other side. This understanding, from the perspective of Turkey, has brought additional obligations for harmonization in the field of competition, state aids, monopolies, intellectual and industrial property rights and common trade policy.

In this connection, harmonization to Community trade policy and preferential trade agreements concluded with third countries. For instance, since 1996, Turkey has been negotiating on the basis of mutual benefit, free trade agreements with the third countries that are similar to the preferential trade agreements concluded by the European Union. At present, free trade agreements have been signed with 18 countries (EFTA, Israel, Macedonia, Croatia, Bosna-Herzegovina, Palestine, Tunisia, Morocco, Syria, Egypt, Albania, Georgia, Montenegro, Serbia, Chile, Jordan, Lebanon, Mauritius). Secondly, technical barriers to the trade of industrial products have been abolished. At present, more than 90 percent of the technical legislation has been harmonized. Thirdly, harmonization of competition policy and the intellectual property rights started. Finally, attempts have been made to ensure harmonization to the Community Customs Legislation. In this framework, harmonization of the rules in the following fields has been achieved: origin, customs value, goods entering customs union territory, customs declaration, release for free circulation, customs regimes with economic impact, circulation of goods, customs debts, right to reclaim.

Apart from the positive contributions of the Customs Union, it has also some challenges. Problems mostly stems from the fact that unlike the other candidate countries, Turkey established the Customs Union before the membership. As Turkey does not have the membership status, it can not participate in the decision-making mechanism of the EU. Turkey is bound with EU Acquis that it is not involved in the adoption process. The best permanent solution would be the EU membership as soon as possible.

Turkey was granted the status of candidate country in December 1999 in the Helsinki meeting of the European Council. The European Council welcomed positive developments in Turkey as noted in the Commission's 1999 Progress Report. It was underlined that Turkey is a candidate state destined to join the Union on the basis of the same criteria as applied to other candidate states. All the Works done under the framework of Accession Partnerships Document which were combined with National Programmes of Turkey, brought Turkey to the accession negotiations.

Finally, on 17 December 2004, European Council concluded that Turkey fulfils the Copenhagen political criteria and the European Union will open accession negotiations to Turkey without delay.

On 3rd October 2005, negotiations are opened with the First Intergovernmental Accession Conference between Turkey and EU.

## Current State of Turkey's Membership Adventure: Achievements and Challenges

The negotiations are opened on the basis that Turkey sufficiently meets the political criteria set by the Copenhagen European Council in 1993. The framework for negotiations has also been agreed by the Council on the basis of a proposal by the European Commission.

During the preparatory analytical phase, the level of preparedness to start negotiations on individual chapters was assessed on the basis of screening reports. Shortly after the launching the accession negotiations, Screening Process started with a meeting on the Chapter "Science and Research" in 2005. Screening meetings were completed for all negotiation chapters in 2006.

So far 13 negotiation chapters out of 33 have been opened. One was provisionally closed. That was the Chapter on Science and Technology. This is not the pace Turkey would like to move forward. There is no doubt that every chapter that is opened brings Turkey one more step closer to the EU standards. However, developments especially since December 2006 proved that political issues (and double standards) tend to dominate entire issues. Most of these external factors are independent of the technical process.

A) Currently only 13 chapters have been opened to negotiations:

1. Science and Research (provisionally closed)
2. Free Movement of Capital
3. Company Law
4. Intellectual Property Law
5. Information Society and Media
6. Statistics
7. Enterprise and Industrial Policy
8. Trans-European Networks

9. Consumer and Health Protection

10. Financial Control

11. Taxation

12. Environment

13. Food Safety, Veterinary and Phytosanitary Policy.

B) The following 8 chapters were suspended due to the reflection of the Cyprus Problem on the negotiation process.

1. Free Movement of Goods

2. Right of Establishment and Freedom to Provide Services

3. Financial services

4. Agriculture and Rural development

5. Fisheries

6. Transport Policy

7. Customs Union

8. External Relations

C) Because of the unilateral demands of Southern Greek Cypriot Administration, the following 6 chapters are completely blocked. We must remember that in a divided county such as Cyprus, Southern Cyprus had been accepted as a member to the EU, without waiting the resolving the Cyprus issue, consequently disregarding the rights of the Cypriots living in the North of the Island.

1. Free Movement of Workers

2. Judiciary and Fundamental Rights

3. Justice, Freedom and Security

4. Education and Culture

5. Energy

6. Foreign Security and Defence Policy.

D) Finally, France is blocking the opening of the following 5 chapters because of their "direct bearing on full membership "which is against the unanimously taken deci-sion of the EU Council of Ministers of 3 October 2005.

1. Agriculture and Rural Development

2. Economic and Monetary Policy

3. Regional Policy and Coordination of Structural Instru-ments

4. Financial and Budgetary Provisions

5. Institutions.

On the Cyprus issue, it is expected that the Member States of the European Union would act in full awareness of their commitments. The EU Council conclusions of 26 April 2004, regarding the lifting the isolations have not yet been imple-mented. Even the Direct Trade Regulation has not been ad-opted. Surely, neither the EU credibility nor the relations be-tween Turkey and the European Union can be held hostage to a single member, that is Cyprus, and its narrow definition of selfish interest. For instance, blocking the "Energy Chapter" because of one country's political ambitions and unilateral de-mands on a completely different topic is an irrational behav-ior. Similarly, "Education and Culture" chapter is also blocked for non-Acquis reasons.

It is evident that Turkey's accession process necessitates mu-tual determination and consistency. There is no doubt that ne-gotiation process is a rocky road where some particular diffi-culties had been experienced by all member states in the past. However, situation of Turkey differs compared to the past can-didate countries, taking into consideration that no other coun-try has so far had more than half of the negotiation chapters blocked for purely political reasons which have nothing to do with their content. Every candidate country has the right to expect from the EU a fair approach on the basis of merit in fulfilling the membership criteria. It is known that none of the previous negotiations had a purely technical character; but no one can easily contest that none of them had been under the impact of political factors to the extent that Turkey's accession process has been until now.

Turkey regards the EU accession process as the most important modernization project after the proclamation of the Republic in 1923 by Mustafa Kemal Atatürk and his friends. The process of EU accession has always been an incentive for reforms. Democratic reforms are more than the preconditions and requirements of the EU membership. Beyond satisfying the European Union, Turkey believes that her people deserve to live in prosperity and in much better standards.

Generally speaking, EU's enlargement policy and its objective of being a global actor have gained utmost importance particularly after the Lisbon Treaty. In this respect, the accession process is a real opportunity for both sides: For Turkey, it is an opportunity to use its immense dynamics for the transformation of the country; and for the EU, it is an opportunity to increase its political and economic power in a more complex global system. This is an irreversible process at the end of which both Turkey and the EU will win as has been the case since the beginning of the negotiations.

The EU, hiding behind the clause of solidarity among member states, has not played a constructive role in encouraging the Greek Cypriots for a comprehensive solution in Cyprus, recognizing the existence of two different communities in the Island, namely Turks and Greeks. There might be other somewhat domestic reasons such as rising islamophobia, the rise of the right-wing considerations, and economic fears, and incertitude. This leads to an overall myopia on the crucial contributions that Turkey makes to Europe now and will make in the future. As to the arguments that Turkey is too Muslim, it has been known from the very beginning of the negotiations and it is not a new phenomenon. However, the rise of xenophobia, racism, prejudices against certain religions and identities to-day threaten humanity in many ways. Turkey, as an EU member would contribute to bringing the EU closer to the Caucasus, Central Asia and the Middle East with its rich historical and cultural heritage.

## Significant Advantages of Full Membership for EU and Turkey

Yet, there are several important reasons why Turkey's application for full membership should be accepted. 1) The first is of economic nature. A young and dynamic Turkey will bring new energy to the tired economies of the EU. As expressed in Turkey's 2011 Progress Report, the EU-Turkey Customs Union continues to boost bilateral trade between the EU and Turkey, which exceeded 100 billion Euro in 2010. 2) Secondly, Turkey is a leading world producer and net exporter of fruits and vegetables with a production level corresponding to 60 percent of that in the EU. About half of Turkey's land area is devoted to agriculture. She is also one of the richest countries in biodiversity, hosting 75 percent of all plant species in Europe. Turkey's accession will double EU's biodiversity and significantly contribute to Europe's agricultural and environmental sustainability. 3) Thirdly, one of Turkey's biggest assets is its educated, young and dynamic human capital. The current average age is 28 years. By contrast, the West European population growth is stable or negative. Turkey's young, well-educated and highly skilled labor force can be a remedy for the structural deficiencies of the EU stemming its aging population. 4) The fourth advantage of having Turkey as full member is her role in securing reliable and affordable energy supplies. She can play a key role in the diversification of energy supply routes to Europe. Thanks to its unique location, Turkey is Europe's energy corridor for central Eurasian, Caucasian, and Caspian oil and gas resources. Over 70 percent of the crude oil and natural gas reserves or the world are located in Russia, the Caspian and Middle East regions surrounding Turkey. 5) Finally, as a secular democracy taken hold within a predominantly Muslim population, the particularity of Turkey underlines the compatibility of Islam and democratic values. Turkey's full membership would create a chance to put an end to the impression that the EU is exclusively a Christian Club. Turkey has also significant potential to help EU in the fight against international terrorism, illegal immigration, trafficking in drugs, arms, even human beings, and criminal activities of all kinds.

Taking these considerations into account, some European leaders would be better advised to develop a forward-looking strategic vision. Europe needs courageous European politicians who will develop a new vision of Turkish-EU relations. What it is expected from the EU is not to show a different approach to Turkey and not to allow some countries with individual cautiousness to hinder the accession process. EU can not be completed without the Turkish full membership. Perhaps it is more important to see that in the EU integration history there is no single country that started negotiations and could not finish the process. It is hoped that Turkey will not be an exception.

## Recent Developments and Privileged Partnership

Privileged partnership is a term which is frequently used in relation with Turkish-EU relations and repeated after since 2004. The aim of the users of this term was to keep Turkey tied up to EU without accepting her as a full member and preventing her taking place at the decision-taking organs at equal status with other member countries. This means that Turkey will be prevented from benefiting the advantages of the full members.

Up to now, privileged partnership is not proposed as the only alternative. But when the full membership negotiations were discussed, all the conditions, exceptions and principles that were put forward by EU were the same with the conditions, restrictions and demands that were mentioned during the discussions and took place in the reports about the privileged partnership. It is obvious that there is a double Standard with regard to Turkey and EU wants to keep Turkey at a different status. But Ankara Agreement which led to Customs Union, in its item 28, says that when the implementation of the Agreement shows that Turkey can realize the obligations arising from the Agreement, the signatory countries will consider the possibility of Turkey's becoming full member.

As a political scientist who has followed Turkey-EU relations for the last 50 years, I have always thought that there is a double standard and a biased evaluation towards Turkey. Can you explain why EU preferred some Eastern European countries, that have recently passed to democracy, rather than Turkey, who, except several short interruptions, had liberal democratic regime for the last 60 years? There is no logical explanation why EU preferred some other countries rather than Turkey in spite of the fact that they were further away from European standards than Turkey in economic and social life. No one can explain why only Turkey had open ended negotiations and some other conditions while other candidates had definite dates for accession. Who can claim that a new candidate is more suitable for full membership than an associate member who has completed the requirements for joining Customs Union many years ago and has realized Customs Union successfully without becoming a full member for years and without using funds that are used by all other members? I can ask a longer list of questions like this; for example, can there be a logical explanation of EU to try to push aside Turkey from the ESDP (European Security and Defense Policy) structures ignoring the fact that Turkey has always been a very active member of NATO for more than half a century and has contributed to every security and defense activity of Europe?

During the last 50 years, Turkey tried to keep up with the economic and social policies of EU. Especially during the globalization and the trend towards the liberalization of imports; contrary to most of the European countries that recommended liberalization to others but continued to protect both their industrial and agricultural sectors, Turkey took liberalization more seriously than those countries and realized it to such an extent that she harmed those two sectors of Turkey. Therefore, I believe that the proposals and the statements of some European leaders, namely Madame Merkel and Mr. Sarkozy are not what Turkey deserves.

Neither those proposals and the statements nor raising the conditions to be met for accession can be explained by the economic recession in Europe because the attitudes of some lea were the same even during the periods without economic recession. What is more, the domestic statements and behaviors of some political leaders and top figures in Europe are in a way brainwashing both their own people and the leaders as well as the citizens of other countries.

Turkey without taking part in decision-making processes carries all the burden of the Customs Union by herself. Turkey is a country that has great potential in many sectors, and if she becomes a full member, she will not only have positive effects on security and stability, but also on economy, foreign policy, culture and many other fields of European Union. Because of the above-mentioned reasons, Turkey rejects Privileged Partnership precisely because it expressly rules out full membership of the EU. Similar models that envisage rather informal relationships with the EU such as Extended Associate Membership or Gradual Integration have not been acceptable by Turkey.

## Concluding Remarks

We cannot say that criticism of EU about Turkey is objective. Most of them originate from domestic political considerations of some member states. And the majority of legal changes they propose are not related with democracy and the welfare of Turkey. They are the changes that will simply serve the benefits or the aims of some European countries. When those proposals are studied carefully, one can easily see that they serve the exploitation of natural resources of Turkey, weakening of the unitary state, exploitation of the minority issues, strengthening the influence of European countries over Turkey, making the implementation of national policies more difficult, and supporting separatist activities in some regions of Turkey directly or indirectly. European Union never criticizes the decrease in investments, they never encourage industrialization and agricultural production. They do this because they have no intention of seeing Turkey as a full member of the European Union. Rather, the members of the EU aim to exploit Turkey and her resources as much as possible by keeping her close to them so that they can have more and more concessions from Turkey.

## Short Bibliography

- Algan, Nesrin and Mengi Ayşegül, "Turkey's Sustainable Develpment Policies in the EU Accession Pprocess", *European Environmental Law Review*, Vol.14, No: 4, April 2005, pp.89-116.
- European Parliament, Report on Turkey's Progress Towards Accession, Committee of Foreign Affairs, Rapporteur Camiel Eurlings, 2006/2118 (INI)
- Hammarberg, Thomas, Commissioner for Human Rights, *Annual Activity Report* 2009, Strasbourg, 14 April 2010.
- Leggewle, Clause, "Privileged Partnership Less Democracy", *Eurozine*, 7.t.2008.

# URBAN TRANSFORMATION

# The Urban Transformation Project of Northern Ankara*

Meltem Yılmaz** and Ruşen Keleş***

## Introduction

The concept of urban transformation is being used in Turkey more frequently during the last several decades. The need to implement upgrading or renovation projects in squatter settlements was the main motive behind it. Although possibilities were provided by various legislation to carry out urban transformation projects in metropolitan cities, economics, social and even political considerations prevented central and local governments until recently from engaging themselves in such endeavors.

The need originates from the pace and patterns of urban development in Turkey, and particularly rural to urban migration. Throughout the second half of the 20th century a rapid urbanization characterized the development process all over the world, including the developing countries. Turkey is one of the countries facing the problems brought about by rapid urbanization mainly due to her structural features. However, urbanization in Turkey had also its own peculiarities.

\*    Erwin Hepperle, Robert Dixon- Gough, *Reinfried* Mansberger, Jenny Paulsson, Franz Reuter, Meltem Yılmaz (eds.), Challenges for *Governance Structures in Urban and Regional Development*, Vdf, ETH, Zurich, 2015, pp.351-362.
\*\*   Hacettepe University/ Faculty of Fine Arts, Ankara, Turkey.
\*\*\*  Ankara University/ Faculty of Political Science, Turkey.

In addition to its features such as its extent, pace and imbalances in the geographical distribution of population and economic activities, Turkey's urbanization manifests itself as an essentially demographic phenomenon, a constant flow of population from rural to urban centers, which caused not by an essentially rapid industrial development that might create extensive employment opportunities in metropolitan centers to justify its pace. Instead, a substantial portion of the population migrating to cities had a chance to begin working in a variety of employments which is called the "informal sector".

The main reasons for rural-urban migration are identified as high population growth, mechanization of the agricultural sector and uneven economic development which have caused disparities among geographical regions and between rural and urban areas. In this respect, while the share of urban population in the total was 25.1 percent in 1960, it rose to 55.4 percent in 1990, and to 76.0 percent in 2013.

Rapid urbanization created numerous bottlenecks in meeting the increased service needs of the migrants as well as those of the existing inhabitants of the cities. These included housing, slum upgrading, urban regeneration transportation, urban infrastructure, environmental protection, public health and education, security, and the like. It was assumed for a long time that most of such unmet needs could be attributed to the imperfections of the market mechanism. Finally, it was realized that uneven income distribution was the main variable causing the crisis and therefore measures of long term had to be taken for their improvement.

Socio-economic marginality seems to be the major reason for huge emergence of squatter settlements in metropolitan centers of Turkey. 50 to 65 percent of the urban population of such cities as Ankara, İstanbul, İzmir still lives in squatter settlements. Despite the fact that squatting was generally regarded a rational action of the homeless poor, attempts have been made to indicate that the expenditures made for building squatter houses were, to a greater extent, a waste on the part of the national economy. If repetitive and sink costs are taken into consideration one could undeniably argue that squatting is not a cheap technique of meeting the housing needs of the poor.

The Dictionary of Town Planning [1] defines "the gece-kondu" (overnight built house) as a dwelling which is constructed without a building licence, in contravention of the building and construction regulations, on the lands owned by public authorities or private individuals, against the will of the landowner, to be used by the poor and lower income families which the State or local authorities are unable to meet their housing needs. These are called elsewhere as "spontaneous", "illegal", "unauthorized" or "uncontrolled" types of dwelling and settlement, and they are, in principle, distinguished from either slums, which are also regarded as non-conventional, or from conventional public or private type of housing.

Slums and squatter houses are the formations which possesses most of the physical and socio-economic qualities attributed to marginal populations. They reflect those characteristics in more pronounced and aggravated measures of magnitude. Although they are often used in the literature interchangeably, the terms of "slums" and "squatter settlements" are entirely different concepts[2].

## Measures taken to upgrade squatter houses and settlements

Up to 1960's, attempts have focused on prevention rather than upgrading because it was assumed that squatting could

---

1   Ruşen Keleş, Kentbilim Terimler Sözlüğü, Imge Pub., Ankara, 1998 (2nd ed.).
2   Ruşen Keleş, Urban Poverty in the Third World: Theoretical Approaches and Policy Options, Institute of Developing Economies, AJİKEN, Tokyo, 1988.

be prevented by strict measures to be implemented by police power of the State and the municipal authorities. The main characteristics of the approaches adopted during the pre-planned period can be summarized as a) the prevention of gecekondu building by providing urban land to be acquired by cities to the homeless, b) the prohibition of the construction of new illegal houses, and c) to legalize the already built ones. During 1960 and 1980, major approaches to the upgrading of squatter settlements have been shaped by the Five Year Developments Plans starting by 1963. The policies implemented in this period aimed at mainly four targets: a) Designating the squatter settlements in the city where upgrading, prevention or demolition works will take place. b) To increase the land stocks of the cities in order to make them powerful enough to help the families to live in decent housing conditions. c) Creation of several funds, one in the control of municipalities and the second at the central government level, to be used for upgrading of squatter settlements and for providing housing credit to build social housing. d) To get the residents of squatter settlements to participate in expenditures incurred to municipalities in connection to such public services as sewerage systems, road construction, water installations, electricity and the like. And finally, e) To demolish illegally built houses.

During the post 1980 period, the fundamental principles adopted by the Law on Gecekondu (1966) did not change substantially. However, new concepts and practices such as the sites and services, and public-private partnership have been added to them. A new Law of 1984 regarding slum upgrading and prevention (No: 2981) provided the transfers of titles, in principle, to the gecekondu owners, if they were built on public lands. The concept of "development and improvement plan" introduced by this law has played a guiding role in transformation of squatter settlements during the following two and a half decades until the beginning of a new stage where municipalities and the Mass Housing Administration (TOKİ) will be cooperating along the lines influenced by past experiences. Other minor steps have also been taken in the direction of upgrading of squatter settlements during the post 1980 period.

## Urban transformation projects for the city of Ankara

A shift was realized by the Metropolitan Municipality of Ankara during the 1990's from the preparation of development and improvement plans to the preparation of urban transformation projects. In this context, Dikmen Valley Project and the Project of Orange Flower Valley have been realized through public-private partnership scheme and through the corporations in connected with the legal personality of the city[3]. The model that was put into effect in connection to the projects initiated by the city of Ankara was called "the consolidation of development right", meaning he amalgamation of existing development rights instituted traditionally on the land parcel basis with those formed on the basis of a project, in order to consolidate them and to redistribute them within the framework of the principle of private-public partnership.

## The transformation project on the northern access to Ankara

The Municipality of Ankara has undertaken to carry out a clearance Project along the highway in the North of the city connecting the center of the city with the Esenboğa Airport that was named as Protocol (VIP) Road. This Project

---

3    Faruk Göksu, "Kentsel Dönüşüm Süreci ve Proje Ortaklıkları" (The Process of Urban Transformation and the Partnership on the basis of Project), Bulletin, Mimarlar Odası Ankara Şubesi Yayını, No:40, May-June, 2006, pp.40-44.

was realized by the enactment of a special law, namely the Urban Transformation Law concerning Northern Access to Ankara of 2004 (No: 5104) and the Law of 2006 (No: 5481), amending the said law. These legislations enabled the City of Ankara to tear down all the gecekondu on both sides of the main road towards the main road to the Airport and to transfer the vacated lands to the municipality to be used according to a new urban design Project to be prepared by the City of Ankara in cooperation with the Mass Housing Administration. It was announced that the Project site which is as large as 3.600.000 square meters, 18.000 units will be built in cooperation with the Mass Housing Administration[4]. In addition to the laws concerning transformation and upgrading of some Ankara squatter settlements during 2006-2006, a more comprehensive law was passed in June 2005 in order to facilitate similar undertakings in other parts of Turkey. This was called the Law on the Protection, Renewal and Utilization of Dilapidated Immobile Historical and Cultural Assets. The aim of the law was to protect, reconstruct, restore, renew the sites of historical and cultural assets, which began to dilapidate, to create districts of housing, shopping, culture, tourism and social amenities and to take measure against the risk of natural disasters. A more recent law was put into force in 2012 (No:6306), while narrowing down the scope of the concept of urban transformation into the renovation of the buildings constructed in disaster prone areas, and enlarging the geographical scope of the transformation undertakings all over Turkeys[5].

4    Ruşen Keleş, (with the assistance of Meltem Yılmaz), "Lessons Learnt from Slum Upgrading and Prevention in Turkey", Report prepared for the United Nations Center for Human Settlements, Nairobi, 2007, p.40.

5    Ruşen Keleş, "Türkiye'de Yerel Yönetimlerde Kentsel Dönüşüm Yönetim Süreci", (The Management of Urban Transformation Project in Turkish Local Authorities), Paper presented to the Symposium on Management of Urban

Recent urban transformation projects which claim to be prepared on the basis of the intentions to develop the culture, social and economic conditions of such areas, are supported not only by local administrations, but also projected and implemented by the Mass Housing Administration (TOKİ) attached to the Office of the Prime Ministry. Urban Transformation Project of the Northern Access of Ankara is one of these projects situated on a land of 1582 hectares and is borders are designated by the abovementioned Law numbered 5104.

Within this Project situated on the Northern Access of Ankara, the road to Esenboğa Airport roughly constitutes the border of the Ankara Metropolitan Municipality. The area on the West of the road remains within the borders of Keçiören District Municipality and the area on the East remains within the borders of Altındağ district Municipality. The whole Project covers an area of 1582 hectares that hosted 10.500 squatter dwellings. The area of the First Stage of the Urban Transformation Project of the Northern Access of Ankara is 324.90 hectares, on which 209.23 hectares belong to private owners and 115.78 hectares to various public authorities and institutions. Although some urban transformation projects were realized previously, like those of Dikmen Valley and Orange Flower Valley, neither the superstructure nor infrastructure work was realized within the urban transformation Project site of Northern access to Ankara. Therefore, this part of the city deteriorated to become the most underdeveloped residential sections of the city. Nevertheless, as the area lies on the highway that connects Ankara to other cities and close to the Esenboğa Airport, it has become an area where important industrial establishment are located.

Transformation in Turkish Local Governments, The Public Administration Institute for Turkey and the Middle East, Ankara, 10-11 December, 2012.

Esenboğa Airport which was put into service in the 1950's increased the importance of the Northern axis of the city. The new Protocol Road starting from the Esenboğa Airport, passing through the district of Pursaklar, Hasköy, Dışkapı and the historical city center called Ulus, continuing along the Atatürk Boulevard, going through the new city center of Kızılay, passing by the compound of Ministries, and running up to Çankaya Presidential Palace. The new location of the Turkish Grand National Assembly also endowed even greater importance to the Northern axis. The construction of a two way highway between the Airport and the city center furthered the significance of the Northern axis. On both sides of the highway appeared illegally constructed squatter settlements. During the process of industrialization which began during the 1970's, establishment in the specialized sectors, like medicine, electronics, furniture, printing, and the like, which needed quick and easy access to the Airport, selected the land on this axis as their place of operation.

Towards the beginnings of the 1980's, the areas had lost its physical attractiveness and its appearance got disfigured. Consequently, it became a must to conduct some work in order to achieve a series of revitalization, rehandling and rehabilitation for the area. A project for this purpose was launched jointly by the Metropolitan Municipality of Ankara and TOKİ and its implementation was started in December 2004. It was planned to demolish the buildings in the area and replace them on a larger land, with 18.000 dwellings, two five-star hotels, cultural buildings, recreational areas, educational and sportive facilities, parks and green areas. As the number of the squatter houses to be demolished is around 10.500, it is decided to carry out the implementation of the Project in two stages, to prevent possible difficulties that may arise. Within this framework, the ownership rights of 115 hectares of land in the area that belonged to public authorities and institutions were transferred to the Metropolitan Municipality of Ankara, free of charge, according to the Law numbered 5104. The remaining land was expropriated in accordance with the agreements separately signed with the other owners of the land, houses, work places and industrial establishments, be them registered or not at the Land Registry.

The agreements signed have it recorded that the entitled parties receive houses or work places in defined square meters that are equivalent to what they owned prior to the implementation and that they receive rental assistance during the construction period to prevent any grievances. Even though the Project will bring some contemporary characteristics to the area in terms of infrastructure and superstructure, it would not be exaggerated to assume that the residents of the area may be regarded as victimized from social and economic perspectives.

The In-site observations demonstrate that the people whose houses were demolished and who are to receive in return an apartment flat complain about the rapidly rising rents in neighboring communities like Mamak due to a rising demand. Against considerably high rents, the symbolic rental assistance they are paid remains insufficient. A further economic difficulty is posed by the prices of the houses constructed by TOKİ for the former land and house owners.

For instance, former squatters, according to agreements they have signed, made an advance payment of 500 TL for a 80 square meter houses located at Karacaören, City of Tebessüm, and committed to pay instalments of 226 TL. /month for the duration of 10 years as principal payment. However, as the agreement signed, this amount increased to 370 TL. / month. In line with the salary increase given to the civil servants as of March 2012. This created financial difficulties for the people of which great majority work for the private sector for quite low levels of remuneration. The people, while they lived in their squatter houses, used to receive a certain amount of heating assistance, but once they moved into their new houses, this assistance was discontinued. Their new houses are hosted by natural gas which brings high-sum invoices to be paid for the heating costs of the new home. On the other hand, the rights of the people who lived in the slum as tenants were not even considered. As the houses were demolished such people had to move out to other districts where rent prices floated at much higher rates. When we review the matter from a socio-cultural perspective, it is observed that the house owners are unhappy and not pleased with the place they are now living at. For example, the people who used to have cordial and strong relationships with their neighbors in their former communities and who were now living at Karacaören (City of Tebessüm) (Smiling City), stated that they are experiencing difficulties in adapting themselves to the new cosmopolitan structure of apartment house life-style.

Another factor that appears to displease and causes difficulties for the residents of the apartments is the plan and layout of the house. In the layout plans of these apartment flats even though a separate stocking area (eg. For coal) is allocated for each family, they are place at the back, thus creating problems in their utilization. Furthermore, the residents of the Karacaören (City of Tebessüm) inform that they schools, job-sites as the TOKİ housing area is distant to the center of Pursaklar and the schedules of the public transportation vehicles are very limited.

Consequently, despite all the constructive and contemporary approaches adopted to constitute its objectives, while it was structed, the Urban Transformation Project of the Northern Access of Ankara creates certain problems since it did not consider the social and economic conditions of the peoples involved. Facts such as the distance between the houses constructed for the peoples whose squatter houses were demolished and various centers, high heating expenses, heavy loan back-payment conditions, placed the people of area under difficulties and caused the Project to deviate from its originally intended objectives. Yet, on the other hand, estranging the people formerly living in squatter settlements from their new residential locations brings forth another socio-cultural problem (Riza Fatih Mendilcioğlu contributed the research by a field study in social situations).

## General overview and concluding remarks

Since the beginning of the process of squatter formation in Turkey, local authorities and the central government have cooperated closely with different degree of involvement in implementation. This was proved reasonably successful. Recently, there have been attempts to concentrate all powers regarding the prevention and upgrading with the central authorities, namely the Mass Housing Administration (TOKİ). It could be more advisable to revise the institutional set up on a power sharing basis not to exclude municipalities. This would not only enable the State to benefit from the experience of local authorities in this field, but at the same time, it would be more in line with the international obligations of Turkey stemming from the European Charter of Local Self Government.

In the power sharing between upper-level and lower-level municipalities in metropolitan areas, initiatives for regeneration, urban renewal, transformation and upgrading should not be used to exclude the district municipalities. At present, urban transformation projects, including those implemented in Ankara, are usually carried out as separated from each other without establishing necessary linkages between them. Partial planning approaches create considerable waste of time, energy and resources. There is also a need to establish a system of cooperation between different tiers of administration together with full consultation with and participation of the residents of squatter settlements.

Perhaps the most neglected aspect of the process of urban transformation is the lack of attention to employment opportunities. Unless measure directed to poverty reduction are taken, physical rehabilitation of squatter zones will not suffice to talk about a real urban transformation and upgrading. Market driven displacement in the upgrading zones within central locations of the cities, as in the case of Ankara, caused great number of low-income families either felt the need to escape prohibitive living expenses in the upgrading new environments or to settle elsewhere in less expensive parts of the city by renting out the flats acquired as a result of transformation of gecekondu settlements.

A particular attention must be paid to the environmental quality of upgraded zones. Resources of municipalities must be complemented by the necessary transfers from the State budget in order to improve the quality of infrastructure.

The approach of public-private partnership has proved to be a workable tool for slum upgrading and transformation. But recent experiences relieve that the real balance in this partnership is rather distorted in favor of the construction firms in the private sector. In order not to allow this distortion to grow to an extent that would jeopardize the public interest, it would be advisable the establishment of housing cooperatives for low-income families in those settlements. Since more than ninety percent of the national territory is situated within the earthquake belts and makes millions of residents subject to immediate risky, any upgrading and prevention schemes and redevelopment plans concerning them must take into account the incorporation of the finding of micro-zoning works together with strict building controls into the planning process.

Allocation or renting out of publicly owned lands by the State and the municipalities must be used in a very restricted manner and an increasing emphasis must be put upon the supremacy of public interest. The method of sharing the incremental value of the land previously occupied illegally by those who violated the legislation concerning building and development would create consequences contrary to the public interest. Because the basic factor behind the increase of the value of the land are infrastructure investments of public authorities and its return directly to those authorities without being shared with private interests would be socially more meaningful. Therefore, the distribution of the plus-value among private interests within the framework of bargains with private individuals under such names as "consolidation of development rights", or "transfer of development rights" would not be in favor of the society as a whole and future generations.

## Short Bibliography

- Ayata, Ayşe, "Industrial Change and Social Stratification in the Urban Context", in Mübeccel Kıray (ed.), Structural Change in Turkish Society, Indiana University Press, Indiana, 1991.
- Bayraktar, Erdoğan, Gecekondu ve Kentsel yenileme, (Gecekondu and Urban Renewal), Ankara, 2006.
- Bademli, Raci, "Forms of Housing in Ankara: Segmentation in the Domain of Housing in a Segmented City", in Ruşen Keleş and Hiromasa Kano (eds.), Housing and the Urban Poor in the Middle East, Institute of Developing Economies, M. E. Series, No: 17, Tokyo, 1986.

- Deliktaş, Gül, "Gecekondu Dönüşüm, Kentsel Yenileme Projeleri: Uygulama Alanları ve Uygulama Süreçleri" (Gecekondu Transformation and Urban Renewal Projects: Their Areas of Implementation and Application Processes), (unpublished paper), The Mass Housing Administration, Ankara, 2007.

- Geray, Cevat, "Toplumsal Konut Yöneltisi ve TOKİ'nin Tutum ve Yöneltilerindeki Son Değişiklikler" (Social Housing Policy and the Recent Changes in the Position and Policies of the Mass Housing Administration), in Ayşegül Mangi (ed.), Ruşen Keleş'e Armağan, Vol.II Kentsel Politikalar (In Honour of Prof. Dr. Ruşen Keleş, Vol. II, Urban Policies), Imge Pub., Ankara, 2007.

- Göksu, Faruk, "Kentsel Dönüşüm Süreci ve Proje Ortaklıkları" (The Process of Urban Transformation and the Partnership on the Basis of Project), Bulletin, Mimarlar Odası Ankara Şubesi, yayın No:40, May-June 2006.

- Keleş, Ruşen, Kentleşme Politikası (Urbanization Policy), Imge Pub., Ankara, 2013 (13rd ed.).

- Keleş, Ruşen, Kentbilim Terimleri Sözlüğü, (Dictionary of Town and Country Planning), Imge Pub., Ankara, 1998 (2nd ed.).

- Keleş, Ruşen, "The Culture of Squatting, Land Rights and the Realities of Globalization", in Ruşen Keleş and Hagen Henry (Eds.), On the Systematics of Old and New Land tenure Rights in Their Cultural Context: Ecological, Economic and Societal Aspects, Peter Lang, Bern, 2004.

- Keleş, Ruşen, Urban Poverty in the Third World. Theoretical Approaches and Policy Options, Institute of Developing Economies, VRF Series, No:152, Tokyo, 1988.

- Keleş, Ruşen, "Regulatory Guidelines for Affordable Shelter: A Case Study of Ankara, Turkey", Geoffrey Payne and Associates, London, 2004.

- Keleş, Ruşen, "Kentsel Dönüşüm Anlayışını Dönüştürmek" (The Need to Transform the Understanding of Transformation), Özel Kalem, May 2007.

- Keleş, Ruşen, (with the assistance of Meltem Yılmaz), "Lessons Learnt from Slum Upgrading and Prevention in Turkey", Paper presented to the United Nations Center for Human Settlemenents (UNCHS), Nairobi, 2007.

- Keleş, Ruşen and Kano, Hiromasa, Economic Development and Social Consciousness: Turkey under Developmentalism, Institute of Developing Economies, M.E. Series, No:17, Tokyo, 1986.

- Payne, Geoffrey K., "Lowering the Ladder", in G. Paynet et al. (eds.), Land, Rights and Innovation: Improving tenure Security for the Urban Poor, ITDG, London, 2002.

- TOKİ, Türkiye'de Konut Sektörü ve TOKİ'nin Konut Üretimindeki Yeri (Housing Sector in Turkey and the Place of Mass Housing Administration in the Production of Housing), 2006.

- Turan, Menaf, "Başkentin Gecekonduları: Kentsel Dönüşüm Projelerinin Arka Bahçeleri", (The Squatter Houses of the State Capital: The Backyards of Urban Transformation Projects), in Ayşegül Mengi (ed.), Prof. Dr. Ruşen Keleş'e Armağan, Vol. II: Kentsel Politikalar, (in Honour of Prof. Dr. Ruşen Keleş, Vol. II, Urban Policies), Imge Pub., Ankara, 2007.

- Yaman, Murat, Türkiye'de Kentsel Dönüş(tür)me Uygulamaları: Sosyo-Politik bir Yaklaşım, (Urban Transformation Works in Turkey: A Social and Economic Approach), MKM Pub., Bursa, 2012.

- Yılmaz, Meltem, Mülkiyet Hakkının Doğal ve Kentsel Çevreye Etkileri (The Impact of the Right to Ownership on Natural and Urban Environment), Siyasal Yay., Ankara, 2010.

- Yılmaz, Meltem, Sustainable Housing Considerations of Turkey-Planning and Design Solutions, Hacettepe University, Ankara, 2008.

# DISASTER MANAGEMENT

# Disaster Policy and
# Management in Turkey*

## Introduction

Dictionaries define the concept of *policy* as a plan of action or a way of management which requires political wisdom. We understand by the term of *management* the act, the art or the manner of managing, controlling, handling or directing. On the other hand, the word *disaster*, reminds an event, such as flood, fire, shipwreck, erthquake and similar natural or man-made problems that cause great harm, distress or damage to many people. To formulate a rational disaster policy and management is one of the extremely important public responsibilities in a country where nearly ninety percent of its territory is prone to earthquakes. According to official sources, in Turkey, 96 percent of the national territory is within the regions exposed to earthquakes in different degrees and 98 percent of the population live in these regions. (TC Bayındırlık ve İskan Bakanlığı, Kentleşme Şurası 2009, Komisyon Raporları I Cilt, p.436). It is reported that during the last century, specifically, between 1900 and 2008, nearly 200 earthquakes took place. The number of death exceeded 100 thousands, and the number of wounded reached 171 thousands. In addition, 600 thousand dwellings were either destroyed or became totally unusable. (p. 436). The possibility of earthquakes that cause serious loss of life and hazards

---

*     2013 International Van Earthquake Symposium, 23-27 October, 2013, Van.

every five years is around 63 percent *in average*. Only during the 1999 Marmara and Düzce earthquakes, 18.000 people lost their lives, 50.000 were wounded, 97.000 dwellings were demolished and many industrial and communication infrastructure of the country were considerably damaged. During the 2011 Van and Erciş earthquakes, the total number of loss of life was 644 and the number of damaged buildings were more than 35.000. (M. Turan, 2012).

According to the evaluation of the Urbanization Council organized by the Ministry of Environment and Urban Development during 4-7 May 2009, the determining factors behind this outstandingly high cost of disasters are the following: a) Risks are too big in the cities as large urban centers are pools of high risks. Risks emanate neither only from the proximity of urban centers to the sources of hazards, nor they are related to the quality of the buildings, but they are also closely related with the settlement patterns, inadequacy of infrastructure and open spaces, spatial distribution of major critical services such as hospitals, schools, communication systems, disaster management centers, and so on. b) Secondly, institutional structure is quite dispersed and organized mainly to address post disaster activities. c) The main goal of the legislation that concern disaster management is not risk reduction. Unfortunately, such legislation does not exist in Turkey. Neither the Law of Disasters of 1959 ( No: 7269), nor the Law on Urban Development of 1985 (No: 3194), including the recent Law on Urban Transformation in Areas Prone to Disaster Risks of 2012 (No: 6306) have the necessary provisions regarding risk mitigation in the real sense (T.C. Bayındırlık ve İskan Bakanlığı, Kentleşme Şurası, 2009 Komisyon Raporları, I.Cilt, p.438).

## General Legal Framework for Disaster Management

Central administration and local authorities, in other words, decentralized administration, constitute two main components of the state apparatus in Turkey, which have considerable powers with respect to disaster management. Functioning of the administration with respect to "the state of emergency" is regulated by the Constitution. According to the 1982 Constitution (Art. 119-122) "In times of wars and *emergency,* public authorities are empowered to take additional measures to maintain public order. Emergency rule is *a legal regime* governed by the principles of legality of administrative acts and the supremacy of law. All emergency measures must be in conformity with special laws that should not be repugnant to the Constitution". (Arts.119, 122, 15, and 125).

The *"state of emergency* is declared in two different situations: a) The event of a natural disaster (like an earthquake, a dangerous epidemic disease (cholera,etc, or a serious economic crisis), b) The emergence of serious indications of wide-spread acts of violence aiming at the destruction of free democratic order or fundamental rights, or a serious deterioration of public order as a result of acts of violence.

In the above mentioned three cases, the Council of Ministers may declare *the state of emergency.* Its maximum period is six months. And it may be extended for periods not exceeding four months. It may be effective either for the whole country or for one or more regions. Decisions of the Council of Ministers concerning *state of emergency* are subject to the immediate approval of the Parliament. The Parliament is authorized to change the duration, totally lift it, or approve any *state of emergency.* During the *state of emergency,* the Council of Ministers may issue decrees with force of law, in other words, *law-amending ordinances,* on matters relating to the *state of emergency* without prior authorization of the Parliament. However, these decrees are subject to subsequent parliamentary affirmation. *The state of emergency* is also subject to judicial review, while the decrees having force of law issued by the Council of Ministers during emergency are excluded from judicial control by the Constitutional Court.

## Institutional Set-up for and Competencies with Respect to Disaster Management

The disaster management is one of the major responsibilities of the government at both central and local levels. The Organic Law of the former Ministry of Public Works and Settlement (No:7116) had charged, in 1958, the then newly established Ministry, "to take all necessary measures before and after the disasters" (art.2). Previously, this task was performed for a long time (between 1937-1958) by the Ministry of Public Works. But a Law-Amending Ordinance of 1983 (No: 180) concerning the organization of bureaucracy, charged the new Ministry of Public Works and Settlement "to manage carrying out of the disaster services in an efficient, orderly and quick manner" (Art.1). During the reorganization of the Ministry in 2011, the Ministry of Environment and Urban Development, in its new name, continued to possess almost all powers of the former Ministry with respect to disaster management, including the working out of the city master plans in areas affected by natural disasters. (Law-Amending Ordinance No: 644, Official Gazette: 4 July 2011, No: 27984).

In addition, organic laws of a number of ministries like the Interior, Defense, Health and Social Welfare, Transportation, Marine and Communication, Forestry and Water Works, Energy and Natural Resources, Science, Industry and Trade are also charged with certain functions in different stages of the disaster management process. Such a broad distribution of powers and responsibilities between numerous ministries, central and departmental authorities cause serious coordination problems in public administration. In order to avoid confusions and overlappings of functions during the natural disasters, legislator empowered the provincial governors, as the agent of the central administration, to take and implement necessary steps immediately following such events, (Law No:7269, Art.1).

One should not forget that field offices of the Ministry of Environment and Urban Development are not adequately organized as to meet the pressing needs. Municipalities and village administrations as units of local authorities are two types of local governments recognized by the Constitution. To set local building regulations and to prepare and carry out city master plans lies, in principle, within the jurisdiction of local authorities. Yet, their capacity to manage great many services connected to disasters is extremely limited. They are poorly equipped to deal with providing guidance and control over planning, building and settlement activities, even under normal conditions. Therefore, reliance on central government in these matters can be regarded as ordinary. The principle of subsidiarity allows the central authorities to assume responsibilities of these duties which are essentially of local character in nature, taking into consideration of "the extent and nature of the task and requirements of efficiency and economy". (European Charter of Local Self-Government, Art.4, Par.3).

As far as their respective legislation is concerned, both cities and metropolitan municipalities are empowered to be active during the rescue, relief, mitigation and other stages of the disaster management process. According to the Municipal Law of 2005 ( No:5393), " Municipalities are in charge of preparing disaster and emergency plans, taking into consideration the characteristics of cities, in order to protect citizens against fires, industrial accidents, earthquakes and other natural disasters" (Art.53). Similarly, their organic law ( No: 5216) empowers metropolitan municipalities to prepare disaster management plans in accordance with the plans prepared at provincial level and to carry out related services" (Art.7).

## The Disasters and Emergency Administration

Due to the inadequacy of the institutional mechanism for disaster management and in the light of the great losses in economy and society, certain steps have been taken after the great Marmara and Düzce earthquakes, in order to ensure the coordination of public services before, during and after the happening of natural disasters. The latest and most important step was certainly the abolishment of the former General Directorate of Disaster Management within the Ministry of Environment and Urban Development and the establishment of a new authority to be in charge at the highest level of administration to formulate the national disaster policy and to coordinate all works to be carried out at central, regional and local levels.

AFAD, *The Disasters and Emergency Administration* was created in 2009, as a central authority attached to the Prime Ministry. (Law No:5902, Official Gazette : 17 June 2009, No: 27261). Its main objective was to organize all public services related to disaster management under one single roof. By its establishment, the existence of 3 former general directorates functioning in the same field have ended. These are the General Directorate of Disasters, General Directorate of Civil Defense, and the General Directorate of Emergency Management. The new administration is in charge of carrying out all the services needed before, during and after natural disasters.

All kinds of plans, programs and reports concerning disasters and emergencies will be approved by *The Highest Council of Disasters and Emergency Administration* which is composed of the Ministers of National Defense, Interior, Foreign Affairs, Finance, National Education, Environment and Urban Development, Health, Transportation, Marine and Communication, Energy and Natural Resources, Forestry and Water Works. The Highest Council meets under the chairmanship of the Prime Minister or one of his deputies.

*A Coordination Council* has been set up in order to assess all data collected regarding the disaster and emergencies, to formulate the measures to be taken and to ensure and control their implementation, and finally to realize the coordination between the public authorities and civil society organizations. This Council is composed of the under-secretaries of all the ministries mentioned above, and the representatives of the State Planning Organization (Ministry of Development), Head of the Disaster and Emergency Administration, and the Director of the Red Cross. It meets under the chairmanship of the Undersecretary of the Prime Ministry.

A third body is *The Earthquake Advisory Council* which in charge of submitting proposals for the protection against earthquakes, to mitigate the damages and the works following the earthquakes and to determine the policies and priorities for earthquake researches. This Council meets under the chairmanship of the Chairman of the Disasters and Emergency Administration and includes representatives or directors of such institutions as the Ministry of Environment and Urban Development, Kandilli Earthquake Research Institute of the Bosphorus University and several other interested authorities, and 10 university staff members proposed by the Higher Educational Council.

The main duties of the Administration are the followings:

1) To prepare emergency, risk management and mitigation plans.

2) To establish data, communication and early warning systems, and to organize training programs in order to raise public awareness in these fields.

3) To work out plans, projects and principles of urban development and to meet the needs of human assistance during disasters.

4) To try to get rid of the effects of disasters by using internal and external resources.

5) To fix the standards for firefighting, searching and rescuing services.

6) To take measures to bring the daily life into normal conditions after the disasters and other emergency situations.

7) To try to plan and implement civil defense services.

Certain responsibilities are left to the field organization of the Administration which functions under the leadership of provincial governors. The duties to be carried out by Provincial Disasters and Emergency Directorates include finding damages, site selection, planning, ownership, debt services, reconstruction, geological and geotechnical researches. There is no doubt that inadequacy of technical staff at the local level and particularly their openness to partisan pressures of all kind make the usefulness of such reorganization efforts highly questionable.

It is obvious that the provisions in the Organic law of Disasters and Emergency Administration has paved the way for a new disorder in the field of urban development planning. In addition, making the public services regarding various phases of disaster management process subject to market-based transactions may contradict the constitutional principle of welfare state.

Although the unification of all the public services related to disaster management under the same roof seems to be positive and rational at first glance, organization chart established by the respective legislation is inadequate and at the same time the new Administration is deprived of the experienced staff of the abolished general directorates. Under these conditions, know-how, experience and knowledge accumulated over the past half century may not be put at the service of the new administrative mechanism.

A National Earthquake Council had been created in 2000, right after the great Marmara earthquake to carry out the following tasks: a) Scientific assessment of earthquake predictions and informing the public, b) identification of priority research areas concerning mitigation, c) consultancy to public bodies and the earthquake prediction (Murat Balamir, "Recent Changes in Turkish Disaster Policy: A Strategical Reorientation", in P. R. Kleindorfer and M. R. Sertel (eds.), Mitigation and Financing of Seismic Risks, Kluwer, Den Haag, 2001, pp.207-234). The Council had published the first national strategy of mitigation in 2002, but it was abolished later on without given any reason for the action. (Ulusal Deprem Konseyi, Deprem Zararlarını Azaltma Ulusal Stratejiisi, Ankara, 2002).

## Planning Urban Development, Building Control and Disaster Management

One of the basic problems in disaster management in Turkey is to link urban development planning to disaster management and to ensure minimum safety conditions for construction. The main concern of the Law of Disasters of 1959 ( No:7269) and its regulations is to provide a formal capacity for intervention *after disasters* and to organize the relief operations (Murat Balamir, "Recent Changes....", Ibid, p. 210). Only a few of the provisions of the Law of Disasters contain any tasks concerning the preparations to be undertaken *prior* to disasters, including the urban development plans. Taking measures to decentralize population and economic activities more evenly over the territory of the country is beyond the immediate concern of the Law. The Disasters Law and its regulations fall short of constituting a contemporary system of disaster management. It does not differentiate between authorized and unauthorized construction and, in one sense, it awards the owners of squatter dwellings at the expense of the safety of the great majority of the inhabitants (Balamir, İbid, p.213).

On the other hand, Urban Development Law of 1985 ( No: 3194) which still is in force, is both outdated and partial in scope. Although municipalities with a population of 10.000 and more and provincial administrations are required to prepare development plans, no consideration is given to integration of geological, geomorphological and seismic data into plans. Attribution of the full responsibility of plan making and implementation in urban centers to municipalities, which are generally deprived of necessary technical and financial resources and the qualified manpower, with few exceptions, causes not only arbitrariness in ensuring environmental and quality standards, but at the same time, it makes following rigorously the principles of reducing the risks difficult. (Balamir, Ibid, p.215). As a result, although the principle of subsidiarity requires that public affairs of local nature, like development planning, must be carried out by the authorities which are closest to the people to increase the autonomy of local authorities to some extent, may have cost to public order and interest that should not be undermined.

Unfortunately, an efficient building control in the system is almost inexistant. Building control is usually carried out by a professional with technical liability, who usually hired either by the owner or by the developer. This decreases the reliability of the whole process of planning. Normally, municipalities issue building permit on the basis of projects submitted to them by landowners. These projects are supposed to meet the requirements of both the building and disaster regulations, which comprise mainly dimensional standards, requirements for heating, lighting, landscaping, parking, fire-fighting, etc. Few of these regulations are covered in the section of the Disaster Law concerned with structural safety standards in buildings (Balamir, Ibid, p.216). As described by Balamir, "The practice of land-use planning and zoning, transportation and infrastructure planning, procedures for density assignment, planning the open spaces, participation processes, strengthening and devising new methods of monitoring building- use control, etc., all of these are distinct aspects of disaster concerns which naturally need to be covered in the Development Law" (Balamir, Ibid, p.216).

## Recent Changes in Disaster Management Regulations

Certain steps have been taken during the post disaster period following the Marmara earthquake. The first was a Law-Amending Ordinance put into effect in 1999 (No:595). It aimed at ensuring the life and property safety in buildings, preventing unplanned, uncontrolled and low-quality construction which causes waste of resources, ensuring proper construction, protecting the rights of those whose property is damaged, and compensating the loss occurred.

This Decree has been criticised for several reasons. Firstly, it focused on individual buildings, but neglected widespread abuses in the construction industry. It also delegated municipal building regulation development to private firms, failed to link construction regulation to maco-economic policies, and did not involve professional organizations in construction control. Another criticism is that the Decree introduced concepts such as *building inspection firms, certified architects,* and *certified engineers.* It was argued that the Decree thus created a "privileged professional group" that breached the constitutional principle of equality before the law (Hasol, "Yapı Denetimi Kararnamesi, Yapı, 2000).

This Law-Amending Ordinance was invalidated by the Constitutional Court in 2001. This was followed by the enactment of a new Building Control Law (No: 4708) in the same year. There were no major changes in the aims of the Law. However, provisions concerning the establishment and functioning of building inspection firms were reformulated. Building inspection firms were defined as private firms to be established by eligible architects and engineers with the aim of supervising projects and construction activities and reporting to local authority responsible for issuing construction and occupation permits. The Building Control Law modified the respective provision of the Urban Development Law (No: 3194) and authorized the building inspection firms to take over from the administration, the task of technical liability mentioned in the Urban Development Law.

Another measure taken in 1999 was the adoption of a Law-Amending Ordinance (No: 587) on Obligatory Eartquake Insurance. (A law on Natural Disasters Insurance was put into effect in May 2012). By the same ordinance, a Natural Disasters Insurance Administration was established under the auspices of the Treasury. All residential buildings are to be covered by obligatory earthquake insurance. Only official, industrial and public buildings in villages are exempt from this compulsory system. According to the official statements, no more than 5 percent of all the buildings in the country are, at present, insured against earthquakes (Keleş, Kentleşme Politikası, 2013, p. 601).

A third attempt has been made in 2000 by another Law-Amending Ordinance (No: 601) and covered proficiency in the construction professions. Existing legislation on Engineering and Architecture and the Law of the Union of Chambers of Engineers and Architects were amended by this ordinance, in which requirements for improved professional competence in the fields of engineering and architecture are detailed. A minimum of five years of professional experience, attendance at training courses, and passing written exams organized by both concerned Chambers are the required conditions Balamir, Ibid, p.226).

A new stage was started by the new Law on Disasters and Emergency Administration. Among its priorities were the preparation of National Earthquake Strategy and Action Plan for the period 2012-2023 and the National Disaster Intervention Plan. The first defined the measures to be taken prior to earthquakes and the respective roles of the public and private institutions during the events. The second includes the tasks of the ministries and other institutions that will perform during and following the disasters.

In 2012, a new law called the Law of Urban Transformation in Areas prone to Disasters, while narrowing down the scope of the concept of urban transformation into the renovation of the buildings constructed in disaster prone areas and enlarging the geographical scope of transformation undertakings all over Turkey (R.Keleş, "Türkiye'de Yerel Yönetimlerde Kentsel Dönüşüm Yönetim Süreci", TODAİE, Türkiye'de Yerel Yönetimlerde Kentsel Dönüşüm Süreci Çalıştayı", Ankara, 10-11 Aralık 2012). As one of the pre-disaster measures, this laws aims at tearing down nearly 6 million dwellings all over Turkey, which are supposed to be vulnerable to earthquakes. At the same time, from a macro-economic point of view, the government plans to contribute to the revitalization of the economy in this way.

## Concluding Remarks

Despite its relatively long experience in natural disasters, even today, Turkish public administration does not seem to be ready to cope adequately with the various aspects of disaster management.

Measures taken after the Marmara, Düzce and Van earthquakes reflect a view that considers disaster management as a question of quality and strength of buildings and adequate construction control. Such an approach has led to the neglect of more important and broader dimensions of the question.

The preservation of life and property is closely related to patterns of urbanization and excessive population concentrations in metropolitan centers. The density of population and buildings affect the efficiency of disaster management adversely. Reducing population density and decentralizing economic activities through regional planning, therefore, is essential to decrease loss and damage.

On the other hand, additional measures have to be designed and incorporated into the responsibilities of local authorities. Yet, recent experiences show that excessive centralization in policy and administration is the main choice of the decision-makers. The measures needed relate to early warning systems and the inclusion of integrated hazard and micro-zonation maps into the development planning process. (Balamir, 2002; UN, 1993: 13-17; UN 1997: 20-28). Efforts to improve construction regulation and the introduction of an obligatory earthquake insurance scheme should not lead to the postponement of a comprehensive revision of the urban development system within a regional framework.

Within the disaster cycle, an increasing number of non-governmental organizations play a role in the rescue efforts. Their uncoordinated involvement makes it difficult to achieve harmonization in rescue and relief operations. It is important to ensure that partnerships do not become additional obstacles in achieving an efficient control and coordination system. Recent experience also shows that in the distribution of national and international donations for relief and recovery programs, the public administration, as a whole, deviated from the fundamental principle of impartiality.

Strengthening the capacity of local governments in terms of authority, financial resources and technical capability to play a more efficient role in all stages of the disaster management process is highly critical. Providing them with training in the issues discussed above would not only increase their role in guiding and controlling urban development, settlement and planning, but allow them to operate more effectively during natural disasters (Keleş, 1993, pp.13-17).

I would like to end up with sharing the suggestions made by the Integrated Urban Development Strategy and Action Plan produced by the Urbanization Council assembled in 2009 by the Ministry of Environment and Urban development: 1) Legislative arrangement have to made to ensure an integrated and effective disaster management system. 2) The processes intended to reduce risks have to be made effective by identifying disasters hazards and risks. 3) The urbanization and planning legislation has to be arranged so as to cover hazard and risk analysis and mitigation planning to ensure mitigation of disaster and settlement risks. 4) Improving of the insurance system against natural disasters has to be ensured so as to cover all types of disasters. 5) For effective response to disasters, communication infrastructure has to be strengthened and facilities such as evacuation corridors, gathering site, temporary shelter, disaster assistance support centers and emergency facilities have to be ensured.

## Bibliography

- Abant İzzet Baysal Üniversitesi, Ulusal Deprem Sempozyumu (National Earthquake Symposium), 11-12 November 2009.

- Balamir, Murat, "Microzonation for Earthquake Risks Mitigation", Background Report on Sustainable Implementation, Legal and Organizational Bases of Land-Use Management in Turkey", Unpublished Paper, October, 2002.

- Balamir, Murat, "Recent Changes in Turkish Disasters Policy: A Strategic Reorientation", in P. R. Kleindorfer and M. R. Sertel (eds.), Mitigation and Financing of Seismic Risks, Kluwer, 2001, pp.207-234.

- Balamir, Murat, Painful Steps of Progress from Crisis Planning to Contingency Planning: Changes for Disaster Preparedness in Turkey", Journal of Contingencies and Crisis Management", Vol.10, No:1, March, 2002, pp.39-49.

- Balamir, Murat, "Türkiye'nin Deprem Yanlışları" (Earthquake Mistakes of Turkey), Cumhuriyet, 15 November 2011.

- Balamir, Murat, "Deprem ve Anayasa" (Earthquake and the Constitution), Cumhuriyet, 30 December 2011.

- Balamir, Murat, "İstanbul'un Yeşili, Silueti, Depremi", (Green Spaces, Silhouette and Earthquake of İstanbul), Cumhuriyet, 2 May 2013.

- Balamir, Murat, "Deprem Yanlışlarını Düzeltmek" (To Correct Earthquake Mistakes), Cumhuriyet, 18 November 2011.

- Bayındırlık ve İskan Bakanlığı (Ministry of Pubklic Works and Settlement), KENTGES, Kentsel Gelişme Stratejisi 2010-2023 (Integrated Urban Development Strategy and Action Plan 2010-2023), Ankara, 2010.

- Bayındırlık ve İskan Bakanlığı, Kentleşme Şurası 2009 (Urbanization Council 2009), Komisyon Raporları (Commission Reports), Vol. I, Ankara, 4-7 May 2009.

- Comfort, Louise, and the Research Center for Urban Safety and Security, "Complex Sytems in Crisis: Anticipation and Resilience in Dynamic Environments", Annual Meeting of the American Political Science Association, Atlanta, Georgia, September 2-5, 1999.

- Demeter, Katalin, Erkan, Nihal Ekin, and Güner, Ayşe (eds.), The Role of Local Governments in Reducing the Risk of Disasters, The World Bank and the Center for Local Government Studies and Training, Marmara University, 2004.

- Ergünay, O, and Gülkan,P., "Land-Use Planning as Instrument of Earthquake Hazard Mitigation", Proceedings of Workshop I on Seismic Hazard Assessment, Cooperative Project for Seismic Risk Reduction in the Mediterranean Region, Genoa, Italy, 1990.

- Ergünay, O. and Gülkan, P. "Legislative and Institutional Framework Relative to the Reduction of Seismic Risk in Turkey", Report submitted to the U.N. Regional Activity Center, Priority Action Program, UNEP-MAP, Split, 1990.

- Gülkan, P., Balamir,M. And Sucuoğlu, H. Et al, The Revision of the Urban Planning and Building Control System in Turkey for the Mitigation of Disasters Effects, Final report of research prepared for and submitted to the Ministry of Public Works and Settlement, supported by he World Bank, Ankara, 1999.

- Gülersoy, Çelik, "Deprem Fiziksel Ama Daha Çok Sosyal" (Earthquake is Physical, but More Social", Cumhuriyet, 11 Eylül 1999.

- Hasol, D., "Yapı Denetimi Kararnamesi", (Building Control Ordinance),Yapı Dergisi, 2000.

- Keleş, Ruşen, Kentleşme Politikası (Urbanization Policy), İmge Pub., Ankara, 2013 (13th ed.).

- Keleş, Ruşen, Yerinden Yönetim ve Siyaset (Decentralization and Politics), Cem Pub., İstanbul, 2012 (8th ed.).

- Keleş, Ruşen, 100 Soruda Kentleşme, Konut ve Gecekondu (Urbanization, Housing and Squatting in 100 Questions), Cem Pub., İstanbul, 2013 (in press).

- Keleş, Ruşen, "Increasing Efficiency in Disaster Management", Paper presented to the U.N. Interregional Seminar on Disaster Management, Jakarta, 1993.

- Keleş, Ruşen, "Turkish Government Structure from Disaster Management Perspective", in Demeter, Erkan and Güner (eds.), The Role of Local Governments in Reducing the Risk of Disasters, 2004, pp.3-13.

- Keleş, Ruşen, "Türkiye'de Yerel Yönetimlerde Kentsel Dönüşüm Yönetim Süreci", (Urban Transformation Management Process in Local Governments in Turkey), TODAİE, Türkiye'de Yerel Yönetimlerde Kentsel Dönüşüm Süreci Çalıştayı, 10-11 December,2011, Ankara.

- Keleş,Ruşen, "Çarpık Kentleşme, Deprem ve Ötesi..." (Unplanned Urbanization, Earthquake and Beyond...), Cumhuriyet,

- Şengül, Mihriban and Turan, Menaf, "Erciş Depremi Öncesinde Afet Sonrası Geçici Yerleşim Alanlarında Yönetim Uygulamaları ve Sorunları" (Before Erciş Earthquake Practices and Problems of Management in Temporary Settlements), Mülkiye, No:274, Bahar 2012, pp.113-148.

- Şengün, Hayriye, "Yerel Özerklik Bağlamında Türkiye'de Değişen Afet Yönetimi Yapısı" (Changing Structure of Disaster Management within the Framework of Local Autonomy), 5. Ulusal Yerel Yönetimler Sempozyumu (5th Symposium of Local Autonomy), 21-23 Kasım 2011, Ankara, 2013.

- Şengün, Hayriye, "12 Kasım Depreminin Etkilerinin ve Sonuçlarının Kamu Yönetimi Açısından Değerlendirilmesi" (The Assessment of the Impact and Effects of the 12 November Earthquake from the Standpoint of Public Administration), Abant İzzet Baysal Üniveritesi, Ulusal Deprem Sempozyumu, Bolu, 2009, pp. 91-102.

- Tezcan, Semih, "Depremin 11. Yıldönümünde İstanbul Uyuyor" (İstanbul Sleeps in the 11th Anniversary of the Earthquake), Cumhuriyet, 17 August 2010.

- Tezcan, Semih, "Tehlikeli Bekleyiş", (Dangerous Expectation), Cumhuriyet, 4 March 2010.

- Tezcan, Semih, "Deprem Konusunda Tüm Türkiye Uyuyor" (The Whole Turkey is in Sleep vis-a vis Earthquakes), Cumhuriyet, 16 August 2011.

- Turan, Menaf, "Lessons Learnt from Van-Erciş Earthquakes 2011, Turkey: An Evaluation of Earthquake Management", International Journal of Business and Social Sciences, Vol.3, No:22, November 2012 (Special Issue).

- U.N., "Interregional Seminar on Disaster Management", Jakarta, 1993.

- U.N., "International Conference of the Integration of Public Administration and the Science of Disasters", Beijing, 1997.

- Ulusal Deprem Konseyi (National Earthquake Council), Deprem Zararlarını Azaltma Ulusal Stratejisi (National Strategy for Earthquake Risk Mitigation), Ankara, 2002.

# The Administrative Structure of Government in Turkey (Central and Local) From the Perspective of Disaster Management*

The principal characteristics of the State has been described in the Articles 1-3 of the Constitution, according to which Turkey is a republic. It is a democratic, secular and social state, governed by the rule of law. Turkish State is an indivisible whole with its territory and nation. The provisions of these articles are especially protected by the Article 4, according to which the above-mentioned fundamental principles of the Republic can not be amended; nor shall their amendment be proposed to the Parliament.

Free and competitive elections based on universal suffrage (Art.67), the existence of more than one freely organized political party, respect for fundamental human rights and freedoms reflect the basic features of a modern liberal democracy.

The Constitution of 1982 vests the legislative authority in the Turkish Grand National Assembly of 550 deputies who are elected by direct and universal suffrage. Legislative authority of the Parliament can not be delegated to any other branch of government. All members enjoy classical parliamentary

*   Draft paper to be presented to the Workshop on **The Role of Local Governments in Reducing the Risk of Disaster**, organized by Marmara University, the Local Government and Public Service Reform Initiative of the Soros Foundation, Disaster Management Facility and the World Bank Institute , April 28-May 2, 2003, İstanbul, Turkey

privileges such a freedom of speech and freedom from arbitrary or politically motivated detentions or arrests.

The executive branch of the government is composed of the President of the Republic and the Council of Ministers. The first has no political responsibility while the latter is politically responsible. The Council of Ministers is composed of the Prime Minister designated by the President from among the members of the Parliament nd the ministers. Ministers are nominated by the Prime Minister and appointed by the President of the Republic. The Constitution does not require the ministers to be chosen from among the members of the Parliament. In Practice, most of them are. The Prime Minister is the head of the executive branch and enjoys certain constitutional privileges not shared by other ministers.

The ministers assume a collective responsibility for the general policy of the government, shared by all ministers, jointly and equally. At the same time, each minister is individually responsible for matters within the jurisdiction of his own ministry and for the acts of his subordinates. As in all other modern states, the executive also participates in the law-making functions. The regulative power of the executive includes the enactment of regulations, by-laws and law-amending ordinances. The latter, that may also be called ordinances or cabinet decrees, can amend existing laws. They entitle the executive with a certain delegated legislative function.

According to the principle of the independence of the judiciary that is protected and safeguarded by the Constitution, both legislative and executive authorities must comply with court decisions. A system of judicial control of constitutionality of laws is in force since 1961, and is performed by a Constitutional Court. Legality of administration means that the executive function must be exercised and carried out within the framework of law. Without legislative authority, the Administration can not undertake any activity. Only a relatively small part of administrative functions are connected with law enforcement. A much greater part of them, like, education, health, planning, housing, disaster management and public order, are related to the practical and technical demands of the society. Administrative matters falling outside the scope of regulation by law constitute matters of "administrative discretion" The Administration has to deal with these matters in a consistent and not an arbitrary manner. Judicial control of administration requires that Public Administration be controlled by the judiciary, namely administrative courts [1].The activities of the Administration is subject to judicial review (Arts. 125, 155 and 157 of the Constitution).

The Constitution devotes an entire chapter to the rights and duties (Arts.41-65) connected with the concept of the social state. The realization of the social and economic rights is a governmental duty, although not the exclusive responsibility of the government[2]

## Centralization and Decentralization

Administration in Turkey is built upon two main principles: centralization and decentralization. These two separate administrative styles or branches constitute a single piece, that is the Administration. This is a result of the unitary character of the State. According to the Article 123 of the Constitution, the central agencies and departments, and decentralized (geographically or functionally) agencies form a whole. Unity and indivisibility as well as integrity with harmony and

---

1    Arif Payaslıoğlu, *An Introduction to Law and the Turkish Legal System*, (2nd ed.), Ankara, 1993

2    Ergun Özbudun, "Constitutional and Adnistrative Law", T.Ansay and D.Wallace (eds.), *Introduction to Turkish Law*, Ankara, (2nd ed.), 1993

cooperation between various parts of the Administration is secured through the central government (and its power of administrative supervision tutelage) over the acts and organs of the decentralized agencies. Administrative tutelage function is exercised by the central government according to the Article 127 of the Constitution for the following purposes: 1. Ensuring the functioning of local services in conformity with the principle of the unity of the Administration, 2. Securing uniform public services, 3. safeguarding the public interest, and 4. Meeting local needs in an appropriate manner.

The Administration is composed of two branches, namely a) central administration and b) decentralized administration. Both has extensive powers with respect to disaster management. The central administration includes the central departments, individual ministries and the Office of the Prime Minister.Ministeries are established on a functional basis by law to carry out certain public services such as the Public Works and Settlement, Environment, Internal Affairs, and the like. Provincial administration of each ministry is established according to the Article 126 of the Constitution. Turkey is divided into provinces on the basis of geographical situation, economic conditions and the requirements of the public services. Provinces are further divided into lower steps of administrative districts. The administration of provinces is based on the principle of deconcentration.

The head of the province is the governor. He is appointed by the Council of Ministers. Branches of ministries carry out their duties under the orders, directives and hierarchy of the governor and sub-governors. The governors are authorized to make certain decisions independently from the central departments. The Article 126 also provides for regional organization.

Centralized and decentralized administrations complement each other. The importance of decentralization is increasing by numerous factors. Decentralized administrations, local authorities and functionally decentralized organizations provide various local and common public services to the inhabitants of a particular geographic area. Provincial local administrations (departments), municipalities and village administrations are the three basic types of local authorities. They are public corporate bodies, enjoying administrative and financial autonomy. Their decision-making organs are elected by universal suffrage every five year. Their formation, powers and functions are regulated by law in accordance with the principle of decentralization [3].

Special local administrative arrangements may be introduced for larger urban areas (Art.127). A special law established a two-tier federative municipal system in metropolitan areas. Out of 3300 municipalities, 16 has this status at present. Duties such as physical planning, intracity transportation, large-scale infrastructure investment planning, water supply and solid waste disposal projects are within the domain of the metropolitan municipality.

## Functioning of the Administration with respect to the State of Emergency

The power to make administrative act is a great privilege of the Administration. Administrative acts are executory in nature. This privilege enables administrative authorities to create unilateral rights and to impose unilateral obligations that will bind persons without their consent.

As a consequence of the supremacy of the Parliament, the Constitution prohibits expressly any delegation of the

3    Ruşen Keleş, *Yerinden Yönetim ve Siyaset*, (Decentralization and Politics), Cem. Yay., İstanbul , 2000 (4th ed.)

legislative power to the executive (Art.7). Although the Parliament has the monopoly to legislate, this does not deny a rule-making power of the executive and the subordinate administrative authorities, such as issuing regulations, by-laws, orders, tariffs, city plans, and circulars. All these rule-making acts are subject to judicial review as to their conformity to the superior laws and rules. The competent court may invalidate any administrative act contrary to a superior rule or law, or to public interest, or in violation of the fundamental rights of individuals.

In times of wars and *emergency*, public authorities are empowered to take additional measures to maintain public order. Emergency rule is a *legal regime* governed by the principles of legality of administrative acts and the supremacy of law. All emergency measures must be in conformity with special laws that should not be repugnant to the Constitution (Arts. 119, 122, 15, 125).

The State of Emergency is declared in two different situations: 1) The event of a natural disaster (like *an earthquake*), a dangerous epidemic disease (cholera, etc.), a serious economic crisis. 2) The emergence of serious indications of wide-spread acts of violence aiming at the destruction of the free democratic order or fundamental rights, or a serious deterioration of public order as a result of acts of violence.

In the first three cases, the Council of Ministers may declare state of emergency. Its maximum period is six months. And it may be extended of periods not exceeding four months. It may be effective either for the whole country or in one or more regions. Decisions of the Council of Ministers concerning a state of emergency are subject to the immediate approval of the Parliament. The Parliament is authorized to change the duration, totally lift, or approve any state of emergency.

During the state of emergency, the Council of Ministers may issue decrees with force of law, in other words, law-amending ordinances, on matters relating to the state of emergency without prior authorization of the Parliament. However, these decrees are subject to subsequent parliamentary affirmation. The state of emergency is subject to judicial review, whilst the decrees having force of law issued by the Council of Ministers during emergency are excluded from judicial control by the Constitutional Court.

## Institutions for and Competencies with respect to Disaster Management

The disaster management is one of the major responsibilities of the government at both central and local levels. The Organic Law of the former Ministry of Public Works and Settlement (No:7116) had charged, in 1958, this newly established Ministry (Art.2) "to take all necessary measures before and after the disasters". Previously, this task was assumed for a long time (between 1937-1958) by the Ministry of Public Works. But a Law Amending Ordinance (No:180) that was put into force in 1983, in connection with the reorganization of bureaucracy, charged the new Ministry of Public Works and Settlement (Art.1), "to manage the carrying out of the disaster services in an efficient, orderly and swift manner". More specifically, the basic duties of the General Directorate of Disasters (Art.11) includes, 1) determination of likely disaster regions and the technical conditions for building in them, and ensuring their implementation 2) determination of the measures and principles to reduce the damage to life and property and ensuring their implementation 3) making an effort to prevent likely disasters, 4) providing immediate assistance and coordination during the disasters, 5) taking immediate short and long-term measures in disaster affected regions and meeting the requirements for service delivery in those regions in cooperation with the State Planning Organization and other public agencies, and finally 6) undertaking all preparatory, implementation, management and control functions for development and resettlement of all regions prone to natural disasters or already affected by them [4].

In addition, organic laws of a number of ministries like the Interior, National Defense, Health and Social Welfare, Transportation, Forestry, Energy and Natural Resources, Industry and Trade are also charged with certain functions in different stages of the disaster management process. Such a broad distribution of powers and responsibilities between numerous ministries, central and departmental authorities cause serious coordination problems in practice. In order to avoid confusions and overlapping of functions during the natural disasters, legislator empowered the governors in the provinces to take and implement necessary steps immediately following such events as the agent of the central administration. (Law No: 7269, Art.1). It was assumed that under his leading and coordinating role, inefficiencies in disaster management would be avoided.

Field (provincial) offices of the Ministry of Public Works and Settlement is not so effectively organized as to meet the requirements. Municipalities and village administrations as two types of local authority that have specific duties during disasters. To set local building regulations is, in principle, within the jurisdiction of local authorities. Yet, their capacity to manage great many services connected to disasters is extremely limited. They are poorly equipped to deal with providing guidance and control over building and settlement activities, even under normal conditions.

---

4    Ruşen Keleş, *Kentleşme Politikası* (Urbanization Policy), İmge, Ankara, 2000, (7th. Ed.)

In order to mitigate damages to life and property, to put into effect post-earthquake rescue, relief and housing programmes, to determine the real magnitude of losses, and to provide immediate assistance in the fields of financial means, health,etc., rescue and relief committees are formed under the leadership of the governor. In the State Capital, a Central Coordination Board functions. The governor manages and supervises all kinds of disaster services during the event through a crisis desk. Each governorate must have a pre-prepared Disaster Management Plan. These plans are implemented by the Sub-Provincial Rescue and Relief Committees.

Two other central agencies provide coordination between the works of the civilian and military authorities. These are the General Directorate of Civil Defense of the Ministry of the Interior and the Prime Ministry's Crisis Center in the National Security Council (MGK). In addition of the General Directorate of Natural Disasters, the Ministry of Public Works and Settlement's General Directorates of Construction Works, and Technical Research and Implementation assume certain responsibilities in the field of building and settlement. By the addition of the Central Disaster Coordination Board in the Ministry of Public Works and Settlement (1978), the Emergency Coordination Center of the Prime Ministry (1989) and the Prime Ministry's Crisis Center (1997), the existing complexity of organizations and powers grow much further.

Following the 1999 Marmara Earthquake, two more central agencies have been created in 2000 by a new Law-Amending Ordinance (No: 600): The first was the General Directorate of the Management of State of Emergency and the second the General Coordinating Office of Disasters. In order to complete this complicated picture, the names of three more institutions that were created following the great Marmara earthquake , have to be mentioned : 1) General Directorate of the Civil Defense for Rescue and Emergency attached to the Ministry of the Interior (Law-Amending Ordinance No: 586 and 596, December 1999 and April 2000), 2) The General Directorate of Emergency Management attached to the Prime Ministry (Law-Amending Ordinance, No: 588, November 1999) , and 3) The Independent National Earthquake Council (March 2000).

Multiplicity of authorities in charge of various aspects of the disasters cause numerous inconveniences in administration. With the creation of the National Earthquake Council in 2000, comprising twenty experts specialized in disaster management, coordination difficulties increased considerably. The tasks of the Council are identified as: 1) scientific assessment of earthquake predictions and informing the public, 2) identification of priority research areas concerning mitigation, 3) consultancy to public bodies and the development of policy and strategies, 4) ethical matters concerning earthquake prediction[5]. The Council has published the first national strategy of mitigation in 2002[6] .

## Planning Urban Development, Building and Disaster Management

One of the basic problems in disaster management in Turkey facing Administration is to link urban development planning to disaster management and to ensure minimum safety conditions for building. The main concern of the Law of Disasters of 1959 (No:7269) and its regulations is to provide a formal capacity for intervention after disasters and to organize the

5   Murat Balamir, "Recent Changes in Turkish Disasters Policy: A Strategical Reorientation", in P.R.Kleindorfer and M.R.Sertel (eds.), *Mitigation and Financing of Seismic Risks*, Kluwer, Den Haag, 2001, pp.207-234

6   Ulusal Deprem Konseyi, *Deprem Zararlarını Azaltma Ulusal Stratejsi ( National Strategy of Mitigation)*, Ankara, 2002

relief operations[7]. Only a few of the provisions of the Law of
Disasters contain any task concerning the preparations to be
undertaken prior to disasters, including the urban development plans. Taking measures to decentralize population and
economic activities more evenly over the territory of country is beyond the immediate concern of the Law. As noted
by Balamir, the Disasters Law and its regulations fall short of
constituting a contemporary disaster management system. It
does not differentiate between authorized and unauthorized
construction, and in one sense, it awards the owners of unauthorized buildings at the expense of the safety of the great
majority of the inhabitants[8].

The present Urban Development Law of 1985 (No: 3194),
on the other hand, is outdated and partial in scope. Although
municipalities with a population of 10.000 or more and provincial administrations are required to prepare development plans, no due consideration is given to the incorporation of geological, geomorphological and seismic data into
the plans. Attribution of the full responsibility of plan-mak-
ing and implementation in urban centers to municipal administrations, which are deprived of necessary financial and
technical means and the qualified manpower, together with
the diffusion of the planning controls , causes not only arbitrariness in environmental standards and quality, but at the
same time , makes difficult following rigorously the principles of reducing the risks .[9] As a result, although the principle of subsidiarity requiring that public affairs of local nature , like development planning , must be carried out by the
authorities closest to people increased the autonomy of local

---

7    Murat Balamir, "Recent Changes...", *Op.cit.,p.21oo*

8    Ibid., p.213

9    Ibid. , p.215

authorities to some extent, its cost to public order and interest has not been negligible.

Building control is almost non-existent in the system. Building control is supposed to be carried out by a professional with technical liability, who is either hired by the owner or the developer. This decreases the reliability of the whole process of planning. Normally, municipalities issue building permit on the basis of projects submitted to them by the owners. These projects are supposed to meet the requirements of both the building and disasters regulations, which comprise dimensional standards, requirements for heating, lighting, landscaping, parking, fire regulations, etc. A few regulations from several of these regulations are made to the regulation of the Disaster Law concerning structural safety standards in buildings[10]. As competently described by Balamir, "Practice of land-use planning and zoning, transportation and infrastructure planning, procedures for density assignment, planning of open spaces, participation processes, strengthening and devising of new methods of monitoring building use control, etc., are all distinct aspects of disaster concerns that need naturally be covered in the Development Law.[11] The present legislation is far from being designed in such a way as to cover all these details.

## Recent Changes in the Regulations on Disaster Management

Three steps taken during the post 1999 period can be devising of mentioned in this respect. The first is the adoption of a law-amending ordinance (No:595) that was put into force in 2000. It aims included ensuring the life and property safety in buildings, preventing unplanned, uncontrolled and low-quality

10    Ibid., p.216
11    Ibid, p. 21

construction which causes waste of resources, ensuring the control of construction, to protect the rights of those who suffered from damages to their buildings and to compensate their losses". This decree has been criticized on the grounds that its main concern was on individual buildings, neglecting building production, delegating the building control powers of the municipalities to private firms, not linking issues of building with macro-economic policies and finally not involving the professional organizations in the process of building control. Another criticism was made in connection to it introducing the concepts such as "building inspection firms", "certified architects" and "certified engineers". It was also argued that the decree was creating "a privileged professional group" [12], in contravention of the constitutional principle of equality before the law.

This Law-Amending Ordinance has been invalidated by the Constitutional law in 2001. This was followed by the enactment of a new Building Control Law (No:4708) in the same year. There were no major changes in the aims of the law. However, the provisions concerning the establishment and functioning of the building inspection firms were reformulated. Building inspection firms were defined as the private firms to be established by eligible architects and engineers with the aim to control all projects and building activity and report to the local authority responsible for both the construction and occupation permits. Building Control Law modified the respective provision of the Development Law (No.3194) and authorized the building inspection firms to take over the task of technical liability mentioned in the Development Law against the Administration.

12    Doğan Hasol, "Yapı Denetimi Kararnamesi", (Building Control Ordinance), *Yapı*, 2000

The second measure taken in 1999 was the adoption of the Law-Amending Ordinance (No:587) on the Obligatory Earthquake Insurance. A Natural Disasters Insurance Administration is established by the same Ordinance and it was attached to the Treasury. All residential buildings are to be covered by the obligatory earthquake insurance. And only the official, industrial and public buildings in the villages are exempted from the compulsory system[13].

A third novelty was brought about by another Law-Amending Ordinance (No:601) adopted in 2000, concerning the proficiency in constructional professions. The existing Law on Engineering and Architecture and the Law of Union of Chambers of Engineers and Architects have been amended by this recent Ordinance through which requirements for improved professional competence in the fields of engineering and architecture were described. A minimum of five years of professional experience, attendance in the training courses and success in written examinations organized both by the concerned Chambers are the essential conditions[14].

## Conclusions

1. Despite its relatively long experience in natural disasters, Turkish Public Administration does not seem ready to cope with various stages of disaster management adequately.

2. Measures taken after the Marmara earthquakes in the late 1990's reflect an understanding which tends to wiev the whole issue as a question of the quality and strength of buildings, and inadequacy of building control. Such an approach caused neglecting other more important and broader dimensions of the question.

13   Balamir, *Op.cit*, p.220
14   Ibid., p.226

3. The security of life and property is closely related with patterns of urbanization and excessive concentration of population in metropolitan areas. Density of population and buildings affect the inefficiency of disaster management in a number of ways. Therefore, decentralization of population and economic activities through regional planning is essential in order to reduce the losses and damages.

4. At a lower and more micro-level, measures are needed to develop and submit to the service of the administration early warning systems and to incorporate integrated hazards and microdonation maps into the development planning process.[15] Efforts to improve the building control system and the introduction of an obligatory earthquake insurance scheme should not end up with postponing a comprehensive revision in the system of urban development planning within a regional framework.

5. In addition to the existence of too many central and local institutions in charge of numerous tasks to be dealt with in pre and post-disaster phases, and during disaster, an increasing number of non-governmental organizations have played a certain role in the last earthquakes in an uncoordinated way, which made the aims of harmonization of rescue and relief operations even more difficult to achieve. Therefore, partnership should not be one of the additional factors increasing the number of obstacles before an efficient system of control and coordination.

---

15   Balamir, Murat, "Microzonation for Earthquake Risk Mitigation", Background Report on Sustainable Implementation, Legal and Organisational Bases of Land Use Management in Turkey, (unpublished paper), October, 2002; see also "Report of the United Nations Interregional Seminar on Disaster Management", Jakarta, December, 1993, pp.13-17: and "Report of the United Nations Conference on the Integration of Public Administration and the Science of Disasters", Beijing, January, 1997, pp.20-28

6. Recent experiences showed that in the distribution of the donations provided nationally and internationally to be used for the implementation of the relief and recovery programmes, the public administration as a whole deviated at times from the fundamental principle of impartiality. This was partly due to the nature of the coalition governments that ruled the country during the last ten years.

7. Perhaps a final point has to be made concerning the strengthening of local authorities to enable them in terms of powers, financial means and technical capability with the aim to play a more efficient role in all stages of the disaster management process. Providing them with the opportunities mentioned above would not only increase their role to guide and control urban development, settlement and planning, but also enable them to function more effectively during natural disasters[16]. It is hoped that recent attempts to reform the public administration system in Turkey, including local government, would in fact meet such a need.

## Bibliography

- Balamir, Murat, "Microzonation for Earthquake Risks Mitigation", Background Report on Sustainable Implementation, Legal and Organisational Bases of Land-Use Management in Turkey, unpublished paper, Oct.2002.

- Balamir, Murat, "Recent Changes in Turkish Disasters Policy: A Strategical Reorientation", in P.R. Kleindorfer and M.R.Sertel (eds.), *Mitigation and Financing of Seismic Risks*, Kluwer, 2001, pp.207-234.

- Balamir, Murat, "Painful Steps of Progress from Crisis Planning to Contingency Planning: Changes for Disaster Preparedness in

16  Ruşen Keleş, "Increasing Efficiency in Disaster Management", Paper presented to the Interregional Seminar on Disaster Management , United Nations, Jakarta, December 1993, pp.13-17

Turkey", *Journal of Contingencies and Crisis Management,* Vol.10, No:1, March, 2002, pp.39-49.

- Comfort, Louise and the Research Center for Urban Safety and Security, Kobe, "Complex Sysrems in Crisis: Anticipation and Resilience in Dynamic Environments", Annual Meeting of the American Political Science Assosciation, Atlanta, Georgia, September 2-5, 1999.

- Ergünay, Oktay and Polat Gülkan, "Land-Use Planning as Instrumant of Earthquake Hazard Mitigation", Proceedings of Worksop I on Seismic Hazard Assessment, Cooperative Project for Seismic Risk Reuction in the Mediterranean Region, Genoa, Italy, 1990.

- Ergünay, Oktay and Polat Gülkan, "Legisative and Institutional Framework relative to the Reduction of Seismic Risk in Turkey", Report submitted to the UN Regional Activity Center, Priority Actions Programme, UNEP-MAP, Split, 1990.

- Erkan, Nihal Ekin, "Yapı Denetimi ve Yerel Yönetimler", (Building Control and Local Authorities", Marmara University, Institute of Social Sciences, The Programme on Local Government and Decentralization, (unpublished paper), 2002.

- Gülkan, Polat, Balamir, Murat, Sucuoğlu, Haluk, et al.,*The Revision of the Urban Planning and Building Control System in Turkey for the Mitigation of Disasters Effects,* Final report of research prepared for and submitted to the Ministry of Public Works and Settlement, supported by the World Bank, Ankara, 1999.

- Hasol, Doğan, "Yapı Denetimi Kararnamesi", (Building Control Ordinance), *Yapı,* 2000

- Keleş, Ruşen, *Kentleşme Politikası (Urbanization Policy),* İmge, Ankara, 2002, (7 th ed.).

- Keleş, Ruşen, *Yerinden Yönetim ve Siyaset (Decentralization and Local Government),* Cem, İstanbul, 2000 (4 th ed.).

- Keleş, Ruşen, "Increasing Efficiency in Disaster Management", paper presented to the Interregional Seminar on Disaster Management, Jakarta, UN, December, 1993, pp.13-17.

- Kubalı, Derya, "Afet Yönetim Sisteminin Verimliliği" (Productivity of the Disaster Management System), Ankara University, The

Institute of the Social Sciences, Ph.D. Programme in City and Urbanization, Ankara 2001.

- Özbudun, Ergun, "Constitutional Law", in T.Ansay and D.Wallace (eds.), *Introduction to Turkish Law*, Ankara, 1993 (2 nd ed.).
- Payaslıoğlu, Arif, *An Introduction to Law and the Turkish Legal System*, Ankara, 1993, 2 nd ed.
- U.N., "Interregional Seminar on Disaster Management", Jakarta, 1993.
- U.N., "International Conference of the Integration of Public Administration and the Science of Disasters", Beijing, 1997
- Ulusal Deprem Konseyi, *Deprem Zararlarını Azaltma Ulusal Stretejisi (National Strategy for Earthquake Risk Mitigation)*, Ankara

# SMART CITIES

## Smart Cities in Emerging Economies: Reflections from Turkey*

## Introduction

We are living in an age of industrial development and technological progress creating far-reaching consequences which were unimaginable about hundred years ago. Accomplishments in information technology opened up unlimited horizons in almost all aspects of life all over the world. Current progress in information technology made it possible also the emergence of a new mode of socio-technical organization that was called by Manuel Castells as the *informational mode of* development.[1] Technological change can be better understood in the context of the social structure in which it takes place. Therefore, manifestations of the interaction between technology and the other elements of social structure in a process that shapes the society, consequently the space is of utmost importance.[2] Technology has been defined elsewhere as" the use of scientific knowledge to specify ways of doing things in a reproducible manner"[3]. It is important to see that what is specific to the above mentioned

---

\* International Forum on Smart Cities and Public Contracting, University of Rosario, Bogota, Columbia, 11-13 April 2012.

1 Manuel Castells, **The Informational City**, Basil Blackwell, London, 1989, p.2.

2 Ibid, p.10.

3 Harvey Brooks, cited in Daniel Bell, The Coming of Post-Industrial Society, Basic Books, New York, 1973, p. 29.

informational mode of development is that here "knowledge intervenes upon knowledge itself in order to generate higher productivity"[4]. Numerous scientific and technological innovations such as progress in microelectronics, transistors, the integrated circuits, the planar process, the microprocessor, computers, and the internet have all contributed to this progress starting from the late 1960's. As rightly mentioned by such sociologists like Alain Touraine and Daniel Bell, the tremendous change we faced is not only the shift from goods to services, but the emergence of information processing as the core, fundamental activity conditioning the effectiveness and productivity of all processes of production, distribution, consumption, and management.[5]

The information age characterized by the mode of informational development has been widely accepted as a great benefit for humanity. However, views have been expressed attracting the attention to the fact that this global change was bringing new ethical dilemmas.[6]

For instance, Florida supported this view arguing that "how information and communication technologies can contribute to the sustainable development of an equitable society is one of the crucial global issues of our time"[7]. Although technology is a powerful instrument affecting all aspects of life, it is only one of the instruments shaping the world. The process of organizational restructuring is essentially dictated by essential economic, social and institutional transformations.[8]

---

4    Manuel Castells, op. cit., 10.

5    Manuel Castells, ibid, p. 17.

6    R. Stichler and R. Hauptman (eds.), Ethics, Information and Technology, McFarland, Jefferson, 1998, p.1.

7    L. Floridi, "The New Information and Communication Technologies for the Development of Education", Invite Address, Unesco World Commission on the Ethics of Scientific Konowledge and Technology, (COMEST), Paris, 31 May 2001.

8    Manuel Castells, op. cit., 126.

Fascinating progress in information technology that was taken place during the last several decades not only caused the restructuring of capitalism starting from the 1980's, but also has changed considerably the nature and the role of the welfare state. From a spatial point of view, this tendency resulted in further decentralization into the suburbs and the rise of the dual city, namely the contrast between the opulence and poverty in shared localities. Despite the tendency toward further decentralization, not only local authorities, but also the national governments are frequently powerless to handle unidentifiable flows made possible by contemporary information technology. One can even argue that the concept of state sovereignty itself has considerably lost its previously absolute character.

Although it is assumed that active citizen participation and a nation-wide or worldwide network of local governments could be implemented most effectively on the basis of new information technologies, it should be kept in mind that technological medium alone will not be able to transform the process of restructuring without social mobilization, political decisions affected tremendously by human element and institutional strategies that would enable local governments to challenge collectively the powers of flows.[9]

## On the Concept of Smart City

The concept of smart city has become one of the widely used concepts during the last decade by academicians and professional organizations and the representatives of local authorities. The concepts like intelligence or smartness are normally used to denote certain characteristics of human beings. Oxford Advanced Learner's Dictionary defines the word *intelligence* as "the ability to learn and think in a logical way about

9    Manuel Castells, op. cit., p.353.

things; the ability to do this well". Briefly, as defined in Webster's New World Dictionary, *intelligence* is the ability to learn or understand from experience; ability to acquire and retain knowledge; mental ability, and the ability to respond quickly and successfully to a new situation; finally, use of the faculty of reason in solving problems, directing conduct effectively. *Artificial intelligence,* on the other hand, is defined "as an area of study concerned with making computers copy intelligent human behavior".

The meaning of the word *smart* in the above mentioned dictionaries is *"clean, neat, intelligent, fashionable, computer-controlled* (controlled by a computer, so that it appears to act in an intelligent way). It is a relatively new phenomenon that we have began to assign such adjectives as smartness and intelligence to objects other than human beings as in the case of smart cities, smart bombs and smart washing machine, and the sentient city.[10]

Numerous cities called smart cities exists both in the US and elsewhere. It was suggested during the 1997 World Forum on Smart Cities that around 50.000 cities and towns around the world would develop smart initiatives over the next decade.[11] Holland attracts our attention to the abundance of similar concepts such as *smart, intelligent, innovative, wired, digital, creative, and cultural.* All the cities qualified with such adjectives try to link together technological informational transformations with economic, political, and socio-cultural change.[12] However, he identifies at least four possible definitions emphasizing on different objectives followed by smart city initiatives. a) The first concerns the application of a wide range of electronic and digital applications

10    Manuel Castells, op.cit., p. 353.
11    Mark Shepard (ed.), **Sentient City: Ubiquitous Computing, Architecture, and the Future of Urban Space**, The M.I.T.Press, Cambridge, 2011.
12    Ibid, p.305.

to communities and cities. In this sense, cities take various names as in the cases of *cyber, digital, wired, informational or knowledge-based city. b)* A second meaning is the use of information technology to transform life and work within a region in significant and fundamental ways. c) A third meaning of intelligent or smart is as embedded information and communication technology in the city. d) A final meaning of smart city is perceived as spatial territories that bring together information and communication technologies (ICT) on one hand and the people on the other to enhance innovation, learning, knowledge and problem solving.

Similarly, Komninos sees smart cities as "territories with high capacity for learning and innovation, which is built in the creativity of their population, their institutions of knowledge creation, and their digital infrastructure for communication and knowledge management"[13]. Another definition has been made by Caragliu, Del Bo and Nijkamp, according to which, smart city is understood "as a strategic device to encompass urban production factors in a common framework, and in particular, to highlight the importance of information and communications technologies in the last 20 years for enhancing the competitive profile of a city"[14]. They also add the following observation in order to complement this definition: "The label smart city should point to clever solutions allowing modern cities to thrive, through quantitative and qualitative improvements in productivity"[15].

A similar concept related to smart city is the smart growth agenda which includes innovative ITC's, architectural planning and design, creative and cultural industries, and concepts

---

13 N. Komninos, **Intelligent Cities: Innovation, Knowledge Sytems and Digital Spaces**, Spon Press, London, 2006, p.1.

14 Andrea Caragliu, Chiara Del Bo and Peter Nijkamp, "Smart Cities in Europe", Journal of Urban Technology, Vol. 18, No:2, April 2011, pp. 65-82.

15 Ibid, p. 66.

of social and environmental sustainability, in order to address serious economic, social and ecological problems facing many cities in the world.[16]

## Main Features of Smart Cities

Main features of smart cities may be grouped around six essential points.[17]

1) The utilization of networked infrastructure to improve economic and political efficiency and enable social, cultural, and urban development. The term infrastructure here indicates business services, housing, leisure, and lifestyle services, mobile and fixed phones, computer networks, e-commerce, and internal services, a wired city.

2) An underlying emphasis on business-led urban development.

3) A strong focus on the aim of achieving the social inclusion of various urban residents in public services.

4) A stress on the crucial role of high-tech and creative industries in long run urban growth.

5) Profound attention to the role of social and relational capital in urban development. This means that a smart city will be a city whose inhabitants have learned to learn, adapt, and innovate. People need to be able to use technology in order to benefit from it.

6) Social and environmental sustainability as a major strategic component of smart cities.

A relatively recent study identified six main dimensions along which a ranking of nearly 70 European middle sized cities ranked.[18] These dimensions were a) a smart economy,

---

16   D. Thorns, **The Transformation of Cities: Urban Theory and Urban Life**, Palgrave, Basingstoke, 2002.

17   A. Caragliu, C. Del Bo and P. Nijkamp, op. cit., pp. 67-68.

18   Cited in Ibid, p.70.

b) smart mobility, c) a smart environment, d) smart people, e) smart living, and f) smart governance.

These six axes connect with traditional regional and neo-classical theories of urban growth and development. Particularly, these axes are based on theories of regional competitiveness, transport, information and communications technology, economics, natural resources, human and social capital, quality of life, and the participation of society members in the city life. In brief, it is generally believed that a city to be smart when investments in human and social capital and traditional (transport) and modern (ICT) communication infrastructure fuel sustainable economic growth and a high quality of life, with a wise management of natural resources, through participatory governance.[19]

Apart from instrumental approaches to the use of digital technology, Japson and Edwards underline the significance of smartness as affecting urban development. According to them, *smart growth* can be understood as an attempt to restrain *urban sprawl*. This is accomplished through a variety of land-use control and other regional and local policy mechanisms that help encourage *compact development, urban revitalization, and re-discovery, transportation and housing diversity, open space protection, and collaborative decision-making.*[20] They also suggest that as preconditions of smartness the following factors of sustainability have to be taken into account in ensuring smart growth:[21] 1) Jobs-housing balance, 2) Spatial integration of employment and transportation, 3) Mixed land-use, 4) Use of locally-produced, clean and renewable en-

19  Caragliu, Del Bo and Nijkamp, op. cit., p. 70.
20  Edward J. Japson, Jr., and Mary M. Edwards, " How Possible is Sustainable Development? An Analysis of Planners' Perceptions About New Urbanism, Smart Growth and the Ecological City", **Planning Practice and Research**, Vol. 25, No: 4, August 2010, p. 419.
21  Ibid., pp. 421-422.

ergy sources, 5) Energy and resource efficient building and
sit design, 6) Pedestrian access (walking and biking) to work
and leisure, 7) Housing affordability (for all income groups),
8)Housing diversity (of style, type and tenure), 9) Higher density residential development, 10) Protection of natural and
biological functions and processes, 11) Resident involvement
and empowerment, 12) Social spaces (Public spaces to encourage social gathering), 13) Sense of place, 14) Intermodal
transportation connectivity.

## On the Smartness of Smart Cities

The smartness of smart cities is generally highlighted with
several contributions they are expected to make to increasing the quality of individual buildings, livability of urban
environments, success of urban development activities and
sustainability of natural resources and the ecosystem in general. Within this framework, the following shared characteristics appear to be reflecting the positive side of the concept
of smart city[22]: 1) The level of exploitation of networked infrastructure to improve economic and political efficiency
and enable social, cultural and urban development. 2) A vision and a strategy for creating the competitive city with the
smart city taking the opportunities to increase local prosperity, competitiveness and sustainability, to signifying to
the presence of a creative class, the quality of and dedicated
attention to the urban environment, the level of education,
multi-model accessibility, and the use of ICT's for public administration to increase urban wealth. 3) An approach to sustainable and inclusive cities, placing the main weight on the
social capital of urban development. At this point, the smart
city knows how to learn, adapt and innovate and the focus

22   Krassimira Antonova Paskaleva, " The Smart City: A Nexus for Open Inno-
     vation?", **Intelligent Building International**, Vol. 3, 2011, pp. 155-156.

could be social inclusion in public service or involving the citizens in service co-design and better services. In this sense, sustainability is considered as the very strategic element of the smart cities; and achieving environmental or social sustainability through participation of the public in local decision-making is key to increasing democracy and governance.

At the lowest level, buildings can be designed or cities can be planned with a view to incorporate into decision-making processes all possibilities of the new information technologies in mind.[23] In this sense, one can imagine how *smart neighborhoods* where media-based social interaction occurs, *smart streets* where new transportation behaviours develop, *smart squares* where civic decisions are taken, *smart museums and parks* where natural and cultural heritage feed learning, and finally, *smart city halls* where mobile e- government services are delivered.[24]

On the other hand, in considering the smartness of smart cities, one should not overlook certain other considerations meaning that the ongoing debate on its principles and strategic policy agenda still continues to be unresolved. In this framework, 1) The first important challenge is that in most of the campaigns for smart city and in using its instruments seems to exist a tendency that such strategies have to be almost *exclusively entrepreneurial*. It is really questionable to what extent a *purely business-led urban development strategy* could meet the real needs of emerging economies of the third world, where poverty is persisting. 2) Secondly, smart cities must seriously start with people and *the human capital* side of the equation rather than blindly believing that information technology itself can automatically transform and

---

23    Rob Moult, "Intelligent Building=Green Building", **Industry and Environment**, Vol. 23, No: 1-2 January-June 2000, pp. 50-53.

24    Paskaleva, op. cit,, p. 163.

improve cities. In other words, there is a real need to create a real shift in the balance of power between the use of information technology by business, government, communities and ordinary people who live in cities, as well as to seek to balance economic growth with sustainability. "In a word, the real smart city might use ICT to enhance democratic debates about the kind of city it wants to be and what kind of city people want to live in"[25]. Human beings can not getting rid of their responsibility to manage their own buildings, cities and environments intelligently simply by delegating it to smart devices produced by modern technology. Non-artificial intelligence of human beings must not be replaced, but complemented by artificial intelligence of information and communications technology.

3) The third consideration has something to do with the specific conditions of emerging economies concerning the preparation to competently use digital information. Since the main focus of our Forum is the emerging economies, it is necessary to see where do stand both the emerging and industrial societies in this respect. We must be remember that the number of computers in developed countries enable them to benefit from the possibilities of digital technology in many fields while corresponding figures in emerging societies are of a nature not to create optimism in this regard. The number of computers in the U.S.A. and other industrial societies are the followings: U.S.A. 164.100.100, Japan 49.900.000, Germany 30.600.000, United Kingdom 26.000.000, France 21.800.000, Italy 17.500.000, Canada 16.900.000, Switzerland 15.900.000, Austria 10.600.000, South Korea 10.600.00. The percentage of internet users is as high as %68 in Sweden, %63 in Denmark, %61 in the Netherlands, %59 in Norway, and %53 in

---

25   Cited in Mark Deakin and Husam Al Waer, "From Intelligent to Smart Cities", **Intelligent Building International**, Vol. 3, 2011, p. 142.

South Korea. On the other hand, the percentage of the total population using internet is as low as %0.2 in Morocco, %0.1 in Algeria, %0.3 in Egypt, %0.4 in Saudi Arabia, %5.3 in Kuwait, %0.2 in Iran and %1.8 in Jordan. In addition to effect of digital inequality, its perception may not just ownership or access to information and communications technology but also the lack of confidence or skill in being successfully use.[26] We must add that even within the United States one quarter of the citizens are "truly disconnected", having no direct or indirect experience with the internet, whilst another 20 percent of Americans were "net evaders", that is people who live with someone who uses the internet from home. Net evaders might use the internet by having others send and receive e-mail or do on-line searches for information for them.[27] 4) A final but related issue is that the information society poses fundamental ethical problems whose complexity and global dimensions are rapidly evolving. As Florida pointed out how information and communications technology can contribute to the sustainable development of an equitable society is one of the most crucial issues of our time.[28] He points to the digital divide in particular as the source of many of the ethical problems emerging from the evolution of the information society. The digital divide disempowers, discriminates and generates dependency. It can engender new forms of colonialism and apartheid that must be prevented, opposed and

26  Lynn McAllister, Helen Hall, Helen Partridge and Gillian Hallam, "Effecting Social Change in the Smart City: The West End Connect Community Project", Paper presented to the Social Change Research Quensland University of Technology, 28 October 2005.

27  Ibid, p. 5.

28  L. Floridi, "The New Information and Communications Technology for the Development of Education", Invite Address. UNESCO World Commission on the Ethics of Scientific Knowledge and Technology (COMEST), Paris, 31 May 2001.

ultimately eradicated.[29] It is generally believed that unequal access of some segments in the society, between men and women, well to do and the poor, to information and communication technology and the acquisition of necessary skills, as in most of the emerging economies, has also tremendous ethical implications for the society as a whole.

## Efforts to Initiate Cases of Smart City in Turkey
## General Profile of Urban Turkey

Turkey is a rapidly urbanizing country in the Middle-East, with 76.6 percent of its total population (76 million) living urban centers. The level of urbanization was only 20 percent in 1950 and 43.9 percent in 1980. The number of cities having 10.000 or more population is 528, and those with 100.000 population is 138. There are 7 cities with a population of one million and over. The distribution of cities among various size categories seems to be rather unbalanced, in the sense that more than three fourths of the urban population is concentrated in the size category of 100.000 and over. A similar inequality exists between the level of urbanization in different geographical regions. For instance, while the degree of urbanization is as high as 91 percent in the Marmara Region with Istanbul at its center, and 83 percent in central Anatolia, it is not higher than 55 percent in such regions as Eastern Anatolian and Black Sea Regions. There is no doubt that such inequalities reflect at the same time relative underdevelopment of the regions concerned.[30]

On the other hand, the Constitution of Turkey requires designing a territorial organization based on the principles of

---

29   L. Floridi, "Information Ethics: An Environmental Approach to the Digital Divide", **Philosophy in the Contemporary World**, Vol. 9(1), 2001, pp.39-46.

30   Rusen Keles, Kentleşme Politikası (Urbanization Policy), Imge Publishers, (12th Ed.), Ankara, pp.60-76.

centralization and decentralization (Art.123). Decentralized institutions, in other words, local authorities are the departments, municipalities and village administrations. Municipalities which are established in settlements with 5.000 and more inhabitants are in charge of meeting the common service needs of local communities. At present there are 2.950 municipalities in Turkey. In view of the fact that Turkey is a developing economy with 12.500 US Dollars per capita GNP, local authorities have to find necessary resources to finance the construction of urban infrastructure, major urban facilities and services without increasing dependency upon the central government funds. However, a certain amount of funds from the national budget is allocated to local authorities every year, in accordance with the constitutional principle requiring that they have to be provided with necessary financial means in proportion to their competencies (Art .127).[31]

To the extent that they are equipped with the opportunities provided by the age of information and communications technologies, increasing number of municipalities have recently initiated smart city programmes in order to carry out local public services more efficiently. Several examples may be worth to mention in this connection. However, one should keep in mind that one of the preconditions of the success in this matter is the capacity of the society to benefit from information technology. In Turkey, the percentage of the households having access to internet is only 30 percent, which does not mean that internet subscribers' range in Turkey is 30 percent of the population. The latter is much lower than 30 percent of the population. This is certainly a considerably low value in a country like Turkey which has a young population density. Besides the low ratio of Internet

---

31    Rusen Keles, **Yerinden Yönetim ve Siyaset** (Decentralization and Politics), Cem Publishers, istanbul (7th ed.).

subscribers, the mobile phone subscribers are nearly 65 million which means 92 percent of the total population.[32]

## The State Planning Organization

First of all, The Liaison Office of the European in Ankara, in cooperation with the State Planning Organization has launched an ICT Policy Support Programme as a part of its Competitiveness and Innovation Programme. In order to implement the Digital Agenda for Europe, this Support Programme aims to enhance development of a competitive and innovative information society, support public-private partnerships.

"Smart cities", "e-governance", "energy efficiency", "environmental protection" and "intelligent mobility" are the main project fields being supported ICTPSP.[33] Istanbul Metropolitan Municipality and Odunpazarı Municipality (Eskişehir) are cooperating with partner local authorities abroad to develop urban information systems, geographical information systems and information systems for governance at local level. These programmes are based on the Lisbon Strategy which aims to make the European Union the most competitive and dynamic knowledge-based economy in the world by 2010.[34]

The State Planning Organization Information Society Department has been established in 2003 to coordinate the Project of e-Transformation Turkey. According to the Information Society Department of the SPO the strategic priorities starts with social transformation and aims at providing a citizen-focused approach, service transformation, communication management and e-government applications.

32   Mobile Democracy Associaton, **Draft Concept Note, Mobile Democracy Academy**, Ankara, 2012.

33   State Planning Organization and the European Union, **ICT Policy Support Programme (2007-2013), Competitiveness and Innovation Reference programme**, Ankara, 2011.

34   The State Planning Organization's e-Transformation Turkey Project.

## Mobile Democracy Academy

Secondly, a Mobile Democracy Association has been set up in Turkey in 2005 to bring forth the understanding of being a real citizen and having an urban consciousness. This Association is a "social living technique", which provides citizens with an efficient means to contact their local administrations in a rapid fashion. The technique used by the Association also increases social sharing and supports the acquisition of social responsibilities of the citizens for their own habitats. Nearly 40 municipalities have joined so far the Mobile Democracy Association as members. A free broadcast channel has been created by the Association in order to form an "information framework" for raising the consciousness level of the city as a whole by determining sub users of the services of various departments of local government, such as the Directorate of Public Health, Directorate of Culture, Directorate of Public Security, and the like. Through the Mobile Democracy Broadcast Channel (Cell broadcast Channel) (888), local authorities get the chance to inform the citizens who live within the surrounding areas of the city, related with road construction, traffic jam, water shortages, cultural and touristic activities.

A second channel (3870) established by the Association is called Democratic Participation Channel through which citizens get a chance to transmit their requestes, suggestions or complaints to local authorities using their mobile phones from everywhere and every moment only by sending SMS's to 3870 service number. It is an interactive channel which aims to raise the level of participation in urban culture and contributes to the formation of a democratic environment. With this system, local authorities become able to receive feedbacks from citizens regarding any local issue. Thus, they can be informed about the views of people who elected them.

The system helps the formation of a participatory urban culture, with applying mobile referenda. The feedbacks that are collected into the municipality's data base through 3870, are automatically forwarded to the concerned sub-departments. By this way, the coordination between different sub-departments can be provided with increasing efficiency.

Mobile Democracy Platform also carries out surveys and referenda through the 888 Cellbroadcast Channel in which municipalities get the opportunity to measure the quality and efficiency of their services and plan their operations effectively for the future course. Thus, it becomes possible to transform the gains of mobile technologies in general as well as in the case of Turkey into the advantages, in the challenge of achieving democracy. Indeed, cell phones as a product of mobile technology, which makes democratic participation independent from the limitations of time and space, and which achieves direct participation of citizens by eliminating any organization or person as a tool to participate, are used by individuals from all age groups and socio economic strata.

## Efforts of Individual Municipalities Initiating Smart City Applications

### 1) The City of Yalova

The municipality of Yalova, located in the Marmara Region, put into effect a new programme that is called *Public Administration Independent of Time and Space*. This model combines an Internet-based administrative information system with practices of total quality management. The basic elements of the model is monitoring, participation and constant improvement of the service provision processes in an interactive manner. The provision of public services such as urban development, issuing of building licence, tax payments is no longer dependent upon space, in the sense that municipal officers can now produce and provide local public services not necessarily from public buildings, but from everywhere.

The system tends to exclude personal initiative in service provision by relieving the service provider of partisan pressures on one hand, and by safeguarding the clients against the risk of partial treatment on the other. Service desks in other words, service information centers, established in each quarter of the city, assist citizens to transmit their applications, suggestions and demands to city administration. Inhabitants of Yalova have the opportunity to submit their applications to municipality either through phones, internet, fax, or by visiting the service desks in the quarters.

## 2) The City of Beyoğlu

The city of Beyoğlu is one of the largest district municipalities of Metropolitan İstanbul. The municipality has recently set up a computer-based management system, which is called as the Smart City Automation System, enabling citizens to reach the city administration and look for solutions to their problems. Management Geographical Information System (MGIS) is the outcome of the integration of two different systems existed before: One was the Management Information System (MIS) and the other was called Geographical Information System (GIS). This interactif new system aims both to provide better quality public services to citizens and at the same time to increase the level of public participation in the administrative processes. By using the smart reception center in the municipality, residents of the city benefit from the services concerning registration, urban development, archives, reaching the service file, tax information, etc. Social assistance services, technical services, environmental services, security affairs, urban development and planning, traffic and tax issue are the most widely used smart services of the municipality. A free, constant and wireless internet system accelerates further the interaction between the citizens and administration.[35]

## 3) Seferihisar (İzmir)

A similar system has been established in Seferihisar Municipality, a touristic town at a distance of nearly 50 kilometers South of Izmir, through which citizens easily can reach "The Municipal Solution Desk", either through internet or SMS's by their mobile phones. This Desk operates in close cooperation with municipal automation system on one hand and the e municipality system on the other. Once a complaint or a demand is taken by the smart telephone of the chief of a municipal division, the service is provided in accordance with the existing rules and the taxpayer is informed about the result. Most of the tax payments in the city are made through this system. Municipality also uses this system of automation to monitor the degree of efficiency of its own vehicles with respect to their fuel consumption.

## 4) Karasu (Sakarya)

Karasu Municipality, again a small town on the Black Sea, in North Western Turkey, has initiated a Smart City Project in order to collect all kinds of statistics concerning the city under one single data base and to enable citizens to benefit from local public services in a fast manner and interactively through such devices as the internet and mobile phones. The data base mentioned above includes all detailed and reliable information regarding the households, buildings and

---

35   Beyoğlu Belediyesi (Municipality of Beyoğlu), Bilge Şehir Beyoğlu (Smart City Beyoğlu), **7/24 On-Line Belediye** (Municipality), (no date).

streets in addition to information with respect to the characteristics of the population, land registry and the real estate. Training programmes have also been organized with a view to educate the municipal personnel in related matters and to qualify them to establish necessary ties with the citizens. A *Service Desk,* meeting the demands, *E Municipality* practices, providing citizens to reach the administration, *S Municipality* device, creating the links between the citizens and the municipality, and finally the *T-Municipality* practice, enabling them to reach the administration 24 hours a day are the main elements of the smart city system in Karasu. All financial resources needed to keep the system continue to operate are provided by the municipality itself with no transfer from the center.

There are several other medium-size cities which created similar on-line service systems and realize other smart city practices. These are Fatih (istanbul), Melikgazi (Kayseri), Meram (Konya), Aksaray, and some others. ETransformation Project at the central level, Local Information Project, Local Network Project, and Partnership Project with private firms, are the examples of the attemps, with similar characteristics, supported by the central government agencies and international donor organizations.[36]

## Conclusion

The smart city concept has been developing during the last three decades and its various configurations appear to be adopted and implemented in an increasing number of cities all over the world. As far as the benefits to be gained from the

---

36  EU Commission, Directorate General for Information Society and Media, On-Line Availability of Public Services: Hoıw is Euope Progressing? Web-Based Survey on Electronic Public Services, Report of the 5th Measurement, October, 2004.

application of the smart city concept in local governance justify its increasing use, that should certainly be encouraged. In
addition to its contribution to the rationalization of service
provision process at local level, it is even assumed that there
is a close relationship between e-governance and e-democ-
racy.[37] However, several other factors have to be taken into
account before this assertion is generalized. First of all, there
are striking differences between the developed and industrialized countries and instruments made available by advanced
information technology differ greatly from one country to
another depending upon their level of economic and technological development. There are also great differences between countries with respect to their preparedness to the demands of the age of information. The ratio of preparedness of
different countries in Europe is as the followings: Denmark:
5.71, Sweden: 5.66, Switzerland: 5.56, Holland: 5.54, United
Kingdom: 5.45, Turkey: 3.86. On the other hand, while the
average European ratio of internet usage is as high as 4.67,
this ratio is only 2.52 for Turkey.[38] These and similar com-
parisons suggest that there will be tremendous discrepancies between nations in benefiting from the ICT. Of course,
these inequalities have something to do with the prevalence
of poverty conditions and imbalances in income distribution
in general in the so called Third World countries.

Secondly, as we look at the smart city practices in Turkey, we observe that almost all cities initiating such innovations are located in the developed western regions. There
is no doubt that such inequalities can be regarded as a direct consequence of regional socio-economic disparities.

---

37   Nur Şat, A Medium for Democracy? E-Municipality (Unpublished Ph.D.
      Dissertation written under the guidance of the author), Marmara University,
      Institute of Local Government, İstanbul, 2008.
38   Nur Şat, op. cit., p. 175.

Furthermore, the number of the cities that are engaged in such endeavors is negligible and no more than 50 out of a total of 2.950. The fact that smartness is actually restricted to a few urban settlements, to well-to-do and to relatively developed regions in the country, neglecting the ultimate goal of maximizing the public interest, would result certainly ethical problems in public administration.

Thirdly, smart city strategies, following the experiments in developed countries seem to be exclusively entrepreneurial. Such a business-led approach may meet the requirements of a neo-liberal age, but it may not suffice to solve pressing urbanization problems of emerging economies.

Sustainable development often is perceived in the sense of ensuring sustainability of capitalism itself without much interest in meeting human needs. Urban populations of emerging economies are faced with serious problems of survival. Meeting the needs of social housing, creating an appropriate traffic infrastructure, building cities based on recycling by setting up comprehensive waste disposal and recycling facilities, planning and urban structure which is able to withstand natural and man-made disasters can be regarded as major macro issues of rapidly urbanizing cities. Particularly in a world with continually rising land prices it would never be economically rational to abandon public land ownership. No matter what instruments are used, digital or non-digital, by smart cities, efforts of city administrations must necessarily focus on these and similar macro-issues of urban development. As mentioned earlier, natural intelligence of human beings can not and should not be replaced, but simply complemented by artificial intelligence of information and communications technology.

## Short Bibliography

- Bell, Daniel, The Coming of Post-Industrial Society, Basic Books, New York, 1973.

- Beyoğlu Belediyesi (Municipality of Beyoğlu), Bilge Şehir Beyoğlu (Smart City Beyoğlu), 7/24 On-Line Belediye (Municipality), (no date).

- Caragliu, Andrea, Del Bo, Chiara, Nijkamp, Peter, "Smart Cities in Europe", Journal of Urban Technology, Vol. 18, No: 2, April 2011, pp. 65-82.

- Castells, Manuel, The Informational City, Basil Blackwell, London, 1973.

- Deakin,    Mark and  Al Waer,   Husam, "From Intelligent to Smart Cities", Intelligent Building International, Vol. 13, 2011.

- European Commission, Directorate General for Information Society and Media on-Line Availability of Public Services: How is Europe Progressing? Web-Based Survey on Electronic Public Services, Report of the 5th Measurement, October, 2004.

- Floridi, L.,"The New Information and Communication Technologys for the Development of Education", Invited Address, Unesco World Commission on the Ethics of Scientific Knowledge and Technology (COMEST), Paris, 31 May 2001.

- Floridi, L.,"Information Ethics: An Environmental Approach to the Digital Divide", Philosophy in the Contemporary World, Vol. 91 (1), 2001, pp. 39-46.

- Holland, Robert G.,"Will the Real Smart City Please Stand Up?", City, Vol .12, No: 3, December, 2008.

- Japson, Edward J. And Edwards, Mary M.,"How Possible is Sustainable Development? An Analysis of Planners' Perceptions About New Urbanism, Smart Growth and the Ecological City", Planning Practice and Research, Vol. 25, No: 4, August 2010.

- Keleş, Ruşen, Kentleşme Politikası (Urbanization Policy), Imge Publishers, Ankara, 2012 (12th ed.).

- Keleş, Ruşen, Yerinden Yönetim ve Siyaset (Decentralization and Politics), Cem Publishers, İstanbul, 2012 (8th ed.).

- Komninos, **N., Intelligent Cities: Innovation, Knowledge Systems and Digital Spaces**, Spon Press, London, 2006.

- **McAllister, Lynn, Hall, Helen, Partridge, Helen and Hallam, Gillian**, "Effecting Social Change in the Smart City: The West End Connect Community Project", Paper presented to the Social Change Research Queensland University of Technology, 28 October 2005.

- Mobile Democracy Association, **Draft Concept Note, Mobile Democracy Academy**, Ankara, 2012.

- **Moult, Rob**, "Intelligent Building-Green Building", **Industry and Environment**, Vol. 23, No:1-2, January-June 2000.

- **Paskaleva, Krassimira Antonova**, "The Smart City: A Nexus for Open Innovation", Intelligent Building International, Vol.3, 2011.

- **Shepard, Mark (ed.), Sentient City: Ubiquitous Computing, Architecture and the Future of Urban Space**, The M.I.T. Press, Cambridge, 2011.

- **State Planning Organization and the European Union, ICT Policy Support Programme (2007-2013), Competitiveness and Innovation Reference Programme**, Ankara, 2011.

- **Stichler R. And Hauptman, R. (eds.), Ethics, Information and Technology**, McFarland, Jefferson, 1998.

- **Şat, Nur, A Medium for Democracy?: E-Municipality**, (Unpublished Ph.D. Dissertation completed under the supervision of the author), Marmara University, The Institute of Local Government, Istanbul, 2008.

- Thorns, D., TheTransformation of Cities: Urban Theory and Urban Life, Palgrave, Basingstoke, 2002.

# COOPERATIVE LAW

# Laws On Cooperatives*

Law No. : 1163
Date of Approval : 24.4.1969
Official Gazette of Publishing : Date: 10/5/1969, No: 13195

## PART ONE
## Cooperative And Establishment Thereof
### A) Description:

**Article-1:** Cooperatives are bodies with variable members, variable capital, and legal identity that are established by natural and public legal entities and private administrations, municipalities, villages, societies and associations in order to ensure and maintain certain economic interests and especially the needs of their members toward professional life and living standards by means of mutual assistance, solidarity and service as trustees to each other.

### B) Establishment, Terms of Validity, Authorization for Using Name

**Article-2:** A cooperative is established through an Rules to be signed between 7 members. The signatories in the Rules should be notary-attested.

---

\* The titles of the cooperatives and their superior institutions cannot contain the names of public bodies and institutions (Article 1 of the Law 3476 and addendum thereof)

The undertakings in the Rules of the other cooperatives the scope of which include the transfer of immovable properties, pertaining to the fact that immovable properties will be transferred to members are deemed as valid irrespective of other official procedure.

While establishing cooperatives, the capital of the cooperative cannot be confined of to a certain amount. The name 'cooperative' can solely be used by the bodies that have been established in accordance with this law hereby.

## C) Permission, Registration, And Announcement

**Article-3:** The Rules is submitted to the Ministry of Trade. Should the Ministry permit the establishment, it is registered with the local Trade Registry Office and announced accordingly. The particulars to be registered and announced are as follows:

(*) The members of the Board of Directors of the cooperatives and their superior institutions that violate Item 4 are sentenced to penalties such as imprisonment from 1 month up to 6 months and heavy fines such as fifty thousand to five-hundred thousand Turkish Liras depending on the type and degree of the act as Per the Article 26 of the Law 3476 and the appended Addendum 2/2.

1. The date of the Rules,

2. The scope, the field of activity and the duration, if any, of the cooperative,

3. The title and the registered office of the cooperative,

4. The capital of the cooperative, and the minimum amount paid in return for the cash portion thereof and the value of the share of each membership,

5. The fact that the membership share documents are prepared in names,

6. What the capital in kind and the valuable assets taken over consist of and the values designated for these,

7. How the cooperative shall be represented and audited,

8. The names of the members of the Board of Directors and the people authorized to represent the cooperative,

9. How the announcements to be made by the cooperative shall be made and how the decisions to be made by the Board of Directors shall be notified to the shareholders, if there are any provisions about this in the Rules,

10. Branch offices of the cooperative: Cooperatives can establish branch offices within and out of the country, should they deem it as necessary. Branch offices are registered with the local registry authorities of the city they are established in with reference to the registered head office thereof.

The Ministry of Trade cannot abstain from permitting the establishment of the cooperative claiming that it is in poor conformity with the optional provisions of the Law.

The amendment of the Rules depends on the procedures of the organization.

## The Provisions to Be Contained by The Articles of Association Obligatory Provisions

**Article-4:** The Rules of the cooperatives have to contain the provisions pertaining to the following particulars.

1. The name and the registered office of the cooperative,

2. The purpose and the field of operating of the cooperative,

3. The states and conditions that result in the gain or loss of the position of membership,

4. The value of the shares of the members and the way the cooperative capital is paid; cash payment of at least ¼ of the cash capital,

5. Whether the members shall deposit capital in kind or not,

6. The state and the degree of responsibility of the members with regard to the liabilities of the cooperative,

7. The duties, authorities, and responsibilities of the managing and controlling organs of the cooperative and the way they are elected,

8. Provisions concerning the representation of the cooperative,

9. The ways to calculate and utilize annual income / expenditure differences,

10. The names, surnames and the residence addresses of the founders.

## Optional Provisions

**Article-5:** The Rules may also contain the following provisions:

1. The provisions concerning the meeting of the General Assembly, the way decisions are made, and the way of voting,

2. The procedures concerning the way the cooperative is operated,

3. The relations of the cooperative as to the associations,

4. The provisions concerning the merging of the cooperative with another cooperative,

5. The duration of the cooperative.

## Construing Provisions

**Article-6:** In case there are no provisions in the Rules pertaining to the particulars written in the lines 1 and 2 of Article 5, the following provisions are applicable:

1. The General Assembly is called for meeting through letters signed by the persons authorized to represent the cooperative, or local newspapers, or through written and signed notices if in villages.

2. The activities of the cooperative: These are restricted to the purpose and the field of operation of the cooperative.

## The Acquisition of Legal Identity and Responsibilities There of

**Article-7:** The cooperative acquires legal identity through registry with the Trade Registry Office. The persons acting for and on behalf of the cooperative before registry are personally and successively responsible for their actions.

## PART TWO
## Acquisition and Loss of Membership Position

## Terms Of Entering Membership and Additional Payments

I-Terms of entering membership and the number of members (modified by Article 2 of the Law 3476):

Article-8: Natural persons need to be able to use the civil rights in order to be eligible for entering cooperative membership. Natural and legal entities that are eager to enter membership apply to the Board of Directors of the cooperative along with a written notice documenting that they fully agree with the provisions of the Rules along with all rights and duties thereto. Should the cooperative be assigning certain personal responsibilities or additional payments other than its own assets to its members, then the intention to become a member is valid solely on the condition that such liabilities are agreed to in writing.

Board of Directors: is obliged to inspect whether the members and those applying for membership are eligible as per the Rules. (*)

The number of housing units, offices (or work places), and members is specified by the General Assembly in construction cooperatives. The Board of Directors cannot have enrolled more members than specified by the General Assembly. (**)

## Membership of legal entities

**Article-9:** Legal Public entities such as private administrations, municipalities, villages, societies and associations, state economic enterprises, and cooperatives may support, have a leading role in, or become members to the establishment of the cooperatives with respect to their purpose of operation.

## Termination Of Membership

I-Freedom of withdrawal from membership – indemnity thereof

(*)  The members of the Board of Directors of the cooperatives and their superior institutions that violate Item 2 are sentenced to penalties such as imprisonment from 1 month up to 6 months and heavy fines such as fifty thousand to five-hundred thousand Turkish Liras depending on the type and degree of the act as Per the Article 26 of the Law 3476 and the appended Addendum 2/2.

(**) The members of the Board of Directors of the cooperatives and their superior institutions that violate Item 3 are sentenced to penalties such as imprisonment from 1 month up to 6 months and heavy fines such as fifty thousand to five-hundred thousand Turkish Liras depending on the type and degree of the act as Per the Article 26 of the Law 3476 and the appended Addendum 2/1.

**Article-10:** Each member has the right to withdraw from membership. In case the act of withdrawal endangers the presence of the cooperative, a provision stipulating that a just indemnity be paid to the cooperative by the withdrawing member can be included in the Rules.

## Restriction of withdrawal from membership

**Article-11:** The usage of the right to withdrawal from membership can be restricted through the Rules up to a maximum term of 5 years.

A provision can be put into the Rules stipulating that any member can withdraw from membership prior to the end of this term provided that s/he has rightful and important reasons. Bindings stipulating that a member can in no way withdraw from the cooperative are invalid.

## Notification period and time of withdrawal

**Article-12:** Members may withdraw only as of the end of the fiscal year and with a prior notification of at least 6 months. Should a shorter period be specified in the Rules, withdrawals within the fiscal year can be permitted.

## Abstinence from accepting withdrawal from membership

**Article-13:** Should the Board of Directors abstain from accepting the withdrawal of any given member from membership in spite of a withdrawal request made in compliance with the Rules, the member notifies his/her request of withdrawal through a notary-public. The withdrawal is realized as of the date of such notification.

## Death of the member and the tranRsfer of membership

**Article-14:** The position of membership is terminated upon the death of the member.

As per the provisions stipulated in the Rules, the position of membership can be passed on to the heirs of the member.

**Membership may be transferred. If the person taking over the membership is eligible for membership, the Board of Directors accepts the membership of such person(s) (modified by Article 3 of the Law 3476).**

**Termination of duty or service; membership in return for immovable properties or enterprise**

**Article-15:** If the position of membership depends on the execution of a particular duty or service, the position of membership is terminated upon the termination of such duty or service. In such cases, the position of membership can be perpetuated through the addition of a particular provision to the Rules.

The acquisition of the position of membership can be connected by the Rules to the enjoyment of certain rights in connection to the ownership of a given immovable or to the operation of a given enterprise. In such cases, the Rules can include provisions that the ownership of an immovable property or the enterprise, or the position of membership can be transferred to third persons as a right to the new owner in case of transfer of them or their rights. The validity of such immovable property acquisition against third persons is dependent on the conditional delivery made in this manner to the Title Deed Registry.

**Principles Of Dismissal from Membership, And Objection Thereof**

**Article-16:** The reasons necessitating dismissal from cooperative membership are specified clearly in the Rules. Members cannot be dismissed from cooperative membership for reasons other than those specified in the Rules (modified by Article 3 of the Law 3476). (*)

Dismissal from membership is decided upon by the General Assembly upon the proposal of the Board of Directors. The Board of Directors can be authorized by the Rules with respect to the reservation of the right of the dismissed member to apply to the General Assembly.

The decision about dismissal is written with cause in the written reports as well as in the members' book. The attested copy of the decision is delivered to the notary public within ten days, for being notified to the dismissed member. The said member can open a lawsuit of objection within three months as of the date of notification. If the notified decision has been made by the Board of Directors, the member can as well forward his/her objection to the General Assembly within the three-month period. This objection is realized through a notary-notification in writing to the Board of Directors, for being submitted to the first meeting of the General Assembly. If the objection is forwarded to the General Assembly, a lawsuit of objection cannot be opened against the decision of dismissal by the Board of Directors. The right to open a lawsuit of objection against the decision to be made by the General Assembly is reserved. The decisions of dismissal against which no objections are forwarded either to the General Assemblies or to the courts within a three-month period become definite.

**The members, the decisions of dismissal about whom have not become definite, cannot be replaced with new ones. The membership rights and liabilities of such persons continue to be valid until the decisions of dismissal about them become definite (Article 4 of the Law 3476 and addenda). (\*\*)**

(\*) The members of the Board of Directors of the cooperatives and their superior institutions that violate Item 1 are sentenced to penalties such as imprisonment from 1 month up to 6 months and heavy fines such as fifty thousand to five-hundred thousand Turkish Liras depending on the type and degree of the act as Per the Article 26 of the Law 3476 and the appended Addendum 2/2.

(**) The members of the Board of Directors of the cooperatives and their superior institutions that violate Item 5 are sentenced to penalties such as imprisonment from 1 month up to 6 months and heavy fines such as fifty thousand to five-hundred thousand Turkish Liras depending on the type and degree of the act as Per the Article 26 of the Law 3476 and the appended Addendum 2/1.

## Period Of Settling Accounts with The Members Who Have Withdrawn or Been Dismissed, And Liabilities Thereof

**Article-17:** Regarding the members that have withdrawn or been dismissed from the cooperative, particulars as to whether or not they or their heirs possess any right on the assets of the cooperative and what these consist of are specified in the Rules. These rights are designated according to the balance sheet of the year of their separation from the cooperative, excluding the reserves.

The returns and the payments which tend to endanger the presence of the cooperative can be delayed by the General Assembly for a period of not more than three years, even if shorter periods are specified in the Rules. In such cases, the right to ask for a just indemnity from the cooperative is reserved. The credits and the rights of the withdrawn or dismissed members and their heirs are prescribed in case they are not asked for within a period of five years as of the date of acquisition of such rights.

The terms stipulating that the withdrawn or dismissed member shall be totally deprived of their capitals or credits are invalid.

## PART THREE
## Rights and Liabilities of the Members
### Deed Of Membership

**Article-18:** It is obligatory for the membership rights of each of the members to be represented with a deed of membership bearing names. The title of the cooperative, the name and surname and business and residence addresses of the owner of the bill and the dates of entering into and parting from the cooperative are borne by the said deed of membership. The owner of the deed of membership and the persons authorized to represent the cooperative sign these particulars. The money deposited or withdrawn by the member is recorded in order of time. If these records are related to the money paid by the cooperative, the member signs the related documents. The signed deed of membership is regarded as a receipt for payment. The said deed of membership can be prepared in the form of a membership account book, on the condition that it includes the Rules. The deeds of membership are not regarded as valuable assets, but do have the influence of an evidence document.

### Membership Shares – Personal Credits

**Article-19:** It is required to collect at least one membership share from every member entering into a cooperative. The Rules may permit the collection of more than one shares by a member within a maximum limit to be specified in the Rules

**The value of a single membership share is 10.000 TL. Those entering into a cooperative can guarantee a maximum of 1000 shares. On the other hand, those entering into a superior institution of a cooperative guarantee a minimum of 50 shares. The value of a single membership share can be increased up to ten times within the decision**

of the Council of Ministers. (Modified by Article 5 of the Law 3476). (*)

**Several shares can be represented on one single deed of membership. The shares not represented by deeds of membership are regarded as equivalent to 10.000 TL. (Modified by Article 5 of the Law 3476).**

The loan demands of each cooperative are covered up with priority by the banks, institutions, or companies, depending on the field of operation of the cooperative.

**The investment activities of the agrarian cooperatives are supported by low-interest loans to be delivered via allotments to be spared from the budgets, within the principles of the legislation prepared by the related Ministry.**

(*) The value of a single membership share has been increased to 100.000 (a hundred thousand) TL with the Decree 93/4507 dated 12.6.1993 of the Council of Ministers published on the Official Gazette 21618 dated 25.6.1993.

The personal creditors of any member can only seize the amount equivalent to the share of the member arising from the interests and income - expenditure differences and the share to be paid to the member upon the dissolving of the cooperative.

## Capital In Kind
**Article-20:** The placement of the same kind of capital or the taking over of a present enterprise or the capitals in kind can be accepted by the Rules.

## I- Evaluation, expert
**Article-21:** If the value of the capital in kind is not specified in the Rules, this designation is realized by the expert to be elected by the majority of the members representing two

thirds of the number of members at the first General Assembly to be called for by the founders.

In case the members entering into the cooperative following its foundation are to put capitals in kind, this call for a meeting is made by the Board of Directors.

In cases where it is not possible for two thirds of the members to come to a unanimous decision, the election of the expert is requested from the Civil Court of Peace.

The report submitted by the expert or experts can be objected at the Civil Court of Peace within one week as of the date of notification. The decision to be made by the court is definite.

## I-Decision quorum, acceptance of the reports

**Article-22:** The subject is discussed after the expert assigned in accordance with Article 21 prepares the reports and submits them to the General Assembly meeting. A copy of the expert report is annexed to the letters of invitation.

Following the reading and examination of the expert reports on the condition that at least half of the number of members are present at the meeting either in person or as represented and if deemed necessary after listening to the explanations of those who have put capitals in kind or the owners of the enterprises or the capitals in kind to be taken over, decisions are made through majority with respect to the approval or refusal of the same values or their evaluation upon the consent of related persons.

## Equality In Rights and Obligations

**Article-23:** The members are equal in rights and obligations within the principles accepted by this Law.

## Right of obtaining information, balance sheet

**Article-24:** The annual work report including the proposals of the Board of Directors about the form of distribution of the income-expenditure differences and the balance sheet and the report to be prepared by the auditors in accordance with the provisions of Article 66 are presented for examination by members at the headquarters and the branches if any for a period of one year, as of 15 days prior to the annual General Assembly meeting.

It is obligatory to present one copy each of the balance sheet and the income - expenditure difference accounts.

The right of the members to obtain information cannot be confiscated or restricted either by the Rules or by the decision of one of the organs of the cooperative.

## Provisions on the confidentiality of commercial books and secrets and penalty thereof

**Article-25:** The examination of the commercial books and the conditions about the communication of the cooperative is possible upon the clear permission of the General Assembly or by the decision of the Board of Directors. None of the members are authorized to be informed about the business secrets of the cooperative, except for those to be informed from the books and documents which they permitted to examine. Every member is obliged to always keep the business secrets which they happen to find out by any means, even in the case they later lose membership position. The member who does not conform to this obligation is sentenced to imprisonment up to one year or with a heavy fine from 500 TL to 10.000 TL or both upon the complaint of the cooperative, even if any kind of losses were not expected, apart from being responsible for the losses to arise against the cooperative

## Right of attending General Assembly meetings (modified by Article 6 of Law 3476)

**Article-26:** Except for the members who were not members three months ago, every member possesses the right to attend General Assembly meetings. With construction cooperatives, such condition is not required for attending General Assembly meetings.

## Obligations And Responsibilities of The MembersTerm of membership and termination thereof

**Article-27:** The amount of money that can be paid by the members for the shares undertaken is specified in the Rules. The cooperative demands the realization of these obligations from the members indebted with capital or other payment obligations through letters personally submitted or via registered posting or by announcements if this is not possible, by specifying a reasonable term. The memberships of those who do not conform with the provision that their obligations should be realized within one month following the second request will automatically terminate. The termination of the memberships of such persons does not necessitate the removal of the debts arising with respect to the Rules or otherwise.

## Responsibility of the Cooperative

**Article-28:** Unless there exists a provision on the contrary in the Rules, the cooperative is only responsible for its creditors with the patrimony.

## Unlimited responsibility

**Article-29:** In case the assets of the cooperative are not adequate to cover up the debts of the cooperative, The Rules can include an article providing that the members can be obliged to be responsible in person and in an unlimited manner. In such cases, in case the creditor cannot obtain whole of their credits upon the liquidation of the cooperative either through bankruptcy or other reasons, the members of the cooperative shall be responsible in succession and with all their assets due to the debts of the cooperative.

## Limited responsibility

**Article-30:** A provision may be introduced into the Rules rendering each member liable from the cooperative debts in excess of his own share in person and up to a certain amount after the cooperative. The amount that the members will be personally liable may also be shown as proportional to the amount of their shares in the cooperative.

The liability is set forth by the bankruptcy administration until the end of the bankruptcy.

## Additional payment burden

**Article-31:** The Rules may put a burden of additional payment on the members. However, it is obligatory to use the additional payments only for the purpose of covering up the balance deficits. The additional payment burden may not only be unlimited but also limited as proportional to specific amounts or volume of work or shares.

In case of bankruptcy of the cooperative, the right of demanding the additional payment belongs to the bankruptcy administration.

## Non-permitted limitation

**Article-32:** The provisions of the Rules postponing the liability to certain time or putting this burden on some member groups are not valid.

## Procedure in case of bankruptcy

**Article-33:** In case of bankruptcy of the cooperatives the members of which are liable in person or are responsible for additional payments, the bankruptcy administration demands for the payment of the debts corresponding to the share of each member, as well as preparing the sequence schedule.

The amounts that are not collected are shared between the other members. The active remainder is returned following the definite designation of the share schedules. The recourse rights of the members against each other are reserved. The members reserve the right to object to the temporarily specified debts and the share schedules, in accordance with the provisions of the Execution and Bankruptcy Law.

## Modification of the provisions on responsibility

**Article-34:** The modifications about the liability of the members and the additional payment burden are only possible through the modification of the Rules. The placement of liability and additional payment burden or the increasing of these expresses a provision in favor of the entire credits of the cooperative upon the registry of the related decision. The decisions about the reduction of the liability do not cover the debts arisen prior to registry.

## Liability of the members entering the cooperative

**Article-35:** In a cooperative where the members are liable in person or obliged with additional payments, any individual newly entering the cooperative being aware of his condition becomes equally responsible as the other members for the debts previously arisen. Contract terms contrary to this and the contracts between the members are not valid for third persons.

## Liability following the withdrawal of a member or the dissolving of the cooperative

**Article-36:** As of the date a member with limited or unlimited responsibility dies or it becomes definite that s/he withdraws from the cooperative for any other reason, in case the cooperative goes bankrupt within one year or a longer period if specified in the Rules, the member cannot avoid responsibility for the debts arisen prior to his withdrawal.

The burden of additional payment continues to be present under the same conditions and within the same period. If a cooperative dissolves, in case it is decided upon announcing the bankruptcy of the cooperative within one year as of the registry at the Trade Registry Office or within a longer period if specified in the Rules, the members are likewise responsible for the additional payments.

## Prescription in responsibilities

**Article-37:** The demands of the creditors for rights arising from the personal liabilities of the members can be put forward by each of them for a period of a further year, as of the termination of the bankruptcy transactions, if not invalidated sooner with the enforcement of a legal provision.

The recourse rights of the members against each other are prescribed are prescribed within one year as of the realization of the payment forming the basis of this right.

## PART FOUR
## Cooperative Accounts

### Income-Expenditure Differences – Division Thereof and Application of Interest to Shares

**Article-38:** In case there are no provisions stipulating the contrary in the Rules, the entire income obtained at the end of a one-year activity as a result of the transactions made with the members is added to the reserves of the cooperative as the income-expenditure difference.

If the distribution of the income-expenditure difference between the members is anticipated, this distribution is realized proportional to the level of operation of the members.

**A provision can be introduced to the Rules stating that an interest can be paid for the capital shares of the members after the distribution of at least 50% of the income-expenditure difference upon the decision of the General Assembly, to be not more than the maximum interest rates applied for the State Bonds. (Modified by Article 7 of Law 3476)**

**A provision can also be introduced to the Rules stating that the revenues obtained from the non-member transactions can be distributed to the members proportional to their capital shares. If not distributed, these are accumulated in a special fund to be used for work that will assist the development of the cooperative. (Modified by Article 7 of Law 3476)**

In case the results of the one-year activity are negative, the deficit is covered up from the reserves and incase these are not adequate, by additional payments or by joint capital shares.

Unless the negative results are removed, the distribution of income-expenditure differences and interests cannot be realized.

## Sparing Reserves

**Article-39:** In the cooperatives, distribution to the members is not realized unless at least 10% of the income-expenditure difference is spared as reserves; an additional 5%

should be reserved as extraordinary reserves in cooperative superior institutions.

The provisions to be introduced in the Rules about the distribution of the reserves to the members are not valid.

## Charity Funds for The Members and The Personnel

**Article-40:** The Rules may introduce provisions about the establishment of donation institutions for the officials, workers, and the members of the cooperatives and the operation of these.

If the assets spared for donation purposes are specified, these are deposited in a special account for the purpose of realizing the objectives for which they were assigned, thus being separated them from the patrimony of the cooperative.

## Funds To Be Spared with Priority from The Income-Expenditure Difference

**Article-41:** The reserves and the money to be deposited in other funds founded in accordance with the Rules and the Law are spared with priority from the income-expenditure difference that is to be divided. The methods and conditions for using the reserves and special funds are specified in the Rules.

## PART FIVE
## Cooperative Organs

## A) GENERAL ASSEMBLY

## I-Authority

**Article-42:** The General Assembly is the organ of the cooperative with maximum authority which represents the entire members. The General Assembly cannot transfer or renounce from the following authorities:

1. Modify the Rules,

2. Elect the Board of Liquidation whenever deemed necessary as well as the members of the Board of Directors and Auditors,

3. Decide upon the division of the operation account, balance and whenever deemed necessary income - expenditure difference.

4. Acquittal of the Board of Directors and Auditors,

5. Decide upon the subjects imposed on the General Assembly by Law or by the Rules,

6. Designate the qualification, location and the maximum price of the immovable to be sold, within the methods to be followed in the purchasing and selling of an immovable (appended with Article 9 of Law 3476),

7. Designate the method of realization for manufacturing and construction works (appended with Article 9 of Law 3476),

8. Designate number of buildings and work-places and the number of the members of the cooperatives in construction cooperatives (appended with Article 9 of Law 3476).

## Call

### I-Those authorized for calling

**Article-43: The Board of Directors and any other organ authorized in this matter by the Rules, the Board of Auditors whenever deemed necessary, the association with which the cooperative is connected and the liquidation officials hold the right to call the General Assembly for a meeting. However, in case the General Assembly cannot meet as stated above, the related Ministry bears the authority to call the General Assembly for a meeting.**

## II-Request of the members, call from the Ministries, permission of the court

**Article-44:** The General Assembly is called for a meeting with the request of at least 10% of the number of members, on the condition that the number is not less than four members. In case the General Assembly does not comply with this request within a minimum of ten days, the General Assembly can be called for a meeting upon the application of the requestors or directly by the related Ministry.

In case the General Assembly does not still meet, the requestors can collect the permission to call the General Assembly for a meeting in person.

## I-Form (modified by Article 11 of Law 3476)

**Article-45: The General Assembly meets ordinarily or extraordinarily whenever deemed necessary. It is obligatory to hold the ordinary meeting within six months as of the end of each of the account periods and at least once in a year. (\*)**

**The General Assembly is called for a meeting within the form and method specified in the Rules.**

**The meeting quorum is specified in the Rules. However, it is obligatory for at least one fourth of the members to be present in person or as represented in the construction cooperatives.**

**The date, place, and the agenda of the General Assembly meeting is notified to the related Ministry and the civil Administrative Officer in writing, at least 15 days prior to the meeting.**

**The chairmanship and the administration of the General Assembly is realized by the chairman and the members**

elected from within the members or the representatives of the superior institutions.

## I-Agenda (modified by Article 12 of Law 3476)

Article-46: The agenda is written on the meeting invitation and the announcement. If the modification of the Rules is in question, it is sufficient to designate the numbers of the articles to be modified in the announcement to be made.

It is compulsory to include in the agenda the conditions to be notified by at least one tenth of the members, on the condition of not being less than four, in writing at least twenty days prior to the General Assembly meeting.

(*) The members of the Board of Directors who do not call the General Assembly for the ordinary meeting are sentenced to imprisonment from three months up to two years and to a heavy fine of between 100.000 TL up to 1.000.000 TL, depending on the type and degree of the act as Per the Article 26 of the Law 3476 and the appended Addendum 2/2.

The topics that are not included in the agenda cannot be discussed. However upon the written request of at least one tenth of the members registered in the cooperative prior to the commencement of the discussion of the agenda subjects, the election of the account examination commission, the leaving back of the examination of the balance sheet and the acquittal, the decision-making about the withdrawn or dismissed members, the calling of the General Assembly to a new meeting, the annulment of the decisions of the Board of Directors claimed to be conflicting the General Assembly decisions as per Law, the Rules and the good intention principles and the subjects regarding the dismissal of the members of the Board of Directors and replacement thereof are included in the agenda upon the consent of one more than half of those attending the meeting.

## The condition of presence of the entire shareholders

**Article-47:** As long as all of the members of the cooperative are attending the General Assembly meeting and as long as there are no objections, decisions can be made even if the provisions related to the meeting invitation are not adhered to, on the condition that the other provisions about the General Assembly meetings are reserved. It is obligatory for such decisions to be signed by the members or by the representatives to be elected unanimously by the members at the meeting.

## Right to vote

### In general

**Article-48:** At the General Assembly, each member has the right to use only a single vote.

### Representation

**Article-49:** If there is an explanation in the Rules, any member can transfer the right of voting at the General Assembly meeting to another member by permitting accordingly in writing. No members can represent more than one member at the General Assembly.

In the cooperatives the number of members of which are over 1.000, the Rules may include provisions allowing each member to represent up to nine members at the most at the General Assembly. For the spouses and the first-degree relatives, the membership condition is not required with regard to representation.

## Those who cannot vote

**Article-50:** Those who have in any manner participated in the realization of the cooperative works cannot participate in voting with regard to the decisions on the acquittal of the Board of Directors. This provision does not apply to auditors.

None of the members can use the right of voting in the discussions about a business article, or a case between the cooperative and him/herself or his/her spouse or ancestors and descendants.

## Decisions

### In general

**Article-51:** Unless there is a provision conflicting the Law or the Rules, one more than half of the votes are required for the decisions of the General Assembly and the elections.

Two thirds of the practically used votes are required for the decisions upon the liquidation of the cooperative or the modification of the Rules. The Rules may introduce heavier provisions regarding the majority of the votes necessitated for making these decisions.

**The increasing of the shares of the members modified by Article 1 of Law 2475 dated 8.6.1981)**

**Article-52: For the decisions upon the hardening of the personal responsibilities of the members or the introduction of additional obligations, the consent of three fourths of the entire members is required.**

However, this condition is not required for the decisions to be made for the purpose of benefiting from the increase in the amount of credit, for the cooperatives obtaining credits from state institutions and the provisions dictated in Item 1 of Article 51 is applied.

These decisions do not bind the members who have not participated in the decision-making and who have notified the cooperative that they have withdrawn from the cooperative within three months as of the date of advertisement. Under such circumstances, the declaration regarding withdrawal from the cooperative takes effect as of the date of validity of the decision. The utilization of the right of withdrawal from the cooperative in this manner cannot be related to the payment of withdrawal indemnity.

## The cancellation of decisions and, terms thereof

**Article-53:** The following persons can apply to the court against the decisions of the General Assembly, where the cooperative headquarters is located, with the claim that the decisions are in poor compliance with the Law, the provisions of the Rules and the principles of good intention, within a period of one month as of the date of the meeting:

The shareholders who were present at the meeting but were against the decisions and who enforced the addition of this term into the written report, who were unjustly prevented from casting their votes and who are claiming that the invitation to the General Assembly meeting was not realized in compliance with the procedures, that the agenda was not announced or notified as it should have been, or that some of the people in favor of the decision were not authorized to attend the General Assembly meeting;

## The Board of Directors;

III-Each of the members of the Board of Directors and the inspectors, in case the fulfillment of the decisions necessitates their personal responsibility.

The date on which the lawsuit of cancellation is opened and that on which the trial will be held is announced by the Board of Directors in accordance with the procedure.

The trial cannot commence prior to the end of the one-month period that results in the loss of rights, as dictated in Item 1. If more than one lawsuit are opened, the cases are merged and a single trial is made.

Upon the request of the cooperative, the court may decide upon the display of a guarantee by the plaintiffs against probable losses. The court specifies the nature and the amount of guarantee.

The cancellation of a decision applies to all members.

## Voting by mail and the meeting of representatives

**Article-54:** In the cooperatives with members more than 1.000, the following practices may render a General Assembly, on the condition that such a provision is introduced to the Rules:

1. That all or part of the decisions of the General Assembly was taken by the votes of the members sent by mail,

2. The group of representatives elected from within the members, consisting of divided groups, with a view to cast their votes in accordance with the instructions to be specified by the decisions to be made.

In case of voting by mail, the content of the letters are specified following its examination in front of the Board of Directors and the representative of the related Ministry, and is recorded with a written report. The decision regarded to have been taken according to the written report signed by those present takes effect.

In the General Assembly of the group representatives, each representative possesses votes at the number of members s/

he is representing. The voting of the representative in poor compliance with the instruction s/he has received shall have no effect on the decision.

## Board of Directors
## Obligations and the number of members thereof

**Article-55:** The Board of Directors is the executive organ of the cooperative, managing the activities of the cooperative within the provisions of the Law and the Rules, as well as representing the cooperative.

The Board of Directors consists of at least three members. It is obligatory for these and their substitutes to be members of the cooperative.

Legal entities elected for the Board of Directors notify the cooperative of the names of their representatives.

**The conditions and the fee of membership (modified by Article 14 of Law 3476)**

**Article-56: The following qualifications are required for the members of the Board of Directors:**

**1-To be citizens of the Republic of Turkey,**

**2-Not to be members of the Boards of Directors of other cooperatives with similar fields of activity,**

**3-Not to have been tried and found guilty as per the provisions of the Turkish Punishment law with regard to embezzlement, theft, corruption, bribe, misuse of duties, forgery, thievery, cheating, fraudulent bankruptcy, misuse of trust, and the crimes committed against the personality of the State or as per this Law.**

**The auditors investigate the conditions for membership. The Board of Directors terminate the assigned duties of those who were selected although they did not have**

these qualifications and those who lost such qualifications later. (*)

Although the duties of those against whom public lawsuits are opened for the above-dictated crimes continue until the first General Assembly meeting, a topic is included in the agenda of the first General Assembly meeting by the Board of Directors with regard to the dismissal or the continuation of the duties of such members.

If the Board of Directors loses the meeting quorum due to this reason or any other reason to be specified in the Rules, adequate number of substitute members are invited immediately for the vacant memberships of the Board of Directors by the board of auditors. (**)

One or several of the members of the Board of Directors can be elected as delegate members, with the authority to represent the cooperative. The election and changing of the delegate members should be registered with the Trade Registry Office.

(*) The members of the board of auditors of the cooperatives or the superior institutions violating Item 2 are sentenced to imprisonment from 1 up to 6 months and a heavy fine of 50.000 TL up to 500.000 TL, depending on the type and degree of the act as Per the Article 26 of the Law 3476 and the appended Addendum 2/3.

(**) The members of the board of auditors of the cooperatives or the superior institutions violating Item 4 are sentenced to imprisonment from 1 up to 6 months and a heavy fine of 50.000 TL up to 500.000 TL, depending on the type and degree of the act as Per the Article 26 of the Law 3476 and the appended Addendum 2/3.

No kind of payments under any names can be delivered to the members of the Board of Directors, except for the salaries, attendance fees, (ristourne), and allowances specified by the General Assembly. (*)

## Term of membership

**Article-57:** The members of the Board of Directors are elected for a maximum period of four years.

Unless there is a provision on the contrary, they can be re-elected.

## Administration and representation
## Transfer of authority

**Article-58:** The Rules may transfer the authority of assigning one or several directors or members of the Board of Directors who are not required to be cooperative members, for the partial or entire administration and representation of the cooperative, to the Board of Directors.

## Scope and restriction thereof

**Article-59:** The persons authorized to represent can realize all legal transactions for and on behalf of the cooperative and necessitated by its objective.

The restriction of the said representative authority does not impose any provisions against the third persons with good intentions. The records registered with the Trade Registry Office regarding that the representative authority is detained for only the works related to the basic enterprise or a branch or the usage of the cooperative title together, is reserved.

The cooperative is responsible for the losses arising from the unjust actions taken by the persons authorized to manage or represent, during the execution of their duties.

It is compulsory that the purchase of the immovable properties decided to be purchased by the cooperative via a title deed transfer or an agreement of selling promise with an annotation be delivered to the real estate registry office. (Appended with Article 15 of Law 3476) (\*\*)

(\*) The members of the Board of Directors and the officials of the cooperatives or the superior institutions violating Item 6 of Article 58 are sentenced to imprisonment from 3 months up to 2 years and a heavy fine of 100.000 TL up to 1.000.000 TL, depending on the type and degree of the act as Per the Article 26 of the Law 3476 and the appended Addendum 2/1.

(\*\*) The members of the Board of Directors and the officials of the cooperatives or the superior institutions violating Item 4 of Article 59 are sentenced to imprisonment from 3 months up to 2 years and a heavy fine of 100.000 TL up to 1.000.000 TL, depending on the type and degree of the act as Per the Article 26 of the Law 3476 and the appended Addendum 2/1.

It is required that the immovable to be purchased is in accordance with the objective of the cooperative (appended with Article 15 of Law 3476).

The members of the Board of Directors administration the personnel of the cooperative cannot realize any commercial transactions with the cooperative within the subject of the cooperative in their own names or in the name of others in person or indirectly, except for the membership transactions. (Appended with Article 15 of Law 3476) (\*)

The announcements, advertisements and explanations to be made by the cooperatives and their superior institutions for the purpose of registering members cannot be deficient or untrue and cannot include misleading information and elements. (Appended with Article 15 of Law 3476) (\*\*)

The distribution and the persons authorized to represent cannot use the authorities that the General Assembly cannot transfer. (Appended with Article 15 of Law 3476) (\*\*)

## 1-Signature

**Article-60:** The persons authorized to represent the cooperative can only bind the cooperative by putting their signatures under the title of the cooperative.

## 2-Registry

**Article-61:** The cooperative presents the names and titles of the members of the Board of Directors and the persons authorized to represent the cooperative and samples of the notary-attested decisions based on this authority to the Trade Registry Office.

## 1-Degree of fastidiousness and the liabilities of the members

**Article-62:** The Board of Directors shows the fastidiousness necessitated by the administration of the cooperative works and makes its best efforts for the success and the development of the cooperative.

The Board of Directors is responsible for the preparation, keeping, and the maintenance of its own written reports, the reports of the General Assembly, the necessary books and the list of the members in an organized manner, and for presenting the operation account and the balance sheets prepared in accordance with the legal provisions for inspection purposes. The members of the Board of Directors and the officials of the cooperative are responsible for the losses arising from their own faults. Such persons are punished in a manner.

(*) The members of the Board of Directors and the officials of the cooperatives or the superior institutions violating Item 6 are sentenced to imprisonment from 3 months up to 2 years and a heavy fine of 100.000 TL up to 1.000.000 TL, depending on the type and degree of the act as Per the Article 26 of the Law 3476 and the appended Addendum 2/1.

(**) The members of the Board of Directors and the officials of the cooperatives or the superior institutions violating Item 7, and 8 are sentenced to imprisonment from 3 months up to 2 years and a heavy fine of 100.000 TL up to 1.000.000 TL, depending on the type and degree of the act as Per the Article 26 of the Law 3476 and the appended Addendum 2/1. Similar to the 'State Officials' regarding the actions and behaviors deemed as crime, and especially for the crimes they have committed on money and properties, balance sheets, written reports, reports and other papers, books and documents of the cooperative.

## Works to be performed in case of the inability of the cooperative

**Article-63:** In case there are serious reasons for the inability of the cooperative, the Board of Directors immediately prepares an interim balance sheet on the basis of the current market prices. In case the last year's balance sheet or a liquidation balance sheet prepared letter, or the interim balance sheet dictated above designates that the resources of the cooperative are not any more able to cover the debts, the Board of Directors notifies the related Ministry about the situation and calls the General Assembly for an extraordinary meeting.

In a cooperative where share promissory notes have been forwarded, in case half of the resources of the cooperative remains to be bounced within the last year's balance sheet, the Board of Directors calls the General Assembly for a meeting and presents the situation to the information of the members. The Board of Directors at the same time notifies the court and the related Ministry about the situation. However, in cooperatives where the members are obliged with additional payments, in case the deficiency specified in the balance sheet is not covered up with the additional payments of the members within three months, the related Ministry is notified.

In case it is deemed possible that the financial situation can be corrected, the court may delay the opening of the lawsuit of bankruptcy, upon the request of either the Board of Directors or one of the creditors. In such cases, it takes the precautions related to the protection and the continuation of the resources of the cooperative, such as keeping the resources book or the assignment of an administrative official.

## Dismissal

**Article-64:** The Board of Directors can always dismiss the personnel it has assigned for the realization of the works, the directors it has assigned, or the other representatives and deputies.

Those who are dismissed reserve the right to demand indemnity.

## A) Auditors
## Election

**Article-65:** The auditors inspect the entire transactions and accounts of the cooperative for and on behalf of the General Assembly.

The General Assembly elects one or more auditors as the auditing organ for a period of at least one year. The General Assembly may elect substitutes for the auditors. It is not compulsory for the auditors and their substitutes to be members of the cooperative.

The provisions present in Paragraphs 1 and 3 of Item 1 of Article 56 also apply to the auditors.

## Working
## Obligation of investigation (*)

**Article-66:** The auditors are obliged to examine whether or not the operation account and the balance sheet conform to the books, whether or not the books are kept accordingly, and whether or not the transactions are realized in accordance with the provisions stipulated by the results of the operation and the patrimony. In cooperatives where members are personally responsible for or obliged with additional payments, the auditors are obliged to examine whether or not the list of members is kept in good compliance with the procedures.

The administrators submit the books and the documents to the auditors for this purpose. Upon the request of the auditors, all kinds of information with regard to the content book and the principles with which this book has been organized and any other subject must be presented. (**)

The members are authorized to call the attention of the auditors in issues they deem necessary and to demand for an explanation.

## Preparing reports (***)

**Article-67:** The auditors are obliged to submit their annual proposals to the General Assembly along with their reports.

The auditors are also obliged to inform the related organs and, whenever deemed necessary, the General Assembly of the faults and wrongdoings in the execution of the works, the actions conflicting Law and the Rules that they designate within the scope of their duties. The auditors attend the meetings of the Board of Directors and the General Assembly. However, they cannot cast votes at the Board of Directors meetings.

(*) The members of the board of auditors of the cooperatives or the superior institutions violating this Article are sentenced to imprisonment from 1 up to 6 months and a heavy fine of 50.000 TL up to 500.000 TL, depending on the type and degree of the act as Per the Article 26 of the Law 3476 and the appended Addendum 2/3.

(**) The members of the Board of Directors of the cooperatives or the superior institutions violating Item 2 are sentenced to imprisonment from 1 up to 6 months and a heavy fine of 50.000 TL up to 500.000 TL, depending on the type and degree of the act as Per the Article 26 of the Law 3476 and the appended Addendum 2/2.

(***) The members of the board of auditors of the cooperatives or the superior institutions violating this Article are sentenced to imprisonment from 1 up to 6 months and a heavy fine of 50.000 TL up to 500.000 TL, depending on the type and degree of the act as Per the Article 26 of the Law 3476 and the appended Addendum 2/3.

## Obligation to keep secrets

**Article-68:** The auditors cannot disclose the particulars they have attained during their duties and which are expected to be damage the cooperative or the members upon disclosure, to cooperative members or third persons.

## Special Provisions

**Article-69:** It is possible to introduce broader provisions regarding the auditing organization, to increase the authorities of the auditors and specially to anticipate interim auditing by the Rules and the decision of the General Assembly.

## PART SIX
## Cooperative Associations, Central Associations of Cooperatives, Turkish National Cooperatives Association, Board of Consultants
## Duties and Liabilities

**Article-70:** Cooperative associations, central associations of cooperatives and the Turkish National Cooperatives Association are established for the purpose of realizing the services such as the protection of the joint benefits of the cooperatives, the realization of economic activities for achieving objectives, coordinating and auditing the activities of the cooperatives, organization of the relations with foreign countries, development of the cooperative-business and the realization of training activities and recommendations on the cooperative-business.

The provisions of Article 62 apply to the members and the officials of the cooperative associations and the Turkish National Cooperative Association.

## Obligation

**Article-71:** Obligations in excess of those imposed by Law or the Rules cannot be imposed on the members of the cooperatives joining in the associations.

## A) Cooperative Unions

**Article-72:** The conditions that associations can be established by 7 or more cooperatives the fields of operating of which are either the same or related to each other, can be specified within their Rules. Such associations are established in the form of cooperatives.

**In case the related Ministry specifies regions, more than one cooperatives cannot be established at these regions on the same field of operation. (Appended with Article 15 of Law 3476)**

## I-General Assembly

**Article-73:** The most authorized organ of the cooperative associations is the General Assembly which consists of the representatives of the cooperatives, unless there is a provision stipulating the contrary in the Rules.

It is possible for the members of the Board of Directors to be elected as representatives.

## Board of Directors

**Article-74:** The Board of Directors of the association is elected from within the representatives included in the General Assembly of the association.

It is compulsory for the members to be elected to the Board of Directors not to be representatives of the same cooperative.

**Inspection and training (modified by Article 18 of Law 3476)**

**Article-75: The central associations of cooperatives audit the connected associations and cooperatives and provide the training and education needs thereof. In case the establishment of the central association is not complete, the associations carry out the auditing of the connected cooperatives. The results of the auditing realized by the superior institutions are notified to the related Ministry.**

**The cooperatives and the superior institutions thereof share the expenditures related to the auditing and the training services provided for themselves, within the rules and principles to be specified by its superior institution.**

## Central Unions for Cooperatives

**Article-76:** The cooperative associations establish central associations among themselves in the form of cooperatives.

The General Assemblies of the central associations of cooperatives are established by the representatives to be elected by the General Assemblies of the cooperative associations included in this cooperative central association.

The members of the Board of Directors of the cooperative associations can be elected to the memberships of the central associations of cooperatives.

The cooperative associations having similar fields of operation cannot establish more than one central associations of cooperatives.

## Turkish National Cooperatives Union

**Article-77:** The associations or the central associations of cooperatives can establish a Turkish National Cooperatives Association in the form of a cooperative.

The conditions of participation are specified in the Rules of the Turkish National Cooperatives Association.

The representatives to be elected by the General Assemblies of the central associations of cooperatives establish the General Assembly of the Turkish National Cooperatives Association. The fact that this board is constituted from the Board of Directors of the cooperatives, associations and central associations of cooperatives can be taken under provision with the Rules.

## Designation of The Representatives

**Article-78:** The number of the representatives of the cooperatives, associations, and central associations of cooperatives which depends on the number of members and should not exceed 5 persons, to constitute the General Assemblies of the associations, central associations of cooperatives and the Turkish National Cooperatives Association is specified in their Rules.

**Article-79:** The Associations, the Central associations of cooperatives, and the Turkish National Cooperatives Association prepare their Rules in accordance with the provisions of this Law hereby.

## Board of Consultants

**Article-80:** The participation of the General Board of Directors of the Turkish National Cooperatives Association and one representative each from the State Planning Organization, the Ministry of Industry and Trade, the Ministry of Agriculture Forestry and Rural Affairs, the Ministry of Finance and Customs, the Ministry of Training Youth and Education, the banks financing cooperatives and the Turkish Cooperatives Institution constitute the 'Turkish Cooperatives Consulting Board'. The duties and the authorities and the form and conditions of working of this board are specified within the rules and regulations prepared by the related Ministry.

## PART SEVEN
## Liquidation of the Cooperatives
## A) REASONS FOR LIQUIDATION
## (Modified by Article 20 Of Law 3476)
## Article-81: The cooperatives are liquidated for the following reasons:

1-As required by the Rules,

2-By the decision of the General Assembly,

3-By the opening of the lawsuit of bankruptcy,

4-Upon the decision to be made by the related Ministry, regarding other conditions anticipated by Law,

5-Due to merging with another cooperative or by transfer thereof,

6-In case the ordinary General Assembly meeting is not held in three successive years,

7-By the decision to be taken by the court upon the designation by the related Ministry of the fact that the means of achieving objectives are absent.

The construction cooperatives are assumed to have reached their objective and liquidated, upon the completion of the works specified in their Rules and following the registry of the buildings in the name of the members after it is passed on to individual proprietorship. However, if the Rules is modified in a convenient manner within a period of six months following the date of registry, and if the objective of the cooperative is also similarly modified, the provision on liquidation is not applied.

The individual relations of the members in accordance with the Flat Ownership Law are finalized within one year at the latest, following the gathering of the building usage permission in construction cooperatives.

In case no liquidation officials are elected by the court or by the General Assembly, the Board of Directors carries out the liquidation transactions. A fee to be specified by the authority having realized the assignment is paid to the s of the board of liquidation.

If a special quorum is not specified in the Rules, quorum is not required at the General Assembly meetings of the cooperatives in case of liquidation. The duties of the Board of Liquidation are specified in the Rules.

The members of the Board of Liquidation are obliged to work for the purpose of completing the liquidation transactions as soon as possible.

The provisions stipulated by the Paragraph 3 of Item 1 of Article 56 and 62 do also apply to the members of the Board of Liquidation.

## A) Notification To the Trade Registry Office

**Article-82:** The dissolving of the cooperative for reasons other than bankruptcy is registered and announced by the authorized organs of the cooperative with the Trade Registry Office. The identities of the authorized organs are specified in the Rules.

## B) Division Of the Liquidation Patrimony

**Article-83:** The properties remaining after the payment of the entire debts of the cooperative entering into a state of liquidation and after the return of the member share prices, can only be divided between the members, if this condition is anticipated in the Rules.

Unless another method of solution is accepted in the Rules, the division is realized equally between the registered members and the legal successors at the date of dissolving.

In case there are no explanations in the Rules stipulating that a division is to be realized toward members, then the amount remaining after liquidation is transferred to the Turkish National Cooperatives Association for being used in accordance with the objectives of the cooperative-business.

If such an association has not been established, this amount is deposited in the fund under the command of the related Ministry, to be donated to the institutions aiming to achieve the objectives dictated in Article 94.

## C) Dissolving Through Unification

**Article-84:** If any cooperative is dissolved by being taken over by another cooperative with its entire active and passive, the following provisions are applied:

1- The Board of Directors of the cooperative taking over invites the dissolved cooperative to notify the credits in accordance with the provisions stipulating liquidation.

2- The patrimony of the dissolved cooperative is administered separately, until its debts are bound to payments or guarantees. The administration is taken over by the Board of Directors of the cooperative taking over.

3- The Board of Directors of the cooperative taking over is responsible against the creditors in person and in succession for the separate execution of the administration.

4- During the period of separate administration of the patrimony, the authorized court responsible for the trial of the cases before the dissolving of the cooperative will be responsible for the cases to be opened against the dissolved cooperative.

5- In the relations between the creditors of the dissolved cooperative and the cooperative taking over and creditors thereof, the properties taken over are assumed to belong to the dissolved cooperative within the same period. In case of bankruptcy of the cooperative taking over on the other hand, these properties constitute a different desk. If deemed necessary, these are used to pay the debts of only the dissolved cooperative.

6- The patrimony of both cooperatives can only be unified as of the date after which it is possible to decide upon the properties of the dissolved cooperative.

7- The registration about the dissolving of the cooperative is requested from the Trade Registry Official. Following the payment or taking under guarantee of the debts, the registry of the cooperative is removed.

8- Upon the registration of the dissolving of the cooperative, the members as well join the cooperative taking over, along with the entire rights and debts.

9- As long as the patrimony is registered separately, the members of the dissolved cooperative can only be pursued for the debts of the dissolved cooperative and regarding their responsibilities until then, with the related principles.

10- During the same period, in case the burden of responsibilities or the additional payment obligations of the members of the dissolved cooperative is reduced as a result of unification, this reduction cannot be put forward against the creditors of the dissolved cooperative.

11- In case personal responsibilities or additional payment burdens arise or increase for the members of the dissolved cooperative as a result of unification, the decision for unification can be made only by the consent of three fourths majority of the entire members. The provisions stipulating responsibility and the additional payment burden are not applied to the members not agreeing with the decision for unification and in addition for those who have notified of their withdrawal from the cooperative within three months as of the date of advertisement of the decision.

## D) Being Taken Over by A Legal Public Entity

**Article-85:** The assets of a cooperative can be taken over by a municipality, an economic State enterprise, a public enterprise, or societies or association working for the good of the public. In such cases, it is necessary for the decision to be taken by the General Assembly to be registered and announced, in accordance with the provisions on dissolving.

Under conditions when the assets of such a cooperative are taken over by a municipality, an economic State enterprise, a public enterprise, or societies or association, the General Assembly may make a decision not to realize liquidation.

As of the date of announcement of the decision of transfer, the active and passive of the cooperative are transferred to the possession of the institution taking over. The name of the dissolved cooperative is removed from the trade registry. This particular is announced as well.

Each of the creditors of the unified establishment and the cooperative can raise an objection to the unification by applying to the authorized court within three months as of the date of advertisement. Unless the right of objection is not given up or a decision made by the court refusing the objection becomes definite or the guarantee to be appreciated by the court is not delivered by the establishment or the cooperative, the unification is not valid.

## PART EIGHT
## Duties and Authorities of the Related Ministry

### A) General Duties and Authorities of The Ministry

**Article-86:** The major duties and authorities of the related Ministry over the cooperatives are as follows:

1- To guide the cooperatives, cooperative associations, central cooperatives associations, and the Turkish National Cooperatives Association on their establishment and organizations and to assist them in administration issues and activities,

2- To supervise, inspect and get other bodies inspect the cooperatives, cooperative associations, central cooperatives associations and the Turkish National Cooperatives Association,

3- To notify the court of the reasons necessitating the dissolving of the cooperatives, cooperative associations, central cooperatives associations and the Turkish National Cooperatives Association,

4- To make necessary attempts at the related Ministries and the institutions for the foundation, crediting with priority, and activating in favor of the country of the cooperatives, especially those related to production, and act as a coordinator,

5- To realize organizations in the field of public and social security funds in order to support the application of current regulations with respect to cooperatives and for the cooperatives and superior institutions thereof. (Appended with Article 21 of Law 3476)

## A) Representatives of the Related Ministry and The Condition of Validity of the Decisions

**Article-87:** The related Ministry assigns a representative to be present at the General Assembly meetings of the cooperatives, cooperative associations, central cooperatives associations and the Turkish National Cooperatives Association.

The General Assembly meetings are opened and continued at the presence of a representative from the Ministry. The administration ensures the presence of a representative on the notified day.

**The representatives are in charge of the inspection and the ensuring of the execution of the meeting in compliance with the Law, the Rules, and the agenda. A price to be designated by the related Ministry at an amount not to exceed twice the local daily allowance of the senior first-degree official is paid to each of the representatives. This price is deposited in the treasury of the finance office by the cooperatives and superior institutions thereof, prior to the General Assembly to be delivered to the assigned representative. (Modified by Article 22 of Law 3476)**

The representatives sign the written reports including the decisions of the General Assembly and the list of those attending the meeting. The representative is required to include his opinion on the decisions conflicting Law and the Rules within the written reports.

The qualifications and the duties of the representatives are specified by related rules and regulations.

However, in case the representative does not attend the meeting despite the realization of the application in accordance with the procedure, the local administrative officer is notified of this situation, for rendering the execution of the meeting. If the representative still fails to attend the meeting, the meeting is initiated in an hour.

## B) Preparation Of Sample Rules Document

**Article-88:** The related Ministry prepares sample Rules to be modeled by cooperatives, cooperative associations, central cooperatives associations and the Turkish National Cooperatives Association, on the condition of obtaining the opinions of the institutions in question.

## C) Method of Accounting and Books

**Article-89:** The method of keeping the accounts of the cooperatives, cooperative associations, central cooperatives associations and the Turkish National Cooperatives Association and the books they are obliged to keep may be designated by the related Ministry.

The provisions of the Tax Procedure Law related to these conditions are reserved.

## D) Control and Inspection

**Article-90:** The related Ministry may get the transactions, accounts and assets of the cooperatives, cooperative associations, central cooperatives associations and the Turkish National Cooperatives Association inspected by inspectors or cooperative controllers. The rules and regulations specify the election, the method of working, and the duties ad authorities of the controllers. These organizations are obliged to conform to the instructions to be delivered by the related Ministry, according to the outcome of the inspection. (*)

(*) The members of the board of auditors of the cooperatives or the superior institutions violating Item 3 are sentenced to imprisonment from 1 up to 6 months and a heavy fine of 50.000 TL up to 500.000 TL, depending on the type and degree of the act as Per the Article 26 of the Law 3476 and the appended Addendum 2/2.

**The state institutions, foundations, municipalities, and the related Ministries providing the cooperatives and their superior institutions with loans may inspect whether or not the supplied loans are being used in accordance with the objectives, the conformity with the plans and projects and from the viewpoint of technical features and quality. (Modified by Article 23 of Law 3476)**

**Those who are assigned at the cooperatives and their superior institutions are obliged to display the properties, money, securities, and the books and documents related to these, even if confidential, to the inspectors, cooperative controllers, and the auditing officials of the credit institutions, to assist in the counting and examining processes, to deliver the requested information in accordance with the truth and completely and to forward correct declarations. (Appended with Article 23 of Law 3476) (*)**

## E) Charging With Control and Inspection Activities

**Article-91:** The related Ministry may assign the cooperative superior institutions, related establishments, and independent inspection institutions for the inspection works.

The rules and principles related to these are specified by the rules and regulations to be prepared according to Article 90.

(\*) The members of the Board of Directors of the cooperatives or the superior institutions violating Item 5 are sentenced to imprisonment from 3 months up to 2 years and a heavy fine of 100.000 TL up to 1.000.000 TL, depending on the type and degree of the act as Per the Article 26 of the Law 3476 and the appended Addendum 2/1.

## PART NINE
## Miscellaneous Provisions

### A) Prohibition From Political Activities (Modified by Article 25 Of Law 3476) (\*)

**Article-92: The cooperatives and their superior institutions cannot realize activities that are of political purpose and toward the disturbance of the general security, public security and order; neither the cooperatives nor their superior institutions can be involved in activities of such purposes.**

The cooperatives and their superior institutions can under no circumstances accept any kind of financial assistance from the political parties and organizations or from the persons and organizations who realize the activities dictated in Paragraph 1, nor can they provide them with financial assistance. The Boards of Directors and Auditors of the cooperatives and their superior institutions, as the representatives of these institutions, cannot participate at any kind of meetings to be organized by political parties.

### B) Exemptions

### Article-93:

1-The cooperatives, cooperative associations, central cooperatives associations and the Turkish National Cooperatives Association are exempted from the following:

A) The interests and commissions they have taken from each other and the money they have taken from their members for bailing purposes – from the bank and Insurance Procedures Tax.

B) The certifying of all kinds of books and Rules and the sealing of the at the opening certifications and all kinds of duties and Stamp Tax.

C) All kinds of taxes to be collected from the immovable properties they possess, as long as they are not rented or they are not allocated at places for the purpose of obtaining an income.

D) All kinds of taxes and duties related to the immovable properties the rights of which are to be transferred by the members.

E) The announcement to be submitted in accordance with Article 13 is not subject to stamp tax or other fees and tolls.

**2-**In case the servitude of the immovable properties and the obligation of the immovable properties are put as capitals to the cooperatives, cooperative associations, central cooperatives associations and the Turkish National Cooperatives Association – from the reduced rates as dictated in Article 9 of the Real Estate Purchasing Tax Law.

(*) The founders the cooperatives, the chairman and members of the Board of Directors, and in case this action takes place at a General Assembly meeting, the chairmen of the General Assembly meeting who have tolerated such action are sentenced to imprisonment from 3 months up to 1 year, depending on the type and degree of the act as Per the Article 26 of the Law 3476 and the appended Addendum 2/4.

From the Corporate Tax within the rules and principles dictated in Item 16 of Article 7 of Law 5422 on Corporate Tax Law modified by Law 199.

In case the cooperatives, cooperative associations, central cooperatives associations do not join the superior institutions which have become active, they cannot benefit from

the exemptions specified in this Article, except for those specified in Paragraph (b) of Item 1 and 2.

## A) Fund For Realizing Services Related to Promotion and Training

**Article-94:** 1% of the positive income-expenditure difference realized according to the annual balance sheets of the cooperatives are deposited at a fund under the command of the related Ministry, for services such as guidance related to the promotion, training, and organization of cooperative-business and assisting the cooperatives with recommendations on administration and activities.

## B) Disputes, Arbitration Committees

**Article-95:** The disputes to arise between the organs of the cooperatives and the cooperatives themselves, and the cooperatives and the cooperative associations they are connected to, and the central associations of cooperatives and the Turkish National Cooperatives Association due to the conditions related to the fields of operation can be settled by arbitration committees as set forth in the Rules, on the conditions that the general provisions are reserved.

## C) Reserved Provisions

**Article-96:** The provisions of Law 2834 on Agrarian Sales Cooperatives and Associations and Law 2836 on Agrarian Sales Cooperatives and the provisions on the Construction Cooperatives of Law 7116 are reserved. However, in case there is no clarity in the laws dictated above, the provisions of this law are applied. (13)

**Article-97:** The cooperatives and cooperative associations established by Laws, no: 2834 and 2836 can organize in the form of central associations of cooperatives or can enter the Turkish National Cooperatives Association.

13)Law 2834 about the establishment of the Agrarian Sales Cooperatives and Associations has been taken out of force with Law 3186 dated 30.4.1985 which was published and announced in the Official Gazette 18748 dated 8.5.1985, except for Articles 8, 11, 13, and 21.

Law 2836 about the establishment of the Agrarian Loan Cooperatives and Associations has been taken out of force with Law 1581 which was published and announced in the Official Gazette 14172 dated 28.4.1972. In addition, the Articles 4, 5, 6, 7, and 10 has been taken out of force with Law 3223 dated 7.6.1985 which was published and announced in the Official Gazette 18785 dated 15.6.1985 and two additional articles were appended to this Law.

Law 7116 about the establishment and the duties of the Ministry of Development and Accommodation has been taken out of force with the Article 37 of the Decree in Power of Law 180 about the establishment and duties of the Ministry of Prosperity and Accommodation which was published and announced in the Official Gazette 18251/(repeated) dated 14.12.1983.

## A) Reference to the Provisions of Joint Stock Companies

**Article-98:** In cases where there are no explanations on the contrary, the provisions concerning Joint Stock Companies in the Turkish Trade Law are applied.

## B) Nature of Lawsuits and The Method of Trial

**Article-99:** The lawsuits arising from the particulars organized under this Law are deemed as commercial cases, regardless of whether or not the parties are merchants.

Simple trial Methods are applied in such cases.

## C)Annulled Provisions

**Article-100:** Articles 458 – 502 constituting the sixth chapter of the Turkish Trade Law concerning the cooperatives are annulled.

## Related Ministry

**Appended Article 1- (appended with Article 26 of Law 3476)**

**The names of the Ministries mentioned in this Law have been replaced with the term 'Related Ministry'.**

**The term 'Related Ministry' should be understood as the Ministry of Agriculture Forests and Rural Affairs for those cooperatives and their superior institutions with agrarian fields of activity, and the Ministry of Industry and Trade for the other cooperatives and their superior institutions.**

## Penal responsibility

**Appended Article 2- (appended with Article 26 of Law 3476)**

1-The members of the Board of Directors and the officials of the cooperatives or the superior institutions violating Item 3 of Article 8, Item 5 of Article 16, Items 4, 6, 7, and 8 of Article 59, and Item 5 of Article 90 are sentenced to imprisonment from 3 months up to 2 years and a heavy fine of 100.000 TL up to 1.000.000 TL, depending on the type and degree of the act.

2-The members of the Board of Directors who do not call the General Assembly for a meeting and the members of the Board of Directors of the cooperatives or the superior institutions violating Item 4 of Article 2, Item 1 of Article 16, Item 2 of Article 66, and Item 3 of Article 90 are sentenced to imprisonment from 1 up to 6 months and a heavy fine of 50.000 TL up to 500.000 TL, depending on the type and degree of the act.

3-The members of the board of auditors of the cooperatives or the superior institutions violating Item 2 of Article 56, and Articles 66 and 67 are sentenced to imprisonment from 1 up to 6 months and a heavy fine of 50.000 TL up to 500.000 TL, depending on the type and degree of the act.

4-The founders the cooperatives, the chairman and members of the Board of Directors violating the provisions stipulated by Article 92, and in case this action takes place at a General Assembly meeting, the chairmen of the General Assembly meeting who have tolerated such action are sentenced to imprisonment from 3 months up to 1 year.

The punishments binding freedom set forth in this Article cannot be converted into fines.

The related Ministry can demand the right to intervene with the public lawsuits opened due to the crimes committed by the members of the Board of Directors and Auditors and the officials of the cooperatives and their superior institutions with respect to their duties.

## Temporary provision
### Temporary Article 1- (own numberless temporary article of Law 1163 dated 24/4/1969 (14)

The cooperatives which are already established and are currently active are required to adjust their Rules according to the provisions of this Law within two years. The cooperatives that do not adhere to this condition are regarded to have dissolved. In case the persons in charge of liquidation by Law do not initiate liquidation within two months as of dissolving, the related Ministry or the Treasury can request for the assignment of a liquidation official from the court.

## Temporary Article 2- (temporary article introduced with Article 2 of Law 2475 dated 8/6/1981) (15)

The provisions in the Rules of the construction cooperatives established before the publishing of this Law which take loans from Public Bodies, which conflict Article 52 of the Cooperatives Law 1163 as modified by this Law are assumed to have been amended according to the mentioned article, without the need for any other procedure.

## A) Taking Effect

**Article-101:** This Law takes effect after three months following the date of its publication. (16)

(14) It is the numberless temporary article of the Cooperatives Law 1163 dated 24.4.1969 modified by Law 1496, and it has been numbered by Law 3520 published in the Official Gazette 20076 dated 10.2.1989.

(15) It is the temporary article put into force with Law 2475 dated 8.6.1981, again numbered by Law 3520 published in the Official Gazette 20076 dated 10.2.1989.

(16) It is the executive article of Cooperatives Law 1163 dated 24.4.1969, and it has taken effect after three months as of its publication on the Official Gazette 13195 dated 10.5.1969

## İ) Competent Authority to Execute the Law

**Article-102:** The Council of Ministers executes the provisions of this Law hereby. (17)

## The Provisions That Were Not Included in Law 1163 Dated 24/4/1969

### I-Temporary Articles of Law 3476 dated 6/10/1988

Temporary Article 1-The cooperatives and their superior institutions the names of which do not comply with the stipulations of Article 1 are obliged to correct and register their names in accordance with this Law through the modification of the Rules, within six months.

According to the Paragraph (2) of Item 1 of Article 56 which was amended by Article 14 of this Law, those who are members of more than one Board of Directors of cooperatives with similar fields of operation shall choose one of the said memberships and give others up within three months as of the date this Law takes effect. (19)

Temporary Article 2- The superior institutions of cooperatives which have gained legal identity before the date this Law takes effect, are regarded to have been established in accordance with the provisions of this Law.

Temporary Article 3- The cooperatives which are already established and are currently active are required to adjust their Rules according to the provisions of this Law within two years. The cooperatives that do not adhere to this condition are regarded to have dissolved. In case the persons in charge of liquidation by Law do not initiate liquidation within two months as of dissolving, the related Ministry or the Treasury can request for the assignment of a liquidation official from the court.

The General Assemblies to be held by the cooperatives in order to adapt their Rules to this Law, meet and decide in accordance with the methods and majorities of ordinary General Assemblies.

## I-Validity and Execution Provisions of Law 3476 dated 6/10/1988

**Article-27: The provision of Item 2 of Paragraph (4) of Article 2 appended to this Law along with Article 26 shall take effect after six months as of the publication of this Law; the other provisions take effect as of publication.** (20)

**Article-28: The provisions of this Law hereby are executed by the Council of Ministers.**

(17) It is the executive article of Cooperatives Law 1163 dated 24.4.1969.

(19) The date Law 3476 took effect is 25.10.1988.

(20) The date the provision of Item 2 of Paragraph (4) of Article 2 appended to this Law along with Article 26 took effect is 25.4.1989. The date the other provisions took effect is 25.10.1988.

### List Specifying the Date of Taking Effect of The Legislation Appended to And Amending Law 1163

| No. of Law | Articles that take effect on a different date | Date of taking effect |
|---|---|---|
| 1496 (21) | ---------- | 10/08/1971 |
| 2475 (22) | ---------- | 10/06/1981 |
| 3381 (23) | ---------- | 25/06/1987 |
| 3476 (24) | The provision of Item 2 of Paragraph (4) of Article 2 appended to Law 1163 along with Article 26 | 25/04/1989 |
| 3476 | Other articles | 25/10/1988 |

(21) Law 1496 dated 16.11.1971 which modified one article of Cooperatives Law 1163.

(22) Law 3381 dated 8.6.1981 regarding the modification of Article 52 of Cooperatives Law and the addition of one temporary article to the said law.

(23) Law 2475 dated 12.6.1987 regarding the modification of Items 2 and 3 of Article 19 of Cooperatives Law 1163.

(24) Law 3476 dated 6.10.1988 regarding the modification of some articles of Cooperatives Law and the addition of two articles to the said law.

# PROTECTION OF CULTURAL VALUES

# Protection of Historical and Cultural Tissue in Ankara: A Case Study on Urban Transformation in Hacıbayram*

Tayfun Çınar**, Ayşegül Mengi** and Ruşen Keleş**

### Abstract

Many historical and cultural buildings of Ankara are located in the Ulus section of the city, the old town center. There are also squatter dwellings in Ulus. This is also a neglected part of the city. The main objective of the project to be summarized in this presentation is to realize the transformation of this historical and cultural center.

The Urban Transformation Project encompassing Hacıbayram Mosque and its Surrounding has been initiated by the Ankara Metropolitan Municipality in 2005. Hacıbayram Project is one of the three parts of the Renovation Project of the Historical City Center of Ulus. This large-scale project covers Anafartalar Shopping Center, Bentderesi, old Agora and its surrounding, and finally, the Hacıbayram Mosque. It was not possible to implement the first part of the project due to its very busy commercial structure. The second part covering Bentderesi was not realized simply because a proper

---

\*    Erwin Hepperle, Robert Dixon-Gough, Reinfried Mansberger, Jenny Paulsson, Franz Reuter, Meltem Yılmaz (eds.), *Challenges for Governance Structures in Urban and Regional Development,* Vdf., ETH, Zurich, 2015, pp. 363-370.

\*\*   Ankara University, Faculty of Political Sciences, Ankara, Turkey.

urban design project for the squatter houses in the area was lacking. Therefore, only the Hacıbayram section of the projection has been carried out.

The Urban Transformation Project of Hacıbayram Mosque and its Surroundings aimed at renovating the historical city center as an essential component of Ankara's urban identity. During the process of implementation, registered buildings were rehabilitated as a part of street rehabilitation works and those which were not registered were demolished. The project was designed by the Protection Implementation Bureau (KUDEB) of the Ankara Metropolitan Municipality in cooperation with an architectural firm. The project also comprises of indoor parking lots, green spaces and viewing terraces.

It is financed through the public funds. Within the framework of urban transformation activities, some of the real estate needed was obtained through an accelerated expropriation decision taken by the Council of Ministers and some others were purchased through mutual agreement. However, the number of mutual agreements is very limited. The ownership problems encountered can be regarded as the most important bottle necks of the project. The limited number of the cases of mutual agreements and the transfer of the registered buildings to others than their original owners seem also to be important matters.

## Introduction

"Urban transformation" and "urban renovation" concepts as the main focus of today's urban policy have been on the agenda of Turkey especially since 1980s. Rehabilitation of squatter areas, re-organisation of the areas with disaster risk, construction of solid buildings in these areas, renovation of blighted areas in the city centers and re-organisation of historical city centers are the main objectives of urban renovation and urban transformation projects in Turkey. These projects are implemented especially in metropolitan cities through social, economic, cultural and political interferences where the urban land is very valuable (Keleş 2013: 388). It is observed that valuable urban areas reused by the central government and local administrations under the name of urban transformation through urban renovation projects. Due to these reasons, urban transformation has been an important challenge for urban areas in Turkey.

Instead of "urban conservation" which aims at protecting historical and cultural values by not neglecting the economic development, "urban revitalization" approach has been accepted in the urban transformation projects for historical city centers. This rent seeking approach has led to value increases, commercialisation and reconstruction of historical city center to attract tourists. In this regard, "conservation by renovation and actively using" have been promoted in such projects rather than "protection" of the historical tissue.

## Urban Transformation in Ankara

In Ankara there are fifty urban transformation project areas designated by Ankara Metropolitan Municipality which cover squatter areas, blighted areas and historical city center. By declaring these areas as urban transformation project area, the municipality contributes to the increase of the urban land values in these areas. Most of these fifty project areas is shown as project area on paper, but there are neither any implementation is ongoing nor it is allowed to do any urban activity on these areas. In other words, keeping these areas empty eases the municipality to make speculations.

The Urban Transformation Project encompassing Hacıbayram Mosque and its Surrounding is one of the urban transformation projects in Ankara. Hacıbayram Project is one of the three parts of the Renovation Project of the Historical City Center of Ulus. This large-scale project covers Anafartalar Sopping Center, Bentderesi, old Agora and its surroundings, and finally, the Hacıbayram Mosque. It was not possible to implement the first part of the project due to its very busy commercial structure. The second part covering Bentderesi was not realized simply because a proper urban design project for the squatter houses in the area was lacking. Therefore, only the Hacıbayram section of the project has been carried out. As witnessed in other parts of Turkey, this area is also commercialized by being declared as urban transformation area. This led to establishment of new shopping centers in the heart of the historical city center.

## Hacıbayram Mosque Project

Ulus section of the city is the oldest and traditional commercial center of Ankara. Different civilization like Roman, Seljuk and Ottoman brought their cultural, political, and architectural accumulations to Ankara. Thus, many historical and cultural buildings of Ankara are also located in Ulus, the old town center. There are also squatter dwellings in Ulus. This is also a neglected part of the city.

As time passes the area has experienced various fundamental issues regarding urban transformation. In the early years of the Republic, Ulus was the heart of Ankara. However, Ulus lost its central position and prestige. The interest of upper and upper-middle income groups in Ulus has been decreased and the area has lost its central position. In parallel to losing its importance and prestige, Ulus started to be a center basically serving lower income groups.

Although many of the buildings in the area have historical value and they are the symbols of the Republic, they are not protected. The maintenance and repair of the buildings was neglected, thus buildings in this region have been dilapidated. The number of empty buildings increased and this caused escalation of fire and collapse risk. When the region was attracted by lower income groups, they settled down in the empty buildings. Thus, living in these buildings has caused a big threat to the lives of such inhabitants.

The urban problems in Ulus have also impacted Hacıbayram Mosque and its surroundings. In order to preserve this historical tissue, starting with 1980s firstly "protection" and then "renovation" projects have been developed for Hacıbayram Mosque and its surroundings.

## The Importance of Project Area

There are three well-known sages in Turkey: Mevlana, Hacı Bektaş and Hacıbayram. Hacıbayram-I Veli (veli means sage in Turkish) is known as one of these three famous sages in Anatolia. He was born in 1352 in Ankara and died in 1429 also in Ankara. Hacıbayram who wrote in Turkish language is known for his tolerance and wisdom. Hacıbayram's motto was to respect elderly and to be gentle to young people, to keep out evil, to be humble, and to be helpful to the people in need.

In line with Hacıbayram's interpretation of Islamic philosophy and accommodation of Eastern and Western cultures together under its roof, Hacıbayram Mosque is an important cultural heritage. Hacıbayram Tomb is located next to mosque. In the project area, the Mosque Augustus Temple lays side-by-side as an indication of co-existence of Islam and other religions in Anatolia. It is believed that this area encompasses the concepts of sage, tolerance and holiness. Additionally, Hacıbayram Mosque and its surroundings are located on an important archaeological site. For these reasons, it is very important that the protection work to be carried out in the area is planned and designed to reflect these concepts and values.

Hacıbayram Mosque is a place for prayers, funerals and its tomb is visited by many people. The Mosque is considered as the most important religious site in Ankara where many funeral ceremonies are held. People from different cities and different segments of the society visit the area for religious purposes, touristic tours and etc. Therefore, the area is considered as an important public space. Inevitably the commercial activities are also developed in the region. The site gives commercial services to foster religious activities. The bookstores sell religious books about Islam.

## Historical Origins of the Project

The rehabilitation work carried out within the project area is not a new initiative. The policy of protection and preservation of historical and cultural assets according to the identity of the city in harmony with its historical tissue has been emphasized especially since 1980s. In 2000s, the "protection" perspective has been evolved into "renovation" policy. Furthermore, the concepts of "conservation by renovation" and "actively using" have been referred in the relevant laws. It is possible to see this change of mentality and approach in the individual projects. Hacıbayram Mosque and its surroundings are not called as "protection area", but "renovation area".

Ulus region where Hacıbayram Mosque is located has been declared as urban protected area in 1980 (the decision no 12.04.1980/A-2167 of High Council of Immovable Monuments and Antiquities). Between the years 1984 and 1989 a project came on the agenda for the region. However, public support was not ensured, problems with public funding experienced, political will was not strong enough. For these reasons the project was put on hold.

Planning competition for Ulus was launched in 1986 by Ankara Metropolitan Municipality in order to find solutions for conservation and rehabilitation problems for the area. This project is called as "Hacıbayram Mosque and its Surrounding Urban Design Project" covering 1989-1994. The objective of the project was to transform Ulus into an important city center as it was in the past.

In 1990 Ulus Historical Center Conservation and Improvement Plan was ratified by the Ankara Metropolitan Municipality (decision no: 15.01.1990/33). This plan was cancelled by decision of the City Council of Ankara Metropolitan Municipality in 2005 until a new plan is designed (decision no: 14.01.2005/2010).

In 2005, the decision that designated Ulus Historical City Center as "Renovation Area" was approved by the City Council of Ankara Metropolitan Municipality (decision no: 2005/9289). This area covers Roman Bath, Hacıbayram Mosque and its surroundings and Ankara Citadel. It is argued that one of the reasons for cancelling Ulus Plan and designating this area as urban transformation and development area have been to demolish the enregistered, but protected buildings in the framework of Ulus Plan (Erkal et. Al. 2005. 42).

The Master and Implementation Plan with protection purposes prepared for the renovation area were approved by the City Council of Ankara Metropolitan Municipality in 2007 (decision no: 15.06.2007/1619 and 17.08.2007/2127).

## Legislative Ground of the Project

The legislative ground of the Urban Transformation Project of Hacıbayram Mosque and its Surroundings is the Law on Renovating, Conserving and Actively Using Dilapidated

Historical and Cultural Immovable Assets numbered 5366 (Official Journal no: 05.07.2005/25866).

The purpose of the Law is to reconstruct and restore, in a manner consistent with area development and to create zones of housing, business, culture, tourism and social facilities in such areas, and to renovate, conserve and actively use historical and cultural immovable assets. According to the law, the power of planning and implementing renovation projects for historical parts of cities is given to local administrations. Designation and all control of renovation areas are under the responsibility of the Metropolitan Municipalities within their boundaries. Municipalities may impose temporary restrictions of construction, utilization or operation on the existing immovable properties. The law also specifies that mutual agreement shall be the fundamental rule in dealing with the evacuation, demolition and expropriation of buildings located in the renovation area.

The Protection Implementation Bureaus (KUDEB) have been established by law numbered 5226 under the municipalities, metropolitan municipalities and governorships. KUDEB's function is to carry out all the operations regarding immovable cultural and natural property, implementation and inspection of the construction. In renovation areas the Bureau is responsible for project appraisal and operations related to the permissions and housing. In 2007, KUDEB of the Ankara Metropolitan Municipality was established under the Construction and Urbanisation Department of the Municipality. KUDEB is responsible for the implementation and inspection of the Renovation Project of the Historical City Center of Ulus. The project was designed by KUDEB in cooperation with an architectural firm.

## Project

The area of the Urban Transformation Project of Hacıbayram Mosque and its Surroundings covers approximately 11 hectares of land. If the ownership details of the land is considered: 3,5 hectares are public land; 3,2 hectares belong to Ankara Metropolitan Municipality and 4,4 hectares, which equal to 40%, belong to the individual people. Most of the buildings are wooden and without a skeleton structure. In 2007, 30 individual building lost and 1.454 m2 land were acquired by Ankara Metropolitan Municipality through mutual agreement. The total payment amount is 1,689,260 Turkish Liras. However, 245 individual building lots and 42.815 m2 land obtained through accelerated expropriation by identifying the value of the real estate. In this framework, 54,114,877 Turkish Liras transferred to land owners' accounts by court decision. 82 buildings were demolished by the Ankara Metropolitan Municipality.

Although it is regulated by the law that mutual agreement should be the fundamental rule, only approximately 11% of the buildings were obtained through this way. 89% of the buildings were obtained through accelerated expropriation.

In addition, the newly constructed buildings as part of urban transformation are transferred to the new owners rather than their original owners.

In the framework of Hacıbayram project there are three staged projects that were designed and tendered. Some of the objectives of street rehabilitation projects are; to protect the natural, cultural and architectural identity of the region, to regenerate economic activities and daily life in the region. These projects aim at rehabilitation of the area by preparing and implementing measured drawings, restitution and restoration techniques.

## Concluding Remarks

Main problems experienced around Hacıbayram Mosque are mainly related to the religious and commercial activities and traffic and parking issues. The limited prayer area, the crowds spreading outside the Mosque's garden during prayers, the crowded funeral ceremonies, street peddlers, nonexistence of indoor parking lots for visitors and the bookstores mostly selling only religious books can be listed among these issues. Due to these problems, the project could not meet the expectations. Main critics against the project can be summarised as follows:

- There are no satisfactory developments regarding the completion of the project. It is not easy to get information about the project, thus the transparency is questionable.

- There are critics that the participation aspect of the project is very weak. The landlords, tenants, shop owners, muhtar and municipality staff did not come together in project preparation and implementation. This caused to ownership issue. One the other hand, it would have been expected that not only the stakeholders in that area, but residents of Ankara as the owner of historical and cultural heritage would have been taken in part in the project.

- The project was not implemented through participatory and transparent mechanisms, and has not been designed in the framework of a plan. In this regard, it is argued that the project is implemented in line with the initiative of the mayor of Ankara Metropolitan Municipality.

- Almost all of the buildings in the region have been defined as in need of heavy maintenance or under the threat of collapse. Thus, in the project instead of protection of the historical buildings stock by renovation, these buildings were demolished and reconstructed.

- The ownership problems can be regarded as important bottlenecks of the project.
- Based on all these criticisms, it is obvious that the project is not an urban renovation project. It is clear that the economic, social and environmental aspects of sustainability is lacking.

As a result, the following assessment can be made for the project:

- The "protection" perspective has been evolved into "renovation" policy. Hacıbayram Mosque and its surroundings are not called as "protection area", but "renovation area".
- The project puts forward the symbols of Islam and Seljuk and eliminates the spatial identity of other periods.
- As witnessed in other parts of Turkey, this area is also commercialised by being declared as urban transformation area.
- The project was not implemented through participatory and transparent mechanisms, thus social reaction and opposition existed.

## References

- Bademli R. [2002], Hacıbayram Camisi Çevresi Kamu Proje Alanı (KPA-2) Kentsel Tasarım Planı Çalışması Tespit ve Değerlendirme ve Açıklama Raporu (Hacıbayram Mosque Surroundings Public Project Area Urban Design Plan Study Identification and Evaluation Report), METU.
- Bademli, R., Ülkenli Z. K., "Hacıbayram Çevre Düzenleme Projesi" (Hacıbayram Urban Environment Design Project).

http://www. Kentselyenileme.org/dosyalar/Hacıbayram.pdf (last visited 13/06/2013).

- Erkal, F., Kıral, Ö., Günay, B., [2005], "Ulus Tarihi Kent Merkezi Islah İmar Planı: 1986-2006 Koruma Planından Yenileme Planına" (Ulus Historical Center Rehabilitation and Construction Plan: 1986-2006 from Conservation Plan to Renovation Plan), Planlama (Journal of Planning), 4: 34-50.

- Keleş, R., [2013], Kentleşme Politikası (Urbanization Policy), Ankara, İmge Kitapevi.

- Osmançavuşoğlu, A., [2006], Urban Transformation Process: Ulus Historical City Center Planning Project, Unpublished Master Thesis, The Graduate School of Natural and Applied Sciences, METU, Ankara.

- Özden, P. P., [2001], "Kentsel Yenileme Uygulamalarında Yerel Yönetimlerin Rolü Üzerine Düşünceler ve İstanbul Örneği" (Thoughts on the Role of Local Governments in Urban Renewal Pratices and Istanbul Case), İ. Ü. Siyasal Bilgiler Fakültesi Dergisi (Istanbul University, The Journal of Faculty of Political Sciences), No: 23-24: 255-270.

- Şen, B. [2006], "Ekonomik Gelişmelerin Kültürel Stratejileri: İstanbul Kent Merkezleri ve Tarihi Kentsel Alanların Yeniden Yapılandırılması" (The Cultural Strategies of Economic Development: Regeneration of Urban Centers and Historic Urban Areas in Istanbul), Planlama (Journal of Planning), 2: 65-77.

- TMMOB Mimarlar Odası Ankara Şubesi, [2005], "Ulus Tarihi Kent Merkezi" (Ulus Historical City Center), Planlama (Journal of Planning), 4: 51-54.

- Türkün, A., Ulusoy, Z. [2006], "Kentsel SİT Alanlarında Turizm Amaçlı Dönüşüm ve Sorunlar: Ankara Kalesi Örneği" (Transformation of Historic Urban Areas with Tourism and the Possible Problems: The Case of Ankara Citadel), Planlama (Journal of Planning), 2: 129-139.

- Yaman, M. [2012], Kentsel Dönüş(tür)me Uygulamaları: Sosyo-Politik Bir Yaklaşım (Urban Transformation Practices: A Socio- Politic Approach), Bursa, MKM Yayıncılık.

- Yardımcı, S. [2008], Transformation of Urban Sphere: Hacıbayram Square and its Environment-Ankara, Unpublished Master Thesis, The Graduate School of Natural and Applied Sciences, METU, Ankara.
- Ankara Büyükşehir Belediyesi 15.01.1990/33 sayılı Meclis kararı (The decision of the City Council of Ankara Metropolitan Municipality).
- Ankara Büyükşehir Belediyesi 15.06.2007/1619 sayılı Meclis kararı (The decision of the City Council of Ankara Metropolitan Municipality).
- Ankara Büyükşehir Belediyesi 17.08.2007/2127 sayılı Meclis kararı (The decision of the City Council of Ankara Metropolitan Municipality).
- Ankara Büyükşehir Belediyesi 14.01.2005/210 sayılı Meclis kararı (The decision of the City Council of Ankara Metropolitan Municipality).
- Ankara Büyükşehir Belediyesi 15.07.2005/1952 sayılı Meclis kararı (The decision of the City Council of Ankara Metropolitan Municipality).
- Bakanlar Kurulu 2005/9289 sayılı kararı (The decision of Council of Ministers).
- Gayrimenkul Eski Eserler ve Anıtlar Yüksek Kurulu'nun (The decision of High Council of Immovable Monuments and Antiquities) 12.04.1980/A-2167 sayılı kararı.
- Resmi Gazete (Official Journal) 05.07.2005/25866.

# ISTANBUL

# Implications of Urbanisation for Turkey.
## The Case of Istanbul*

Istanbul is the major city of a rapidly urbanising country, Turkey. Physical, environmental, economic and socio-cultural problems facing the city are described and analysed in this chapter, with special emphasis on the local and national impact of policies to be implemented. An attempt is also made to see how future developments in the world in general and in the region in particular will affect the quality of the environment and urban management. It seems almost certain that unless the present rate of population growth is curbed in the coming decades, the hopes for sustainable development may just remain on paper.

### Turkey's Urban Profile

Turkey is one of the most rapidly urbanising countries in the Mediterranean region with more than half (65 percent in 2000) of its population living in urban centers. The annual rate of urban growth, over the last forty years, has been around 6 percent. In absolute figures, the urban population increased from 6. 9 million in 1960 to nearly 44 million in 2000. It is estimated that it will reach 57. 3 million

* Antonio Marquina (ed.), *Environmental Challenges in the Mediterranean (2000-2050)*, NATO Science Series IV, Earth and Environmental Sciences, Vol.37, Kluer, Dordrecht, 2004, pp.345-359.

by the year 2005 (18), increasing the share of urban population to 80 percent.

The socio-economic characteristics of Turkey have been greatly influenced by the demographic trends facing the country. The average rate of increase in the population was 2.49 percent during the period 1960 to 1990, but it has declined slightly during the last decade (25). It decreased to 1.83 percent by the year 2000.

Living and working conditions in the countryside together with the inheritance legislation, which enhanced the fragmentation of rural landholdings, caused a rapid migration to cities following World War II. Rural to urban migration is chiefly directed towards major urban centers, and especially to the five largest cities, including Istanbul, the major city (4). Both rural to urban migration and natural growth played an important role in Turkish urbanization. However, the generally accepted hypothesis that declining birth rates make the migration component of the urban population growth the most significant determining factor does not hold true in the case of Turkey where the birth rates are still quite high even in the metropolitan centers. The relative share in the urban population of the cities with a population of 100.000 or more increased from 45.3 percent in 1960 to 70.5 percent in 2000, and it is estimated that it will be around 80 percent by the year 2010. During the 1960-2000 period, more than 30 million people began to live in cities, and it can be safely assumed that 20 million more people will be living in urban areas in ten years time. Out of these 20 million people, 16 million will be settled in cities of 100.000 and more inhabitants (13). There is a significant increase in the number of cities in the size-category of 100.000 or more inhabitants. The number was 56 in 2000: this figure may reach 80 by the year 2010. This tendency can be interpreted as a process operating at the expense of the prevailing supremacy of Istanbul on the urban scene. Istanbul is still ahead of other cities not only in the number of industrial establishments, but also in all other social, cultural and economic institutions.

Ankara, the State Capital, preserved its secondary position despite its spectacularly rapid growth rate. Although the population of all the larger cities are far below the level where they should be normally according to the so called "rank-size rule", the distribution of secondary regional centers throughout the national territory shows, at the same time, a remarkable tendency towards a more even distribution. In other words, the primacy of Istanbul in the hierarchy of settlements has been weakening since the early 1960's. In fact, a change in the primacy of Istanbul between 1950 and 2000 is noticeable in Table 2 below. This change may be explained by the relative efficiency of the redistributive policies implemented during the First (1963-1967) and the Second (1968-1972) Five Year Development Plan periods. These considerably influenced the number and relative importance of other large cities and have given the spatial pattern of urbanisation a relatively balanced appearance. This does not mean, of course, that the unbalanced pattern of urbanisation has been entirely changed. What it means instead is that some regional centers like Eskişehir, Mersin Bursa, Adana, Gaziantep, Konya and Diyarbakır are gradually becoming counterbalancing magnets in Anatolia, attracting the population flow that it otherwise expected to concentrate in Istanbul and Ankara.

Table 1. Stability in the Ranking of the Five Biggest Cities (1950-2000)

| Cities | 1950 | 1985 | 1997 | 2000 |
|---|---|---|---|---|
| Istanbul | 1 | 1 | 1 | 1 |
| Ankara | 2 | 2 | 2 | 2 |
| Izmir | 3 | 3 | 3 | 3 |
| Adana | 4 | 4 | 4 | 4 |
| Bursa | 5 | 5 | 5 | 5 |

Source: State Institute of Statistics, Population Censuses

This trend is in line with the observation of S. El-Shaks emphasizing that the form of the primacy curve seems to follow a consistent pattern in which the peak of primacy is reached during the stages of socio-economic transition. His reference to the decentralisation and the spread effects in the development process, namely the increasing importance of the periphery, also holds true in Turkey's case, with the minor difference that this has not happened spontaneously, but has come about as a result of deliberate state action.

| Table 2. Change in the Primacy of Istanbul | | | |
|---|---|---|---|
| Share of the Major City (%) | 1950 | 1985 | 2000 |
| Ankara and Izmir (second and third largest) as (%) of Istanbul | 53.8 | 68.1 | 61.3 |
| Ankara, Izmir and Adana (second, third and the fourth largest) as (%) of Istanbul | 65.8 | 82.2 | 74.6 |
| Ankara, Izmir, Bursa and Adana (second, third, fourth and the fifth largest) as (%) of Istanbul | 76.4 | 93.4 | 88.2 |

Source: Rusen Keles, *Urban Poverty in the Third World*, IDE, Tokyo, 1988, p. 5b, and the State Institute of Statistics, Population Censuses

The growth of urbanisation is at the same time a reflection of the pace of urbanisation in the country and in the differential demographic growth of regions. Among the seven geographic regions of Turkey, the Marmara region, which has Istanbul as its center, represents the highest ratio of urban population which was 78.1 percent in 2000. Reciprocal effects of the urbanisation of the region and of Istanbul are not negligible. In the priority list, the Marmara region is followed by the Aegean (57. 8 percent), Central Anatolia (64.8 percent), and the Mediterranean (56.7 percent). The least urbanized regions are the Southeast (61. 6 percent), the East (49.2 percent), and the Black Sea (42.6 percent) regions.

Even after the relative showing down of its rate of population increase, Istanbul is still one of the main urban centers, which attracts migrants from all parts of the country. It is interesting to see that only 37.3 percent of its 1997 population was born in Istanbul. The rest (62.7 percent) is composed of immigrants. Out of 5.5 million inhabitants in 1985, over a million (18.5 percent) originated in the following Black Sea provinces: Kastamonu, Trabzon, Çorum, Ordu, Sinop, Rize, Samsun, Tokat and Gümüshane. Nearly 700.000 (12.2 percent of the total migrants) came from the following eastern provinces: Sivas, Samsun, Kars, Malatya, Erzurum and Erzincan. The fact that more than 60 percent of the inhabitants of Istanbul were born in other provinces seems surprising in view of the observation that, for the whole country, the population born in places other than their place of residence was only 20.9 percent for that year.

Table 3. The Population of Istanbul (000)

| Years | Greater Istanbul (A) | Turkey (B) | (A/B) |
|---|---|---|---|
| 1927 | 705 | 13.648 | 5.2 |
| 1950 | 1.102 | 20.947 | 4.8 |
| 1960 | 1.506 | 27.755 | 5.4 |
| 1970 | 2.203 | 35.605 | 6.2 |
| 1980 | 2.909 | 44.707 | 6.5 |
| 1990 | 6.229 | 56.473 | 11.0 |
| 2000 | 8.803 | 67.804 | 13.0 |

Source: State Institute of Statistics, Population Censuses. The impressive increase in the figure of 1990 is due to the consolidation that was realized in 1984

## Ankara versus Istanbul

The proclamation of the new Turkish Republic in 1923 can be regarded as a turning point with regard to the location of the State Capital. Istanbul was distrusted by the rulers of the new Turkey. It was considered as a symbol of the old regime and of colonial exploitation. Therefore, Atatürk, the founder of the Republic, and his associates wanted to find a new State Capital, whose inhabitants were dedicated to nationalism and the modernisation goals of the Republic, rather than continue with Istanbul with its "cynicism and corruption".

As a result, Istanbul gradually lost its socio-economic and political importance. An indication of this trend was the decrease in the city's population from 1 million at the beginning of the 29 th century to 704.825 in 1827 and to 758.488vin 1935. On the contrary, Ankara was a small Anatolia town and a trade center in 1923 when it was designated as the new State Capital. It was also regarded as strategically much safer than Istanbul. Besides, the latter was regarded by the founders of the Republic as much too cosmopolitan, representing the interest of the imperialists rather than those of the Anatolia people that supported the Turkish liberation movement from when it began in the late 1910's.

Following the transfer of the capital to Ankara, Istanbul remained as the nation's industrial and business center, its greatest port, the focus of the transportation network and the center of cultural and intellectual life. It attracted most of the private industrial and commercial investments during the initial decades of the Turkish Republic. Its population continued to increase rapidly during the 1960's and 1970's. Many of the agencies responsible for economic development and public investments remained in Istanbul, and a large amount of imported goods required for the development of new industries flowed inevitably through Istanbul. This necessitated, in turn, public investment in the city's port facilities which further reinforced its position as the principal channel for foreign trade.

## Istanbul: A Short History of a Ruralising Metropolis

Istanbul served as the capital of the East Roman Empire from 395 A.D. It is the only major city in the world to lie on two continents and the 8 kilometer long Golden Horn cuts through the heart of the European side. Across the Bosphorus lies the Asian section of the city between the Black Sea to the north and the Sea of Marmara to the south (1). This one-time capital of three empires (Roman, Byzantine and

Ottoman) stretches out to embrace a diversity of population and natural and man-made environments (17).

Under the highly centralized Ottoman system, Istanbul grew steadily. By the end of the 18 th century, its population exceeded 870.000. Concern over the rapid increase in the number of its inhabitants led to imperial policies to check the flow from the provinces of migrants. European experts were also invited to work out master plans to guide the city's development. At the same time, foreign capital was channeled into Istanbul as the city's economic dominance over its vast hinterland increased. European businessman and their local agents were heavily concentrated in the metropolis. The city became a European outpost, the place where the imperialist powers had a chance to control their growing share of the Ottoman economy. This was the typical pattern of urban development, called *dependent urbanisation* (urbanisation dependent) by Manuel Castells, taking place in almost all Third World countries which were more or less integrated with the world capitalist system (28).

## The Contemporary City and Economy

Modern Istanbul spreads far beyond the ancient city's seven hills, covering about 6.600 square kilometers on both sides of the Bosphorus. About 67.8 percent of Istanbul's population live on the European side. But, in recent years, the Asian portion of Greater Istanbul has been growing more rapidly. The basic settlement pattern has been linear, with development spreading from the old city north for 40 kilometers on the European shore of the Sea of Marmara, and east for 100 kilometers on the Asiatic Sea coast.

Although the historical business center was located on the European side in the historic city and adjacent areas to the north, Istanbul has become, during the last four decades, a multi-centered metropolis with several business districts located in various parts of its territory, containing institutions of finance, imports and exports, corporations, retail, wholesale, etc. In other words, Istanbul is a mosaic of commercial districts, industrial plants, strip development, residential zones, transportation facilities, military bases and forests that ring the waterways, Industrial development is more intensive in the extreme west and east of city's linear development pattern: Sefaköy, Avcılar, Çekmece in the west and Kartal, Pendik, Gebze in the east. Heavy industry is particularly concentrated in the eastern industrial estates which have suitable transportation connection with the rest of Turkey (8).

While greater Istanbul accommodates about 13.6 percent of the country's population, the GNP it creates provides an important in put into the country's economy. The share of the active population working in industrial occupations in Istanbul increased from 23 percent in 1955 to 41.4 percent in 1985, while corresponding figures for the whole country during the same period were 6 percent and 14.4 percent, respectively. The economy of Istanbul represents 30.3 percent of the whole industry and 47 percent of all the services. The share of Istanbul in per capita GNP is two and a half times that of Turkey (19). The share of Istanbul in total investments in Turkey dropped from 27 percent in 1965 to 19 percent during the 1970's with a view to fostering development in the less developed eastern regions.

The economic sectors in which the share of Istanbul is disproportionately high are paper and paper products (39.5 percent of Turkey's figure), chemicals, petroleum, coal and plastic products (38.7 percent of the total) and metallurgy (35.7 percent). On average, the share of the city in manufacturing industries is 26.7 percent. In these sectors, the number of workshops represented by Greater Istanbul is 50 percent of the total. In fact, Istanbul represented 64.3 percent of foreign trade in 1986. It is also interesting to note that a considerable part (38.3 percent) of the tax revenue in the country is collected in Istanbul. For some kinds of taxes, this percentage is still over 50 percent. In heavy industry, Istanbul represents 43 percent of all the factories in Turkey. As far as the number of workers is concerned, this percentage is 30 percent. It becomes 27 percent in terms of the total economic output. For light industry, on the other hand, the percentages indicating the share of Istanbul in Turkey's total are 24.4 for the number of plants and 30.5 for the number of workers (22).

The share of the active population who work as salaried workers is much higher in Istanbul compared with Turkey's figure in general. Similarly, the ratio of the self employed is three times smaller than the national average. Another indicator of the change in economic structure of the city is the distribution of the active population among economic sectors. As expected, the share of the non-agricultural sectors is incomparably high in the major city. In the distribution of the active population among professions and status categories, several occupations seem to occupy the most important places. These are employees, small businessmen (the self-employed), the retired, and civil servants, in that order.

The main central business district (CBD) is situated on the west side of the Bosphorous, hence creating daily journeys between both sides. Water, together with other modes of transport, plays an important part in mass transportation. In the CBD, which has nation-wide economic importance, there are traditional activities which do not need to be located there. Therefore, the Planning Authority of Istanbul proposed, in the early 1980's, the relocation of such functions to sub-centers to be established along the 100 kilometer length of the metropolitan area. A great many administrative agencies of the many commercial and industrial establishments of the country are active in Istanbul. The CBD, at first located in the historical core, has lately been expanded towards the north. The public sector agencies are also situated in the CBD or in the near periphery.

Despite the tendency to decentralize, encouraged and guided by the planning authorities, the sub-centers are still not sufficiently developed in Istanbul. There does not exist an efficient distribution of activities among these newly structured sub-centers and the main CBD. In practice, all development has been guided by market forces. As a result of the white collar and skilled force being largely concentrated in the CBD, in areas where economic feasibility and prestige value coincide, there emerged an increase in housing demand. As the public sector has not been able to cope with and regulate the demand in time, neighborhoods have emerged with no planning.

Industrial establishments are unevenly distributed through the city. Their locations were not chosen as a result of the optimisation of economic, social and physical location factors, taking into consideration their likely impact upon the environment. The excessive concentration of industrial establishment in the central zones became a matter of concern from the point of view of national security and strategic considerations during the 1960's and, consequently, on the suggestion of the National Security Council, the city council adopted a new industrial settlement plan which aimed at the decentralisation of new industrial establishments to areas away from the center. Although the industries already settled in the central zones are trying to migrate out of the city, this does not result in a considerable decrease in the number of industrial factories within the city. The reason is that the factories are still viable (27).

## Housing and Squatting

Meeting the housing needs of low-income families in Istanbul has been a major task of the governments since the late 1940's when the rural to urban migration began to accelerate. The number of gecekondus, unauthorized dwellings, increased from 10.000 in 1948 to more than a million in 2000. The Governor of Istanbul stated in the early 1980's that the average number of gecekondus built annually was around 22.000 (9). Roughly 60 percent of the city's population live at present in them.

According to the estimates of the Planning Authority of Greater Istanbul, the population of the city is expected to reach 12 million by 2010 (23). This is rather a conservative figure. Because if the annual additions to the present population, estimated to be about 1 million, are taken into account, the city's population may have already surpassed the estimate referred to above (7). When the fact that the number of informal subdivisions have increased from 200.000 to over 3 million since 1975 is taken into account, one could safely assume that the population of the city may double in the first two decades of the 21 st century (7). As to the distribution of the additional population of the city, it is assumed that one third of the increase will take place on the east side and two thirds in the west.

Greater Istanbul has about 1.8 million dwellings with an average household size of 4.5 persons. This leads, together with the yearly increase in population of 250.000 people, to a yearly housing need of about 60.000 dwellings. When added to the number of gecekondus built prior to 1970, one can assume that there exists about 1 million gecekondus in the city, housing nearly 60 percent of the city's population.

Gecekondus are often mentioned and defended as a solution to the acute housing shortage in the metropolis. There is no doubt that they help to fill the gap in the supply of social housing. Gecekondu construction is an outcome of the creative intelligence of self-help efforts of the homeless urban poor. It also reinforces the self-reliance of the community residents. Of course, it ensures the use of the labor force at a considerably low cost, but it is doubtful as to what extent it helps to reduce unemployment. This is a structural illness, as in other Third World countries.

However, the gecekondus are built on lands unsuitable for human habitation with inadequate or no infrastructure and services. Therefore, the need for partial or full renovation or the relocation of their residents requires repetitive investments and makes this method prohibitively costly (10).

In Istanbul, the gecekondu building process is no longer a kind of self-help activity, carried out by the homeless. Rather, it has become partly or totally commercialized during the last three decades, and has lost its social significance entirely. Presently, the urban poor who can barely pay the rent of a gecekondu are no more than tenants of the professional gecekondu builder (13).

## Governing Greater Istanbul

Greater Istanbul is one of the 81 provinces of Turkey. A Governor, appointed by the Council of Ministers, is in charge of establishing law and order. On the other hand, Istanbul is the largest local government unit, a municipality, in the country. Until 1984, it consisted of the city of Istanbul and about thirty smaller municipalities surrounding it. Following the attempt by the government to incorporate peripheral settlements administratively within a single metropolitan administration, the Constitution of 1982 permitted setting up metropolitan municipalities in the largest urban centers. Using this power given by the Constitution, the government that came to power in late 1983 managed to pass legislation through Parliament to create a metropolitan municipality in Istanbul (1984), the same as with two other major cities, namely Ankara and Izmir, based on a two-tier model of administration.

Istanbul originally had a municipal Organisation founded in the middle of the 11850's under Ottoman rule, and modified later in the Republican period in the 1930's, but the structure could not meet the needs of more efficient local services and better participation in the decision-making of today's Istanbul. At present, certain major functions, such as master planning, large-scale undertakings of water supply, transportation, sewerage, central heating, parks, car parks and terminals and the like, are carried out by the metropolitan (upper-level) municipality of Istanbul. All the local services, other than the ones mentioned above and those that are described in the municipal legislation as the duties of municipalities, are left to 32 district (sub-provincial) municipalities and 42 smaller non-district municipalities within the metropolitan area (11). The increase in the number of the smaller municipalities which are not districts in the administrative sense, grew parallel to the increase in the number of squatter settlements which mushroomed without facing strong preventive measures during the 1960's and 1970's. For example, the following non-district municipalities, were set up during the ten years between 1966 and 1977: (1966): Avcilar, Güngören, Yakacik, (1967): Sefaköy, Alibeyköy, (1969): Hadmköy, Celaliye, Soganlik, (1970): Esenler, (1971): Kmerburgaz,

Selimpaça, Yenibosna, Dolayoba, (1972): Çinarcik, (1975): Yesilbag, (1976): Kocasinan, Halkali, (1977): Yahyalar (25).

The municipalities at both upper and lower levels elect their mayors and city councils. All units in the metropolitan area enjoy special revenue sources provided by special legislation. The new system of local administration has achieved its first goal to a certain extent, which consisted in providing better and more efficient public services. However, the goal of participation is still far from being realized. The main reason is that the optimal size of the district municipalities in population and territory is not adequately defined. In almost all district municipalities, the size of the population and the territory exceed the optimum levels that are suitable for active public participation. In fact, it is obvious that there can be no participation, in the real sense of the world, in municipalities such as Bakırköy which had a population closer to two million in 1990. Others like Kadiköy, Fatih, Sisli and Kartal each had a population of between half a million and one million.

The size of district municipalities and the complexity and anonymity of social interactions that characterize these sub-centers are not suitable to producing a participatory atmosphere. This seems to justify the observation of some social scientists that called such a state of affairs "the decline of community and "the decline of citizenship" (2).

There are also important differences in the sizes of the population and territory of these municipalities. Since the number of inhabitants determine the amount of revenue that each district municipality receives from the central government budget, these discrepancies give rise to enormous injustices, in the absence of compensatory mechanisms.

The Council of Greater Istanbul Municipality is made up of the mayor of the metropolis, who is elected by the inhabitants of all of Istanbul for a period of five years, mayors of the district municipalities and one fifth of the members of each of the district councils, who are also elected. The metropolitan council is constituted for five years. The members of the council keep their positions in the lower level councils while serving on the metropolitan council. Istanbul has a metropolitan council which consists of nearly 150 members.

There is no doubt that the quality of the environment in the metropolitan area will be affected in years to come by the extent to which the central government and the local authority cooperate efficiently in carrying out of the public services directly or indirectly related to the environment. It seems that attempts to reform the local government system will enable the sub-national government to respond better in the future to the increasing concern of the inhabitants as to the quality of the environment. In accordance with the goals set by the Rio and Habitat II Conferences, the government is currently trying to put into effect a local government reform which is, to a large extent, in line with the principle of subsidiarity.

## Urbanisation and Environment

Istanbul was one of the cleanest cities in Turkey, not polluted by industry or urbanisation until recently. However, it has changed during the last two and a half decades. The municipality has had to set up a special department of environmental protection to deal with water and air pollution. It has dealt with the removal of more than 4000 unhealthy industrial establishments along the coast. According to the findings of several applied researches, the most important source of noise in Istanbul is the traffic. Measurements of 1986 show that the average $SO_2$ mgm per cubic meter was 193.9 for the European side, and 164.4 for the Asian side. For the whole metropolitan area, the value was found to be around

92 mgm per cubic meter. On selected sites on the historical peninsula, the noise level was 73.9 db for Sisl and, 74.5 db for Kadiköy. As far as solid waste discharged is concerned, the major centers of economic activity like Eminönü, Beyoglu, Sisli and Bakırköy are at the top, with per capita figures well above Istanbul's average figure.

The green spaces of past centuries were rapidly turned into apartment blocks in Istanbul in the second half of the 20th century. Per capita green space, which should not be less than 7 square meters according to the existing planning standards, is only 2.2 square meters. When allowance is made for public squares in the city and cemeteries, the amount of actual usable green space becomes much smaller. Only 33.9 percent of the available green space is actually usable by the inhabitants of the city. There is a definite adverse impact of building activities upon the natural environment.

Squatting itself can be regarded as an environmental problem in the metropolitan area where most of the adverse consequences of unplanned and disorderly urbanisation are reflected. One million out of the two million gecekondus existing in the country are situated in Istanbul. Regardless of their economic and social characteristics, at least three features of squatter settlements in Istanbul affect the environment directly: The first is the visual pollution created by unplanned and unlawful construction; the second is the inadequacy of urban infrastructure; and the third is the deterioration of hygienic conditions in these quarters. In fact, according to the findings of applied research carried out by the State Planning Organisation (20), the percentages of the households in these unauthorized settlements deprived of basic urban public services are quite high, as shown below:

a) Those that do not receive their drinking water from the city's regular water network (9.0 percent)

b) Those whose liquid wastes are not discharged into the city's sewerage system (16.5 percent)

c) Those that discharge their solid wastes into streets or to the sea, but not to the garbage baskets (12.3 percent)

d) Those whose solid wastes are not collected regularly by the city authorities (28.0 percent)

A major environmental issue related to the water supply system is that nearly half of the 7000 kilometer long pipe system is either unhealthy or in need of repair or complete renewal. A considerably large part of the system is broken and suffers leaks. Similarly, almost one third of the population and one fifth of the area of Istanbul is deprived of a modern sewerage system. Accelerated urbanisation during the 1950's and 1960's filled the *Golden Horn* shores with haphazardly located factories, manufacturers, work premises and warehouses. Chimneys started to dirty the air, and water polluted the sea. The quantity of daily liquid waste discharged into the Golden Horn by the industries in the region is approximately 200.000 tons. Of this, 67 percent is chemicals, 27 percent washing water, 4 percent cooling water, and the rest other kinds of wastes. More than half of the industrial premises were found to discharge solid wastes.

It was observed, in the early 1970's that the ratio of sulphur dioxide in the air, pollution during the days where the ratio exceeded the limit harmful to human health, reached 62 percent at Silahtar, 67 percent at Eyüp and 58 percent at Hasköy. Little left of the *Golden Horn* of past centuries, much praised by local and foreign poets and authors like Baron Durand, Pierre Loti, and Charles Diehl. The *Golden Horn* has been reduced to a simple *horn*, no longer possessing the adjective *golden*.

Within one or two decades, Turkey's membership of the European Union could materialize. Starting from the end of

2004, Turkey will probably begin negotiations for full membership. This requires full adaptation to the rules, standards and regulations concerning running water, services, various kinds of pollution, and infrastructures like those prevailing in the member states of the European Union. One can expect, as a result, a sharp improvement in all these and related standards, and in the quality of life in general.

## 8. Impact of Globalisation upon the Environment

Since the early 1970's, the world has witnessed a rapid Globalisation with at the same time a decline in the power of the national state. It is capital that largely determines the success and failure of individual economic sectors as well as the totality of national economies. Since capital recognizes no national boundaries, the traditional concept of national sovereignty has lost much of its meaning. Globalisation requires that all obstacles to the free flow of international capital be removed even at the expense of environmental values. As a result, sustainability is to a considerable degree adversely affected by Globalisation On one hand, it puts all sorts of sophisticated technological opportunities at the service of mankind, but on the other hand, it exerts, directly or indirectly, deteriorating effects upon natural and historical values, because capital has a single, global, *sui generis* logic which everyone is forced to obey. This observation is true not only for transnational capital, but also for national and local capital.

Turkey had to open its doors to the influence of Globalisation as early as the beginning of the 1980's. Since the strategic points of connections are the cities and their economic, financial, socio-cultural and political institutions, Istanbul, as the only city which possessed most of the characteristics of a *world city*, assumed an increasing role in promoting the interest of international capital. For example, according to the

Mayor of Istanbul in the middle of the 1980's, "Istanbul is a city 2.500 years old and has more than 3000 historical buildings. If nearly one hundred of them prevent the construction of a major transport artery serving international and national trade, they must be demolished. We do not share protectionist views which prevent development". (5) This policy began to dominate all aspects of the city's development from the early 1980's: five-star hotels, luxury residential zones, university campuses and the like have been created in the city's green areas but inadequate attention has been paid to the preservation of natural assets and resources. The sites where the Yapi Kredi Plaza, Sabanci Center, Konrad Hotel, Hyatt Regency, Swiss Hotel and the like have been built are a few of the examples of this kind of development.

The services necessary for the Globalisation of capital have been concentrated in the high-rise buildings in the trade centers that were built with no regard to the zoning regulation of the city. It has been suggested that Istanbul is in a position to undertake the activities required by Globalisation , such as banking insurance , legal and accounting services, consultancy, communications, publicity, marketing and engineering services for neighboring countries like Georgia, Azerbaijan, Ukraine or Romania (14,15,16). The same logic emphasizes that unless Istanbul turns its attention to the demands of the new world system, it will face the risk of becoming a marginalized city with a severely curtailed potential for further evolution (14,15,16).

On the other hand, Turkey's international economic policies and its likely membership of the European Union have already adversely affected development of the cities and urban environments. In order to ease conditions favorable to the free flow of capital, important amendments have been made in the Constitution and the corresponding legislation.

For example, the MAI (Multi Party Agreement) that was accepted by Turkey requires, among other things, that "the provisions in the previously signed environmental agreements that are not favorable to free trade be removed". Similarly a new Law on Privatisation (No:4046) in 1999 authorized the newly established Privatisation Authority to work on master plans for the communities where the privatized economic enterprises were located. The condition was that the central or local authorities could not modify the plans for five years. Furthermore, Article 125 and 155 of the Constitution have been amended with a view to permitting international arbitration to resolve legal conflicts that might is from administrative contracts of concessions. In other words, this amendment puts an end to the role played so far by the Council of State for the protection of the environment. Parliament, in its turn, passed the necessary legislation accordingly without much delay (Law No: 4501, October 2000). These examples indicate that the dynamics affecting urban sustainability will no longer be controlled by domestic institutions but will rather be shaped internationally as a result of Globalisation. There is no doubt that the impact of these changes is badly affecting the historical identity of Istanbul and will continue to be detrimental to the environment, as in the last two decades. We believe that it is not possible to agree with the views of the proponents of Globalisation. They prefer integration within international capitalism through a network of global cities which implies sacrificing the cultural, historical and natural identity features of such cities as Istanbul in order to contribute to the successes of world capitalism.

## Conclusion

Urbanisation in Turkey is still proceeding at a considerable speed. Push and pull factors behind rural to urban migration movements are still strong enough to distort the rural- urban balance in favor of the latter. Unless an effective system of regional planning exists, inequalities between geographic regions, particularly between the east and the west, will not be reduced naturally by time. Inequality in the distribution of population in economic activities and investment is the very reason which causes a concentration of pollution in the highly urbanized Istanbul and surrounding settlements. Although the degree of urbanisation in the Marmara region in the west of the country is as high as 78.1 percent, this figure is less than 50 percent in Eastern Anatolia and the Black Sea regions. Such a striking imbalance, that is also reflected in all economic and social indicators of development, requires immediate handling through planning at national and regional levels. This would also ease the task of Istanbul in the long run.

Since the pace of industrial development lags behind the speed of urbanisation, rural migrants in major urban centers face an inescapable problem of unemployment or underemployment. Even in Istanbul, which is supposed to be the most industrialized city in the country, the rates of unemployment and underemployment are much higher than the corresponding figures for Turkey. As a result, the share of the informal sector in the economy of the city grows and the number of inhabitants living in the illegally formed squatter settlements increases. The informal sector and informal settlements become integrated with time, giving the false impression that real integration is taking place in both space and society. In fact, it is happening without spatial and socio-cultural integration. Unemployment, poverty and alienation are the very sources of the deterioration of environmental conditions in general. It seems that it will take at least a decade to overcome such conditions before joining the European Union as a full member.

When mentioning the informal sector one refers to unplanned and disorderly development from the standpoint of City Planning and of urban public services. Plans to upgrade the informal settlements formed through informal initiatives will never lead to a future urban development in the metropolis. These initiatives usually remain on paper and the main course urban development is determined by the pressures of informal forces.

Changing the internal dynamics of the society during the 1980's and 1990's, as well as the effects of Globalisation, formalized the informal sector, and allowed it to acquire a permanent feature [12]. It seems reasonable to assume that the permanent effects of Globalisation on cities and the environment are more negative than positive in nature.

The main characteristics of urbanisation in general are reflected in the general socio- economic, cultural and spatial patterns almost equally. All the features characterizing Istanbul indicate that it is a premature metropolis. The growth of Turkey during the last century has made Istanbul a great city of quantities with insufficient qualitative additions. Istanbul is proud of having spectacularly attractive historical assets and natural beauty, but the city is largely lacking the managerial capacity of providing the basic urban services and infrastructure for its residents. It underwent a phenomenal urbanisation in the demographic sense, during the second half of the 20th century, but too fast to enable it to cope adequately.

As an industrialized city, which still possesses pre-industrial traces in its historical nuclei, Istanbul has been decentralising in an unplanned manner, with the great majority of its residents concentrated in its surrounding peripheries. The core grows relatively slowly, but the periphery receives the lion's share of the increase of both population and industry. Between 1950 and 1990, the center grew by 250%, while the size of the periphery's population increased by 4500%. When the features of the new migrants are taken into consideration, one can admit that Istanbul is a great ruralizing metropolis, not only in terms of the origins of the great majority of its inhabitants, but also in terms of the peculiarities of its daily life, human relations and economy.

Patterns of informal economic mechanisms, as exemplified in gecekondus, dolmuses (shared taxis), and small-scale economic enterprises, prevent Istanbul from maturing into an industrialized world city, serving better the needs of international capital. Old and new, east and west co-exist in Istanbul within the framework of multiculturalism. As a result, its social fabric is composed of many different, and most of the time, contrasting social elements. As such, it basically reflects the prevailing characteristics of the socio-economic and cultural structure of Turkey as a whole.

As far as the implications of urbanisation are concerned, one can see certain points of optimism as well as several points of pessimism. One of the most important factors that allows considerable optimism is that population growth may be stabilized by the year 2020, as estimated by the yearly development reports of the World Bank. It has been estimated that the total population of Turkey will reach 90 or 100 million by 2020 and the annual rate of growth would be reduced to less than one percent. This would consequently affect the amount of surplus population in rural areas and would slow down rural to urban migration considerably. This means that more people may stay in the villages without increasing environmental and other negative externalities in the biggest metropolitan centers like Istanbul.

Another point of optimism is the impact of the Southeast Anatolian Regional Development Project (known as the GAP) that has already begun to check the population flow from the East to the West, and to reduce regional inequalities between geographic regions. No less important than this is the likely membership of the European Union which may produce positive consequences in the improvement of environmental protection standards. Furthermore, the role of international and supra- national Organisations, like the UN, UNEP, UNESCO, UNCHS, is immense in fostering co-operation. Next is the increasing emphasis on the principle of subsidiarity, in other words on the need for public services to be carried out by the authorities closest to the people. Increased emphasis on this principle in European countries may encourage

Members of local communities to take part in efforts to protect the environment more efficiently. Reliance upon people and increasing public awareness may produce beneficial results for the orderly development of cities and towns. It is hoped that the decreasing political and military tensions in the Mediterranean region will help reduce the enormous defense expenditure that could otherwise be used for development purposes. But on the other hand, a considerable part of the geography of the region is vulnerable to natural disasters. Therefore, preparedness of the societies in the region must be increased in order to avoid or mitigate the damages of such natural events.

Similarly, doubts about the role of the state in the society, and an increasing emphasis on Privatisation and deregulation as a result of world-wide Globalisation, seem to create and strengthen an anti-planning attitude towards urban management. Consequently, public land in Turkey and elsewhere is being privatized systematically. This may create negative conditions for the orderly growth of the metropolis. It is assumed that market solutions are the best tools for the effective implementation of urban development schemes. It seems that in the absence of the intervention of public authorities, the natural and historical values of greater Istanbul would suffer most from haphazard development. Sustainable development, which requires harmonisation of economic growth and environmental protection, must be based on the planned guidance of urbanisation. The historical and natural values of Istanbul cannot be sacrificed to an uncontrolled pace of urbanisation.

## References

1. Aru, K. A. (1971) Istanbul, in Rural-Urban Migrants and Metropolitan Development, Laquian, A. Istanbul Technical University, Istanbul.

2. Bookchin, M. (1997) The Rise of Urbanization and the Decline of Citizenship, Sierra Club Books, San Francisco.

3. Castells, M. (1975) La Question Urbaine, Maspero, Paris.

4. Danielson, M. N. and Keles, R (1985) The Politics of Rapid Urbanization: Government and Growth in Modern Turkey, Holmes and Meier, New York.

5. Ekinci, O. (1994) Istanbul'u Sarsan On Yil: 1983-1993 (The Ten Years that Have Shaken Istanbul: 1983-1993), Anahtar Yayinlari, Istanbul.

6. Eussner, A. (1989) Türkiye'nin Avrupa Topluluğu Üyeliğinin Bölgesel Politika Açisindan Etkileri(Effects of Turkey's Full Membership of the EC upon Regional Development Policy), Friedrich-Ebert Foundation, Istanbul.

7. Görgülü, Z. (1993) Hisseli Bölüntü ile Oluşan Alanlarda Yasallaştirmanin Kentsel Mekana Etkileri (The Effects of Legalization of the Process of Informal Subdivision on the urban Space), Yildiz Technical University, Faculty of Architecture, Istanbul.

8. Güvenç M. (1999) Istanbul'u Haritalamak: 1999 Sayımından Istanbul Manzaralari (Mapping Istanbul: Profiles of the City reflected in the 1990 Population Census), Istanbul 36.

9. Istanbul Valiligi (1983) Planlama ve Koordinasyon Müdürlügü, 1. Istanbul Sempozyumu, The Governerate of Istanbul, Directorate of Planning and Coordination, The First Istanbul Symposium.

10. Keles, R. (1988) Urban Poverty in the Third World: Theoretical Approaches and Policy Options, Institute of Developing Economies, Tokyo.

11. Keles, R (2000) Urbanisation and Urban Policy in Balland, D. (ed.), Hommes et Terres d'Islam ,Melanges Offerts a Xavier de Planhol, Tome II, Institut Français de Recherche en Iran, Teheran, 127-133.

12. Keles, R. (2001) Urbanisation, City and the Informal Sector, State Institute of Statistics, Informal Sector (1), Tuncer Bulutay, Ankara, 11-17.

13. Keles, R. (2002) Kentlesme Politikasi, (Urbanisation Policy), Imge, Ankara

14. Keyder, C., and Öncü A. (1994) Istanbul at the Crossroads, Biannual Istanbul, Selections, 93, 2, 1, Turkish Historical Foundation, Istanbul, 38-44.

15. Keyder, C. (1996) (ed.) Istanbul: Küresel ile Yerel Arasında (Istanbul: Between the Global and the Local), Metis, Istanbul.

16. Keyder, C. (1996) Marketing Istanbul, Biannual Istanbul, Selection Turkish Historical FoundationIstanbul, V. 4, 2, 87-91.

17. Kuban, D. (1996) The Growth of a City: From Byzantium to Istanbul, Biannual Istanbul, Selections 1996, Spring. V. 4, 2, 73-76.

18. National Report of Turkey to the Habitat II Conference (1996) Prime Ministry, Istanbul.

19. OECD (1988) Regional Problems and Policies of Turkey, OCDE, Paris.

20. State Planning Organisation (1993) Gecekondu Arastirmasi (Survey on Squatter Settlements), Ankara.

21. Sönmez, M. (1996) A Statistical Survey: Istanbul in the 1990's, Biannual Istanbul, Selections 1996 Spring, Istanbul, V 4, 2, 104-108.

22. Sönmez, M. (1996) Istanbul and the Effects of Globalisation, Biannual Istanbul, Selections 1994 and 1995,Winter, Istanbul, V. 3, 1, 83-85.

23. Tekeli, I. (1994) The Development of the Istanbul Metropolitan Area: Urban Administration and Planning, IULA-EMME, Istanbul.

24. The Increasingly Growing Giant: The Geographic Anatomy of Istanbul (1996) Biannual Istanbul, Selections 1996, Winter, Istanbul.

25. Tuncer, B. (1977) Turkey's Population and Economy in the Future, The Development Foundation of Turkey, Ankara.

26. Turgut, S. (2000) Metropoliten Alanlarda Planlama-Kent Yönetimi Iliskileri ve Istanbul Metropoliten Alaninda Planlama Yönetimine iliskin Bir Model Denemesi (The Relationships between Planning and Urban Administration and a Modeling Experiment concerning Planning Administration in the Istanbul Metropolitan Area), Yildiz Technical University, Istanbul.

27. Tümertekin, E. (1972) Analysis of the Location of Industry in Istanbul, Istanbul University, Geographical Institute, Istanbul.

28. Zevelyov, I. (1989) Urbanization and Development in Asia, Progress Publishers, Moscow.

# COASTAL MANAGEMENT

# Thoughts on Coastal Zone Management in Turkey*

## Introduction

Since most often the values and ideologies of political parties in power are reflected into and shape their policies, an objective rule is needed to guide the practice towards the goal of the preservation of natural assets. In other words, there is a need to find a reliable and operational yardstick by which one can judge the appropriateness of policies of coastal management being implemented in Turkey. Therefore, an attempt is made here to see whether the concept of public interest can be used for this purpose.

## The concept of public interest

It is not surprising to see that some well-known scholars in the field of Political Science, like Charles Lindblom and Robert Dahl had some doubts whether the public interest is a useful and meaningful concept (1) in policy-making, while Monique-Roland Wehly used the term "myth" to describe it (2). On the other hand, for Daniel Bell and Irving Cristal, it is inconceivable to think of a society not guided by the concept of public interest (3). Finally, Gerhard Colm

* Dino Borri, Domenico Lamarda, Laura Grassini, Angela Barbanente, Abdul Khakee (eds.), *Local Resistance to Global Pressure: A Mediterranean Social Environmental Planning Perspective*, L'Harmattan Italy, Torino, 2004, pp. 370-383.

thought that "politicians, statesmen, judges, and those who formulate governmental policies will have to make recourse to this concept at all times" (4). Although it has become one of the most controversial concepts in political science, public interest is still a promising criterion for finding out the right way in public affairs. There is no doubt that the difficulties involved in defining it do not allow us to ignore this concept altogether as a workable and practical instrument.

An individualistic or utilitarian approach assumes that public interest consists of arithmetic sum of the interests of private individuals, and of an attempt to maximize its components for the purpose of maximizing it as a whole. Hobbes, Hume, and Bentham are some of the representatives of this lime of thought. According to them, although it is possible to make individual choice as a collective choice, such an attempt would involve numerous logical problems. It is not always easy to say why $x$ is more in the public interest than $y$.

Hobbes believed that it would be mora rational to give priority to individual interest. David Hume thought that any action, regulation or policy, can be regarded as being in the public interest if it serves the great majority of the people it is affecting. He also emphasized that a certain action that is in the public interest may contradict the interests of the individuals, and that individuals do not spontaneously and naturally respect the public interest while the state apparatus as a whole is, almost always, in favor of the public interest by its nature. Jeremy Bentham, another representative of this tradition, believed that the interest of the society is equal to the sum of the interests of the members constituting it. Bentham argued that any action that is in the public interest must consider how many people, and in what ways, will be affected by such an action.

There is, however, also another approach, which is based on the belief that there exist a different public or general interest, independent of, and superior to the interests of each and every individual. The names of Jean Jacques Rousseau and William Pareto are often associated with this second approach. They believed that the public interest couldn't be regarded as being identical with the interests of the majority. The vote of the majority may be only one of many techniques that can be used for this purpose. Public interest has a normative value, and its content is the common interest of the citizens (5).

A third way of defining the term of public interest is to base it on certain subjective value judgments concerning political choices and moral values as maintained by well-known monist philosophers such as Plato, Aristotle, Hegel and Marx. The latter, for example, saw the public interest in the dictatorship of the working classes or proletariat, while Hegel had simplified the matter by equating the concept with the interests of the State.

A final definition of the concept of public interest is a variant form of the monist conceptualization of public interest that aims to minimize the role of the public sector in economic and social life. Globalization, competitiveness, constant technological innovation, liberalization, deregulation and privatization are the main instruments to achieve its ends. According to this new conception, urban and environmental sustainability can be best realized if they are left to the interplay of the market forces.

Everyone in society, representatives of local and central governments and civil society organizations, tend to consider themselves as authorized to interpret the term, although its content, scope, and boundaries change from one culture to another. The power to interpret the concept of public interest for each country must be clearly stated in each country's respective constitutions and laws. Regardless of the ambiguity of this term, public interest has become more important nowadays as the gradual deterioration of national resources, the degradation of bio-centric value and the violation of the rights of societies have become of worldwide concern. Within national boundaries environmental issues have to be considered within the context of this term since the environmental problems caused by particular groups in order to maximize their own profits and interests have to be confronted and solved by public institutions, in cooperation with citizens themselves.

## Principles of coastal zone management in Turkish legislation

The term public interest is used in the Turkish Constitution of 1982 in several articles, including the one pertaining to the protection of coastal areas. However, there is no clear definition of the concept. It used for example in connection with the reasons for restricting the use of the fundamental rights and freedoms, eminent domain power of public authorities and the right to private property. The specific provision of the Constitution (Art. 43) emphasizes that "Coastal areas are under the possession and supervision of the State. In the utilization of coastal belts surrounding the seas, lakes and rivers, the public interest shall be given priority. The width of the coastal belts shall be regulated by law, and by taking into consideration their use and the possibilities and conditions of their utilization by individuals".

Within this general legal framework, details regarding the coastal management are found in several different acts of Parliament. According to the Article 19 of the Municipal Law of 1930 (n. 1580), powers of possession, management and supervision of coastal areas within municipal boundaries belong to the municipality. The Law on Coastal Areas of 1990 (n.3621, Official Gazette: 17 April 1990, n. 20495) defines the main concepts related to coastal areas. The most important one among these is certainly the concept of coastal belt because of its potential implications for orderly and sustainable development. It is defined in the Law (Art. 4) as comprising the coastal line from the water in the direction of land. The actual extent of land granted to the coastal line varies according to the following criteria:

a) It is horizontally 20 meter wide in the areas for which implementation plans are to be prepared.

b) It is horizontally 50 meter wide in settled areas within and outside boundaries of the municipality or adjacent areas, whether they have a master plan or environmental protection plan or not.

c) It is 100 meter wide horizontally in non-settled areas within or outside the boundaries of municipalities or adjacent areas, whether they have a master plan or not.

d) Coastal areas are, as underlined above, under possession and supervision of the State and they have be accessible to equal and free use of citizens. The Law, following the wording of the Constitution, establishes the principle that in the utilization of coasts and coastal belts, public interest will be given priority (Art. 5).

e) The Law prohibits, as a rule, building activities in coastal areas. Wells, hedges, rails, wire-fences, ditches, stokes and similar obstacles cannot be constructed in these areas and no sand, pebble, ete, can be taken away. No wastes and remnants, which might have polluting effects, like rubber, soil, garbage, and the like, may be discharged into the coast.

In coastal areas, only the following constructions may be allowed, in accordance with the principles of the master plan:

a) Infrastructure like wharfs, harbor installations, shelters, quays, breakwater, bridges, passageways, containing walls, lighthouses, shipping spaces, boat houses, salt pan, fishing nets, refinery and pumping stations, constructed with the aim to protect and to use the coast in the public interest.

b) Special construction like dockyards, spaces used for breaking down the old ships, plants for the reproduction and breeding of underwater products, which can only be built on the coast because of the nature of their operations. These constructions and plants cannot be used for purpose other than the ones stated in their original licenses.

If the implementation plan for the area has not been worked out yet, no construction or factory plant is allowed, either on the coasts themselves or no the coastal belts within the prescribed distances. In case there is an implementation plan, only the following building activities may be allowed:

a) Constructions and plants that serve the objective of protecting and using the coasts in the public interest.

b) Constructions and establishments which could not be realized elsewhere than on the coastal belts.

c) Buildings and establishments for day tourism, excluding residences.

d) Roads, open parking lots, green spaces, playgrounds and social and technical infrastructure. These exceptional constructions cannot be used for purpose other than the ones for which they are permitted. These constructions and establishments cannot prevent access to the coasts.

In cases where the master plans prepared for the protection of coasts and coastal belts fall within the provisions of the Law on the Encouragement of Tourism, because of the characteristics of the region, the plans are to be approved and finalized in accordance with the Article 7 of the said

Law. Municipalities have the power to regulate the implementation of plans that encompass areas within, or adjacent to, their own boundaries. For areas outside these boundaries the power resides with the governor's office. Constructions with no license at all, or conflicting with the principles of the license and its appended documents, are subject to the regulations in the City Planning Law of 1985 (n. 3194).

One of the major sources of the deterioration of coastal areas in recent years have been the construction activities that have taken place on the lands reclaimed from the seacoast or river coast. There are several provisions in the Law on Coastal Areas, which regulate building activities in these areas. Thus, in principle, all demands for land reclamation have to go through the Ministry of Public Works and Settlements, and through the governor's offices, depending on the location of the locality concerned. In case the Ministry finds it appropriate to reclaim land from the coast in that region, a master plan needs to be prepared for the lands thus acquired, in accordance with the City Planning Law. These plans have to be ultimately approved by the Ministry of Public Works, or by the Ministry of Tourism for places within the jurisdiction of the Law on the Encouragement of Tourism.

The territories acquired as a result of land reclamation are also in the possession and under the supervision of the State. The number of construction activities to be allowed in these areas by the respective legislation is limited and comprised of the following:

## Interpretations of the Constitutional Court

The first law on coastal zone management in Turkey was put in effect in 1984 (Law n. 3086, Official Gazette: 1 December 1984, n. 18592). It was followed by a second Law in 1990 (Law n. 3621, Official Gazette: 17 April 1990) because of the cancellation of the first upon recourse to the Supreme Court on the grounds of unconstitutionality. It is rather surprising that the latter too was cancelled partly again by the Constitutional Court because some of its provisions were conflicting with the constitutional principles for the protection of coastal areas primarily in the public interest. As a result, the final Law on Coastal Areas was passed in 1992 (Law n. 3830, Official Gazette: 11 July 1992, n. 21281) in order to regulate the matter in compliance with the Constitution.

The reasons given for the decisions taken by the Constitutional Court have been published in the Official Gazette. Their examination provides a sound view of how the High Court interprets the principle in the Constitution with regards to the protection of coastal zones. According to the Constitutional Court (Official Gazette: 10 July 1986, n. 19160 and 22 January 1992, n. 21120), the definitions of "coast" and "coastline" are not clear, and the principles governing the use of coastal areas are unsuitable for their free and equitable use, and they constitute a potential threat to coastal zones because they allow private ownership and private building rights. Further on, the Constitutional Court argues that provisions concerning the use of coastal strips are not formulated in accord with the principle of public interest, and that the rules allowing for the acceptance of pre- 1972 private ownership as "acquired rights" is incompatible with the principle that no private ownership right can be established in the coastal strips.

It was also added that since the coastal zones are a natural continuation of the seas, lakes and rivers, their use could be made possible only when they are kept accessible to all citizens. The Constitution established a rational and valid criterion in line with contemporary understanding. In this context, reducing the width of the coastal strip to simply 20 meters would contradict the principle of public interest and it should be set at least at 100 meters. In other words, their width has to be large enough to allow for the construction of installations that meet the people's needs such as health, clean air and recreation, and that are convenient for the enjoyment of the sea and the sun, for the building of an appropriate coastal road... This will allow to benefit from the sea as a natural resource of wealth and well-being and finally and to construct installations to be used for this purpose.

One of the most remarkable points in this respect is that the Constitutional Court has based its decisions on the role of the public interest in the protection of coastal zones both in relation to the constitutional principles concerning the coasts (Art. 43) and in relation to environmental concerns (Art. 56). It would be reasonable to assume that the legislator has taken into consideration all of these factors in reformulating the respective provisions of the new Law on Coastal Zone Management.

## The need to identify whose interest is the public interest

The judiciary sector is much less open to controversies in the struggle for power or economic interest as compared with either the executive or the legislative sector. Therefore, leaving the definition of the public interest to its jurisdiction is quite right. It is much more immune from partisan pressures than other powers. In the case of coastal protection, the Constitutional Court insisted on giving priority to the concept of public interest, as states by yhr Constitution, in the sense that coastal areas must be kept open to all citizen at all times. Its interpretation is well reflected in the decisions mentioned above.

However, it is not always that easy to agree on the exact meaning of the concept of public interest. As mentioned above, there are views that private individuals may ensure the prevalence of the public interest if they prove themselves to be conscientious citizens with a high degree of public awareness in environmental matters. More recently, new concepts are being developed to be used as operational instruments, inspired by the influence of worldwide globalization and by liberal world views. These suggest that the interests of individuals and of businesses, on one hand, and those of the market economy, without being forced to utilize the instruments of public regulations. This argument is made, despite the fact that businesses usually constitute the biggest source of pollution. In fact, very few industries, businesses or manufacturers include pollution prevention among their objectives. Nevertheless, production, services, consumption, transportation, construction and other activities, which are the basic factors of a high standard of living, create waste that inevitably results in the degradation of the environment. The axiom "I produce, therefore I have the right to pollute" unfortunately still applies to many aspects of human activity.

Despite these realistic observations, there is an increasing concern among business leaders in may parts of the world to behave consciously enough to comply with their moral responsibilities towards the bio-environment. Their concern has various sources, and some entrepreneurs and enterprises have attempted to include environmental dimensions in their production activities. They perform analyses of the potential benefits of modifying their conduct to adapt themselves to new regulations, with the aim of both rationalizing their costs and improving their productivity. Other enterprises owe their birth, existence and survival to progress in the environmental field. An environmentally conscious market is rapidly growing all over the world. Therefore, many companies specialize in pollution control, waste-treatment, consultation, communication or the production of "green products". These products are either new or result of alterations on old goods and services. For some companies, however, environmentally friendly behavior is merely some kind of "fashion", which allows them to send environmental messages to their clients.

Whatever the reasons may be, the business world is showing signs of increasing concern for the protection of the bio-environment. According to a survey carried out by a French research institute in 1989, for 32 percent of the business leaders interviewed, protection of the environment is a priority, and for 60 percent, even though not a priority, it is still a very important goal. No one admitted that it was an unimportant goal. Furthermore, 85 percent felt the need to be mobilized to do something about the environment, and 57 percent believed they had some responsibility towards it (5).

It is clear that a "green" capitalism is rapidly emerging. There are however as many signs for being optimistic as there are for being pessimistic. Concerns for profit maximization and for the degradation of environmental values are consequences of human behavior. The adverse impact of globalization, in conjunction with a priori considerations, compels us to behave more responsibly. The concepts of autonomy and freedom have to be carefully distinguished from selfishness. Solidarity among members of the same society, among nations, neighboring countries and between present and future generations must constitute an integral component of a new concept of public interest, which is very different from the one required by worldwide globalization. The scope of the word public in the concept of public interest has to be enlarged as much as possible. Since ethical values are considerably integrated within public interest, the question of "profit for whom" has to be constantly asked. It seems that in the 21st century, "business is business" will have to change into "business is no longer simply business". Finally, one must not forget that public interest in its broadest sense can only be protected by effective legal systems and institutions, at national as well as international levels. Moral and legal sanctions have to complete each other in order to guarantee the survival of fundamental bio-centric values (6).

The business world is developing a series of legal and economic instruments that might help achieving the objective of cooperation between public authorities and the private sector in order to save the environment. Contractualization, environmental impact studies, Eco-auditing and Eco-labeling are some of these new liberal techniques. Even the role of the state is changing altogether as a result of globalization. As rightly observed by Breunung and Nocke, "in practice, the state has to stick with what seems likeliest to solve the problem. From being a sovereign authority, it becomes a negotiating partner. Consensus, cooperation and exchange based negotiations often replace unilateral legal commands". Their argument thus continues: "Politics can no longer maintain is monopoly on the definition of the public interest in these conditions. It is at the very least hard to see why general interests should be upheld only because the seal of the law is retroactively placed on the outcome of cooperative state action. Nor is there any spontaneous reason for the assumption that industry, citizen's movements and other participants in negotiating processes will act as representatives of general social interest and not in their own" (7). According to such beliefs, the object of a firm is no longer confined to profit maximization, because as the firms increase in size, the effects of their actions on society also increase. In other words, they begin to have an expanded social function. Breunung and Nocke conclude that "Firms grow into a quasi social institution (8).

On the other hand, Bregman and Jacobson, pointing out the advantages of the self-regulation as a legal system for coordination, distinguish between two types of coordination: developed and underdeveloped. A developed kind of coordination is one that requires individuals to express and take positions in the public interest as part of their projects, while underdeveloped coordination is conceived as one that does not force individuals to formulate and pursue a public interest separate from their own interest (9).

They maintain that in underdeveloped versions of coordination, the public interest appears only as a constraint on individual interests. They simplify the matter further by emphasizing that in the classical theory of contract, public interest means no more than the interest expressed by the State, in other words, it is equated with direct state regulation of contract formation and administration. Another aspect of the concept of public interest according to Bregman and Jacobson is that public interest promoted by regulation is static. It is static in the sense that it does not change from project to project. Self-regulation, by contrast, promotes a dynamic public interest, constantly evolving from project to project.

A closer look at the new approaches to environmental protection suggests that one should be more careful about the opportunities they provide to maximize the public interest. Such an assumption seems to me reasonably valid particularly if the use and protection of coastal regions are at stake. In fact, François Ost drawing the attention to a decision of the French Council of State, underlines the need to be cautious in this respect. He points out that the Council of State decided that "government cannot contractually divest itself of its police powers and the techniques of contractual negotiation would prevent a number of risks in terms of the legal regime of the public service" (10).

One of these is the risk of breakdown in equality between firms.

There is in fact the danger that the most powerful among them would, through contract, secure privileges. Second is the risk that public authorities become captive or end up being bought by the firms that they are supposed to control and regulate. In other words, environmental contracts might bring about collusion between public decision-makers and private entrepreneurs so as to place the former under the influence of the latter. In other words, "the norm protecting natural environments would never go beyond the concessions allowed by industrial sectors. A final risk is the one of reducing the democratic nature of public action by "privatization".

In some of the powerful interest groups there is a very low degree of internal democracy in their negotiation with the State. For some of them, there is the question of representativeness within the sector concerned. More broadly, these observations point out the difficulty inherent in identifying the requirements of the general interest in terms of a process of summation of group interests. There is a real risk, of course, of distorting policies in favor of the short-term and most powerful interests, while the interests of future generations require advocates of the long-term.

It has been pointed out, for example, that Eco-auditing -which is a tool for the firm's environmental administration aiming at the systematic, periodic and objective evaluation of its policy, program and equipment in that sphere- has to be conceived as a complement rather than as a substitute for respect of environmental standards and regulations. Because the tool itself has a purely voluntary foundation, firm conform to it only if they want to, and for the sites and products where they feel that it might be advantageous. This means that private firms will develop and internal system of environment protection in accordance with their own needs and choices. Francois Ost believes that this is to push the "logic of self" very far (11).

On the other hand, Eco-labeling aims at singling out the least polluting products. But the assessment is made throughout the product's lifetime from manufacture to disposal, through transport, treatment and use. This system too is optional Once awarded, the Eco-label can be used only by means of a contract between the firm concerned and the competent authorities. Therefore, we ought to know that the statement eco is no longer necessarily synonymous of environmental protection or of the public interest (12).

## Concluding Remarks

There is no doubt that there may be indisputable advantages of using the tools of the private sector in all environmental matters in general and in the coastal zone management in particular. The general ideology and practice of most of the international institutions, like the World Bank, European Commission and the OECD go in the same direction. However, since the profit maximization goal of the private firms is not changed and will not be changed in the near future, to sacrifice this objective to the concerns of environmental protection does not seem likely. As a result, the interest of the society as a whole and of the environment will always come second. In other words, a concept of public interest defined in accordance with the needs and potentials of the private firms cannot answer the basic question of the coastal zone management that will be on the agenda of the country for a long time to go. The traditional concept of public interest seems to be more useful and operational in this context. It might be harmful to attempt to use it in narrowly economic terms (13). This is another reason why, when it comes to the protection of coast zones as well as of other environmental assets, the assessment of the public interest is too important to be left to stockholders instead of stakeholders.

## Notes

1. Virginia Held, The Public Interest and Individual Interest, Basic Books, New York, 1970, p. 9.

2. Monique-Roland Weyl, Gerçekte ve Eylemde Hukukun Payı (The Role of Law in Reality and Action), Konuk Yay., 1974, p. 130.

3. Virginia Held, Op. cit., p, 11.

4. Virginia Held, Op. cit., pp. 99 and 105.

5. Vatimbella, A. (1992), Le Capitalisme Vert, Syros- Alternatives, Paris.

6. Keleş, Ruşen, An Attempt to Redefine Public Interest and the Bio-Environment, Biopolitics: Business Strategy for the Bio-Environment III, ed. By Agni Vlavianaos Arvanities, Athens, 1996, pp. 72-74.

7. Brennung, Leonie and Nocke, Joachim, Environmental Officer: A Viable Concept for Ecological Management?, Gunther Teubner, Lindsay Farmer and Declan Murphy (eds.). Environmental Law and Ecological Responsibility, John Wiley, New York, 1994, p. 270.

8. Ibid., p. 272

9. Bregman, Eric and Jacobson, Arthur, Environment Performance Review: Self-Regulation in Environmental Law, Teubner, Farmer and Murphy, op. cit., p. 208.

10. Ost, François, A Game Without Rules? The Ecological Self-Organization of Firms, Teubner, Farmer and Murphy (eds.), op. cit., p. 347.

11. Ibid, p. 352.

12. Op. cit., p. 356.

13. Owens, Susan, Interpreting Sustainable Development: The Case of Land Use Planning, Greening the Millennium: The New Politics of the Environment, ed. By Michael Jacobs, Blackwell Publishers, Oxford, 1997, p.89.

## Bibliography

- Bregman. E., Jacobson A. (1994), Environmental Performance Review: Self- Regulation in Environmental Law, Gunther T., Lindsay F., Declan M. (eds.), Environmental Law and Ecological Responsibility, Wiley, New York.

- Brennung L., Nocke J. (1994), Environmental Officer: A Viable Concept for Ecological Management, Gunther T., Lindsay F., Declan M. (eds.), Environmental Law and Ecological Responsibility, Wiley, New York.

- Held V. (1970), The Public Interest and Individual Interest, Basic Books, New York.

- Keleş R. (1996), An Attempt to Redefine Public Interest and the Bio- Environment, Vlavianos Arvanitis A. (ed.), Biopolitics: Business Strategy for the Bio- Environment III, Athens.

- Ost F. (1994), A Game Without Rules? The Ecological Self- Organization of Firms, Gunter T., Lindsay F, Declan M. (eds.), Environmental Law and Ecological Responsibility, Wiley, New York.

- Owens S. (1997), Interpreting Sustainable Development: The Case of Land Use Planning, Jacobs M. (ed.), Greening the Millennium: The New Politics of the Environment, Blackwell, Oxford.

- Vatimbella A. (1992), Le Capitalisme Vert, Syros- Alternatives, Paris.

- Weyl M. R. (1974), Gerçekte ve Eylemde Hukukun Payı (The Role of Law in Reality and Action), Konuk Y.

# ETHICAL DUTIES

## Our Ethical Duties Towards Future Generations in a Globalising World*

Our duties for future generations and the requirements of inter-generational equity have become important issues of Environmental Ethics and Environmental Law during the last several decades. Not only in academic circles and international institutions, but also among the public and in the media, increasing concern is expressed to such concepts as inter-generational equity, ethical obligations, the identity of future generations and the like.

As rightly maintained by Carlo Petrini, the duty to respect the rights of future generations can be defended, using both deontological (Kantian) and utilitarian arguments. Another strong argument is that of responsibility elaborated by Hans Jonas.[1] Jonas argued that the new and increasingly incisive potential of human activities calls for a new approach to traditional ethical principles: The major pillars of rights and freedoms enshrined in traditional ethics should no longer be associated with a prediction of hope, but with the fear of an impending threat, in other words, the worst case scenario.

The Kantian imperative is reformulated by Hans Jonas in the following terms: "Act so that the effects of your actions

\* International Conference on Biopolitics, organized by B.I.O. (Biopolitics International Organization, Athens, Greece), Gijon, Spain, 2013

1 Carlo Petrini, "The Rights of Future Generations in Environmental Ethics", International Journal of Ethics, Vol. 7, No: 3-4, 2011, p. 198.

are compatible with the permanence of genuine human life" (p.199).

The issue of the duties towards future generations creates at least two conceptual problems: The first is identity, and the second one, temporal distance. Future generations do not exist at the time when current generations are concerned with them. For this reason, some writers rightly object to the expression of "rights of future generations" and prefer to use the terms "responsibilities", "duties" and " obligations". Legal tradition holds that "rights" are granted to living subjects who may have the chance to exercise them. On the other hand, the temporal aspect which is related to intergenerational equity poses untold challenges from the legal point of view (p. 200).

From another point of view, intergenerational equity can not be separated from the issue of sustainable development (p. 202) that will be taken up below later.

The significance of the concept of the rights of future generations derives not only from the principles of Environmental Ethics, but at the same time, it has a close bearing on recent development of highly important rules in International Environmental Law.

Starting from the principles of the universal declarations adopted in such international conferences as Stockholm (1972), Rio de Janeiro (1992), the main approach of the Report of the Brundtland Commission, called Our Common Future, established that "the right to development must be fulfilled so as to equitably meet developmental and environmental needs of present and future generations". Similarly, the first principle of the Stockholm Declaration (1972) stressed that "man had the fundamental right to freedom, equality and adequate conditions of life, in an environment of a quality that permitted a life of dignity and well-being, and he bore a solemn responsibility to protect and improve the environment for present and future generations".

A complementary principle of the Brundtland Report is, of course, the one pertaining to sustainable development, which is defined as the kind of development which, meets the needs of the present, without compromising the ability of the future generations to meet their own needs.

Sustainable development is also cited as one of the objectives of the United Nations Millennium Declaration adopted in 2000 to be achieved in 2015.[2] The Declaration urged the member states to support environment al sustainability by including the principle of sustainable development in their national development programmes. This is also the focus of the Final Declaration of the UN World Summit on Sustainable Development held in Johannesburg in 2002.[3] Sustainable development affects future generations considerably. It offers at least two important leads. a) The first is the introduction of an obligatory temporal requisite. It requires that States should not form their policies around shortterm considerations, but must weigh environmental questions in a long-term perspective. b) The second concerns responsibility towards all the parties involved, including as yet unborn. In this connection, we often refer to the proverb implying that "we have not inherited the environment from our ancestors, but we owe it to succeeding generations". The concrete concept referred frequently, when the issues of intergenerational justice as it applies to the environment is debated, is certainly, the expression of common heritage of mankind.

2   UN Millennium Development Declaration. Resolutions adopted by the General Assembly Fifty Fifth Session, Agenda Item 60 (b), 2000.

3   UN., The Johannesburg Declaration on Sustainable Development, New York, 2002.

Having economic and legal origins going back to Roman Law, the concept means the transmission of goods between succeeding generations.[4] It acknowledges man's responsibility to the environment as a "good" (public trust) to be safeguarded, respected and enhanced in the awareness that mankind is himself a part of his environment.[5]

Although there is a substantial agreement that each generation has a moral obligation not to penalise succeeding generations by causing irreversible harm to the environment, there are contrasting views among scientists as to whether this obligation should be defined legally. Similarly, views are expressed emphasizing that the concept of future generations itself can not properly be described without taking into consideration such items as social context, human dignity and living conditions. A further consideration is based upon the assumption that since future generations can not claim their own rights, special mechanisms should be set up in order to defend their interest on their behalf. Here an hypothetical and incomplete participation replace the direct involvement of future generations in decision-making processes.

The questions posed with regard to the concept of intergenerational justice have been addressed not only by environmental lawyers, but also by sociologists, philosophers and ethicists.[6] They have suggested that if the individualistic approach to ethics is abandoned, most of the problems related to the value of the concept could be overcome.

Some of the uncertainties are related with what the concrete obligations are and how we can fulfill these obligations under present circumstances. Principles of prevention and

4    Petrini, p. 200.
5    Petrini, p. 201.
6    Dieter Birnbacher, 1994.

precautionary action developed by the International Environmental Law may be an answer to such hesitations.

The question of how many generations will be included in the notion of future generations in addition to immediate next generation also rises technically difficult problems to solve. Yet unborn individuals (fetuses, embryo), the position of children and mentally unfit groups present no less important technical problems in this respect.

Suggestions of the well-known environmental lawyer, Edith Brown Weiss, seem meaningful for the solution. They include, a) to encourage intergenerational equity by banning inconsiderable exploitation, but at the same time to avoid this being translated into unreasonable obligations to protect future generations, b) to avoid all attempts to predict or quantify the value of future generations, c) to choose principles that are reasonable, clear and practicable, and finally, d) to choose values that are generally shared by different economic and social systems.[7]

Similarly, Aldo Leopold, author of Land Ethics emphasized that an attitude or behavior can be said to be ethically acceptable when it tends to preserve the integrity, stability and beauty of the biotic community.

Although the aforementioned uncertainties lend controversies to the usefulness of the notion of responsibility towards future generations, these can not justify a refusal to acknowledge that responsibility.[8]

There is good reason to deal with our responsibility towards future generations not only as a moral duty, but also as a legal principle. This is the reason why the protection of future generations is mentioned specifically in various

---

7    Edith Brown Weiss, **In Fairness to Future Generations**, UN University and Transnational Publishers, Tokyo, New York, 1988.

8    Petrini, op. cit, p. 207.

international legal instruments, as I mentioned earlier.[9] Because, such a formal recognition can not be left to the development of customary law, but it has to be achieved on the basis of a treaty or convention.

The principle of sustainable development must be integrated into national policies and programmes. The loss of environmental resources has far reaching implications for the welfare of the current generation as well as for the ability of future generations to maintain and improve the welfare and living conditions of human beings. Most of the natural resources are now being rapidly degraded or polluted, or are at risk of further deterioration.

Nearly two billion hectares of cropland, pastures and forests worldwide have been degraded over the past fifty years. Desertification causes economic losses in the areas affected. Half of the world's wetland disappeared in the past century. Biodiversity is often not protected and managed sustainably. It is faced with increasing risk of extinction or genetic erosion. Every year, an estimated one million people throughout the developing world die prematurely from respiratory or other illnesses associated with urban air pollution. Ecological problems emanating from climate change, ozone layer depletion threaten not only the present, but also the future generations. The obligation a) to pursue a preventive and precautionary environmental policy, b) to reduce environmental pollution to a minimum, and c) to develop technologies that do not harm the ecological richnesses of the planet, seem to be a must. The last, but not the least, is of course, to allow for the economic development of the poor countries so as to meet the requirement of equity within the present

9    Lothar Gündling, "Our Responsibility to Future Generations", **American Society of International Law**, Vol. 84, No: 1, January 1990, p. 208.

generation and to solve the problem of poverty based environmental degradation.[10]

The challenges we are faced with are too big for one country to handle alone and too structural in nature to ignore where our expertise needs an update.[11] Therefore, international cooperation and the need to ensure the proper implementation of the principle of International Environmental Law, namely, common but differentiated responsibility must be the guiding principle.

Several countries, like New Zealand, Hungary and Israel, have initiated the creation of a formal mechanism of guardians for the long-term interest, even to the point of giving them the mandate to engage in the legislative processes.[12]

Their status is either a parliamentary commissioner for the environment or a national commissioner for future generations. It is suggested that such a guardian should possess the following characteristics: It should be independent, effective, transparent, legitimate, and it should have access to all kinds of information.[13]

Expansion of the sphere of influence of neo-liberalism, in other words, globalization, dominated the whole world since the end of the 20th Century and put the whole eco-system under its hegemony. This radical change affected the quality of human life, mechanisms feeding the natural resources and even the very existence in a number of ways. Globalization has even affected the sovereignty of the nation-states over their own national territories. At the same time, it tends to increase inequalities between poor and rich nations, geographical regions and social classes.

---

10   Gündling, p. 212.
11   Maya Gügel, "Guarding Our Future: How to Protect Future Generations", **Solutions**, Nov-Dec. 2010, p. 62.
12   Ibid., p. 64.
13   Ibid., pp. 66-67.

New value systems and living patterns strengthened by worldwide globalization jeopardize considerably the rights of future generations over natural, historical and cultural assets. Particularly, the changes in consumption patterns, conspicuous consumption threaten the future of the planet extensively. As rightly suggested by former French Minister of Environment, Mme. Corinne Lepage, in her book Vivre Autrement (Living in a Different Way), we really need to change radically the ways in which we live. Different sections and chapters of the book deal with particular suggestions regarding the need to change prevailing consumption habits and practices in different economic and social sectors such as: to reduce energy consumption, to change the sources of energy, to produce differently, to cultivate and to feed differently, to be housed differently, to move differently, to work differently, to entertain differently, etc., in order to safeguard the future of humanity. French writer and journalist Herve Kempf went even further, in his book entitled as Pour Sauver le Planete, Sortez du Capitalisme (To Safeguard the Planet, Escape Capitalism), by proposing the abandonment of the capitalist system itself.

Egoist and individualistic interests do not transform themselves spontaneously into collective interests, and if followed unconsciously, rapidly end up with creating ecological crises.[14] One can not talk about the public interest without taking into consideration the future. It becomes meaningless, in case it does not go beyond the sum of the private interest of present generation.

This is the reason why rising the quality of life by improving environmental conditions has been, since the beginning, at the center of concern of the European institutions, in addition to the efforts of the United Nations. For example, the

14   Corinne Lepage, Vivre Autrement, p. 22.

principle of sustainable development has been included, as requirement in the Article 37 of the Charter of Fundamental Rights of the European Union (Lisbon Treaty) which stipulates that "A high level of environmental protection and the improvement of the quality of environment must be integrated into policies of the Union and ensured in accordance with the principle of sustainable development". According to the Article 191 of the consolidated version of the Treaty of Lisbon on the Functioning of the EU, "The policy of the European Union in the sector of the environment will seek to achieve the following goals which reflect morally defensible values: a) "The conservation, protection and improvement of the quality of the environment, b) safeguarding of the health of the individual, c) the sensible and rational use of natural resources, and d) promotion, at international level, of measures to deal with regional or global environmental problems, and in particular, to combat climate change".

Of course, the realization of all beautifully formulated goals and principles depends upon the awareness, will and willingness of the people. As we had emphasized, with my distinguished friend and colleague Professor Vlavianos Arvanities, the Founding President of the BIO, in a meeting organized by the World Society of Ekistics in Mumbai, India, "Culture is an essential element of a sustainable city. The environmental conditions are affected by our culture, which is, in turn, shaped by the environment. BIO culture represents a conscious effort to reach interdependence. Aesthetic values, music, science, the arts, politics, economics and determination to changing the existing consumption patterns shaped by contemporary capitalist development and globalization can all come together on the struggle for a better quality of life."

## Bibliography

- Birnbacher, Dieter, La responsabilité envers les générations futures, Presses Universitaires de France, Paris, 1994.
- Bourg, Dominique, *Planete sous Controle,* Textuel, Paris, 1998.
- Bourg, Dominique, *Les scenario de l'écologie,* Hachette, Paris, 1996.
- Bourg, Dominique et Whiteside, Kerry, *Vers une démocratie écologique,* Ed.Seuil, Paris, 2010.
- Brown-Weiss, Edith, *In Fairness to Future Generations,* United Nations University and Transnational Publishers, Tokyo and New York, 1988.
- Gügel, Maya, "Guarding Our Future: How to Protect Future Generations?",*Solutions,* November.-December 2010.
- Gündling, Lothar, "Our Responsibility to Future Generations", *American Society for International Law,* Vol.84, No:1, January 1990.
- Jonas, Hans, *Une éthique pour la nature,* Deschée de Brouver, Paris, 2000.
- Jonas, Hans, *Le principe responsabilité,* Flammarion, Paris, 1995.
- Keleş, Ruşen, "The Quality of Life and the Environment", *Asia Pacific International Conference on Environmental behaviour Studies,* North Cyprus, Eastern Mediterranean University, 2*9 December, 2011.
- Kempf, Herve, Pour sauver la Planete, sortez du capitalisme, Ed.du Seuil, Paris, 2009.
- Lepage, Corinne, *Vivre Autreement,* Grasset, Faris, 2009.
- Petrini, Carlo, "The Rights of Future Generations in Environmental Ethics", *International Journal of Ethics,* Vol.7, No:3-4, 2011.
- United Nations, *The Johannesburg Declaration on Sustainable Development,* New York, 2002.
- United Nations Millennium Development Declaration, Resolutions adopted by the General Assembly Fifty Fifth Session, Agenda Item (60)b, 2000.

# The Political, Legal and Ethical Issues in Urban Planning*

The aim of this paper is not to cover all issues concerning legal, political and political aspects of the planning process, but to make an effort to shed some light into their interrelationship. In other words, I intend to draw your attention to the inadequacies of each of these scientific disciplines in the accomplishment of the planning goals, emphasizing on the need for close cooperation. These and similar subject will be taken up generally first, and an effort will be made to provide some illustrations from the experiences of Turkey.

## Politics

Politics comes from polis, the Greek word for state. Politics and the state are closely related, and the words political and politics are quite generally defined as having to do with the state, more specifically with the government. The state itself may be identified as the social organization having final authority over all persons residing within a specified territory, and having for its primary purpose the solution of common problems and provision of common goods, also with the maintenance or order.

* Edward Gassner and Nazmi Yıldız (eds.), *Interdisciplinary Aspects of Town Planning*, Studies of the European Faculty of Land Use and Development, Vol. 16, Strasbourg, Peter Lang, Frankfurt, 1993, pp. 149-163.

Politics has a dynamic nature. It is the study of shaping of power, which is crucially important in local communities.

Politics refers to all that has to do with the forces, institutions, and organizational forms in any society that are recognized as having the most inclusive and final authority existing in that society for the establishment and maintenance of order, the effectuation of other common purpose of its members and the reconciliation of their differences. "Political" is the corresponding adjective.

The policy-making official, whether an elected representative or not, tries to decide what needs are greatest, relative to their costs, and how to order the priorities of various claims on government.

For a number of reasons, political science, as an instrument to solve all these conflicting issues, has not made rapid or great progress towards scientific accomplishments. The difficulties involved in scientific measurement, the prevalence of bias (partiality), complexity of the social life and the extremely limited extent to which political scientist can direct experiments are major deterrents in this respect.

Human beings desire to preserve their lives and vested interests, and normally they use almost any means that seems to them necessary for the accomplishment of that purpose.

Much of the political theory in the modern period has been based upon the belief that man is highly rational, and from him, irrational behavior can not be expected. However, works of many social scientists proved that human nature was ambivalent, partly rational, and partly irrational. According to this belief, no man is good enough to be trusted with absolute power, but all men have sufficient potentiality for good to be trusted with a share in government.

Within the context of planning activities, the relationships of planners and politicians are of crucially important.

Planners are inherently long-term thinkers, whereas politicians are usually short-range thinkers, often in some close relationship with their terms of office and with their circonscriptions. Planners must deal more adequately with the realities of politics and its inevitable need for compromise, consensus and coalition. On the other hand, politicians need to recognize that there is much in planning that can be used to improve the public good, in other words, to serve the public interest, and make for better politics.

The politician who is not careful about the public condition, is not likely to remain in office, or if somehow able to survive despite such a misstep, is unlikely to be effective. For this reason, politicians tend to be suspicious of planners who are determined to speak for the public interest based on theoretical and, or rational arguments.

The planner should learn the skills of the politician with regard to compromise, conflict resolution, negotiation, and arbitration. This is the only way for the planner to become a significant force in change, instead of the traditional all-knowing interpreter of the public interest. In this connection, it must be stressed that the concept of public interest is diverse, changing and sometimes contradictory. There is rarely, if ever, a unity of public interest in uses with which planners deal. This means that changes and revisions should be eagerly sought rather than avoided.

A related matter is to see whose goals are to be used to formulate planning. The conventional wisdom has been that planners should continue the traditional approach of assessing goals and using them to serve as the basis for plans. With the politicization of some planners, as well as the ideological thrusts from the left into planning, there has been much more evidence that planners bring their own values into the assessment of goals.

According to the Code of Ethics and Professional Conduct of the American Institute of Certified Planners, "A planner's primary obligation is to serve the public interest. While the definition of public interest is formulated through continuous debate, a planner owes allegiance to a conscientiously attained concept of the public interest".

A lawyer-client relationship is one of strict confidence to such an extent that the public interest is considered secondary to the client's interest. Here, ideally, the position of the planner is just the opposite.

## Law

Planning law is a 20th century product. It made its debut as a by-product of the housing reform movement and legislation and was not freed from this context later on. What is essentially significant about planning legislation is that it ventures a perspective of the interdependence of land in any complex industrial society and it attempts to plan for the future by creating legal and institutional framework for a physical environment inharmony with new standards of expectations and demands.

Within the context of city development plans, defining the sites of proposed roads, buildings, airports, playgrounds, recreation areas, allocating areas of land for agricultural, residential, or industrial uses and purposes, and designating the land as subject to compulsory purchase, all concern planning law. Central-local relationships pertaining to the approval of the plans and their revision were also matters to be dealt with the planning law.

The city development plan is intended as a guide to private developers, their architects, lawyers and advisors, as well as a general guidance to governmental authorities dealing with land, especially in the area of the designation of land for expropriation. It presents not only a balance sheet of the allocation of land for foreseeable development in the future, but also it provides a framework within which controls over private development can be tested to see how the controls fit into planned program for the area. It is also an effort to systematize land acquisition and to indicate where the public force will probably come into play.

All these features indicate that, in one way or another conflicts may arise between public authorities in charge of the preparation and enforcement of development plan and the individual interest which are at stake as a result of the proposals of the plan.

The impact of planning upon property rights requires the formulation of just and equitable policies providing decent compromises between the public and the private interests.

In recent years, an animated discussion has been going on in the common law countries about the nature of the planning law. With the wider participation of government in the broad management of the economy, and an acceptance of public responsibility for social services, accompanied by delegation of powers from the aims must be realized in terms of legislature to the executive and administrative branches, the democratic countries have witnessed a considerable agitation over the relationship between the individual and the state. "Rule of law" and "the Principles of natural justice" are the key emotive terms to this eternal struggle between individual freedoms and the efficiency of the administration.

A way must be found to ensure that the state conforms strictly with town planning laws, regulations and schemes and does not exploit its special position to secure short-term advantages at long-term cost.

Planning has little value as an academic exercise. Its aims must be realized in terms of bricks and mortar. But this can only be achieved if planning is equipped with adequate and sensitive legal tools. In the planning field, law has, therefore, a unique opportunity of contributing to the harmonious and dynamic development of the society.

Administrative law has generally been concerned with preventing the executive from over-reaching itself and abusing its powers; it also has, however, an important part to play in working out the means which will enable planning policy to be realized and the many difficulties which separate ideal from reality to be overcome.

Planning can operate through either or both of two kinds of instruments administrative decrees and incentives. The former are typically legal in nature, the latter are typically economic. Administrative decrees as conceptualized in analytical jurisprudence get their validity from one particular normative order, that of state. Inceptives as conceptualized in economic value theory, get their validity from a quite normative order, one which, for want of a better term, we many call the market.

As we know, planning is closely related with the central issues of who is to get how much and who is to enforce the distribution. These two problems, one of them economic, the other legal, point up to a twofold tie which the pure theory of planning has with the disciplines of economics on one hand, and the jurisprudence on the other.

They are finally related with a third discipline which is the politics. Hans Kelsen, eminent German scholar, in his gerneral theory of law and state (Allegemeine Staatslehre und Reine Rechtslehre) had formulated in the early 1920's his views on the nature of law. He had viewed law as a normative order, which is correlative with the government as an ultimate agent of enforcement. Not only Hans Kelsen, but a number of social philosophers like John Austin, Jean Bodin and Hobbes, had likewise recognized the close connection between law and force. This analysis has a significant implication for city planning.

A city plan like all other kinds of plan is the picture of an ideal state. Therefore, it is a normative order rather than a natural order. Indeed, such attributes of planning activities as value, have their being entirely in the propositions of a normative order.

The state is the normative order, an agent of enforcement, which preempts the use of force in the context of "is", and recognizes it in the context of "ought to be "as something that is reserved for the collectivity rather than the discrete individuals. The link between the "is" and the "ought to be" is provided by the basic legal norm. No order can be valid if its norms do not correspond to what can be characterized as realistic. This point is extremely important for the cities of the Third World countries where grandiose and good looking plans with attractive colors designed by planners with no adequate attention to the preconditions of their applicability.

Finally, the form of a city plan may be best described as hierarchical. It is also a dynamic order. Every norm or activity within the whole order of the plan owes its validity to norms which lie somewhere above it. This validity can be traced upward along a chain of increasingly more general and inclusive norms until one reaches a final source, the basic legal norm. In other words, at the beginning there is the basic legal norm, at the end there is the final act of application. Between these limits, every norm within a plan can be viewed, on the one hand, as application of a more general norm, and on the other hand, as a source of more specific norms. Between these limits, there is also a chain of authorities. If the command of the supreme authority be violated, then coercive sanctions ought to be applied by that authority. It would be impossible to carry out the proposal of city development plans without these sanctions, if they are properly implemented.

## Ethics

The concept of "rules of conduct" embraces the norms of a given system of normative regulation that directly express the ideological, political foundations of society, its ideological principles and its dominant moral views.

Law interacts comprehensively with moral norms, which are an important expression of the requirements of the social system, its economic basis and above all, those moral rights and duties which mediate directly the social rights and duties that are taking shape in the given sphere.

Morality is an inalienable aspect of people's intellectual life. So, in morality, the function of regulation and its role as an intellectual factor are inseparable. Moral norms are formed during the assertion and development of moral views, and they are a normative expression of them. They mediate people's conduct, from within to the extent that they have become entrenched in social consciousness. In a society with antagonistic classes, morality is qualitatively heterogeneous.

Although law belongs to the sphere of people's intellectual life, according to its chief characteristics, it constitutes an institutional social regulator, capable of regulating the most diverse relations.

Law and morality are two original, independent instruments of social regulation that interact, but do so precisely as specific, sovereign phenomena, each fulfilling its own special functions and having its own specific value in the mediation of social relations.

These considerations are closely related with modern town planning and ecological concerns. The contemporary ecological situation has prompted greater consideration of ethical notions where morality applies not only to human regulations, bur man's attitude to everything living. In order to exist, man can not restrict himself to adapting to nature. Rather, he must transform its environment to satisfy his constantly growing needs.

Nature viewed in the light of the goals and tasks of man as a social being acquires a value significance. Moral values which motivate man to proceed from vital and long term interest, when ongoing in any kind of activity become of great importance. The concept of morality, resting on the unity of social, collective and individual interests, shapes a responsible attitude to nature.

The most important aspect of morality is its normative part. Its purpose is to talk to man in the language of its own moral existence. In it, the ethical notions of good, evil, duty, conscience, dignity, responsibility, and guilt have a predominantly imperative sense.

An inevitable consequence of political pragmatism in general and at city level, and its initial thesis, namely, everything that is profitable is also moral, is the moral emptiness more inherent in the political ethics and political consciousness of western society. That is inevitably having a negative effect, in turn, on citizen's individual consciousness and morality and on the means they employ to decide their own personal problems.

A scanning of ethical values and application of the laws of the jungle at the level of state policy have a consequence, a devaluing of moral criteria and standards at the individual level

It was in the age of early bourgeois revolutions where ideologists and politicians formulated the universal slogans of liberty, equality, fraternity and justice, and first put forward the thesis that all men were born equal, and that the relations between them at all levels should be built on moral principles. The historical pattern has also been manifested in the socialist revolutions that opened up the way to the building of a new social system without exploitation and alienation of men, and on the basis created a higher type of human ethics which proclaimed the principles of collectivism and cooperation of equal people, free from all forms of social oppression, peace and friendship among nations, as the moral standards of human intercourse.

## The Twilight Zone

Ideally, town planning is a function being performed by political and administrative institutions within the confines of legal norms. Local communities, through their elected organs, carry out the city development plans which are also prepared by themselves. Proposals in the development plans restrict the scope of the ownership rights of individuals. They may postpone, prevent and remove altogether the use of those rights. These are necessary precautions aimed at the orderly and planned development of cities, ensuring the comfort, health and safety of citizens and the performance of urban functions in a more efficient way.

The scope of the restrictions put on the rights and freedoms of individuals by planning authorities is limited by the public interest (Intérêt Général). In cases where the public interest is not the determining factor in restricting the rights guaranteed by the constitution, one is confronted with a forceful usurpation of his rights. This would naturally be incompatible with the ideal of law state.

As stated above, city development plans are products of the planning functions of urban governments. Scholars who believe in the virtues of laissez-faire, maintain that any kind of planning does contradict the free will and freedoms of the individuals. Since they are regarded as a threat to human rights, they are viewed as not compatible with democracy.

This anti-planning attitude which is somewhat outmoded has been largely replaced during the second half of the 20th century by the planning -mindedness flourishing particularly in the less developed countries of the world with the guidance of some international institutions like the UN. Even those who are not sympathetic to the system of centrally planned economy, have become in favor of planning at the local level. Neither the revival of liberalism throughout the world in the 1980's, nor the rapprochement between East and West, are justified excuses for taking a hostile attitude toward local planning. For, plans worked out with a view to optimize the long-range interests and welfare of the society as a whole, can serve only the promotion of democracy in the countries concerned.

Since the aim of the law state is to ensure the protection of the rights and freedoms of individuals against the likely oppressions of the state, it is necessary that those who believe that their interest are harmed by the plan, be given the possibility to recourse to the judiciary. This is why citizens are normally encouraged to participate in the planning process in various stages in Western democracies. This is why civil society organizations are given the opportunity to express themselves in public enquiries. Thus, a just balance is sought to strike between the individual interests and the goals of the plans. The fact that people find the opportunity to express themselves has ultimately the effect to reduce their reaction to the implementation of the plan.

Once approved, development plans are made public in principle. This practice is the major guarantee provided to citizens to examine and evaluate the plan and to have a chance to recourse to the authorized courts, if necessary, against the injustices. Finally, citizens whose ownership rights and other interests are adversely affected by the plan should have the right to ask for its cancellation of the plan, or the regulatory decisions of the administrative authorities.

## Turkey

In Turkey, this function of review is performed by the administrative courts and by the Council of State at a higher level. The right to apply to the mediation of judiciary power helps to minimize or remove the effect of the objections to the proposals advanced by the plans.

In addition, most of the planning controls such as expropriation, zoning, subdivision regulations, and licensing are legal instruments in nature.

Turkey is a law state as stated in the article 2 of its constitution. Again, the article 125 of the Constitution requires that all actions and acts of the administration be subject to judicial review and control. Similarly, there exist a number of clauses in the Constitution, that guarantees for the protection of rights of the communities and citizens against the abuses and misuses of each other and third parties.

1. One is the article 23, which states that the freedom of residence may be restricted by law for ensuring sound and orderly urban growth.

2. According to the article 35/3, the exercise of the right to own property shall not be in contravention of the public interest.

3. Thirdly, the coastal areas are under the sovereignty and at the disposal of the State. In the utilization of the sea coast, lake shores or river banks, and of the coastal strip along the sea and the lakes, public interest shall be taken into consideration with priority.

4. Fourthly, according to the article 56, everyone has the right to live in a healthy and balanced environment. It is the duty of the State and the citizens to improve the natural environment and to prevent environmental pollution.

5. Similarly, the State is charged by the article 57 of the Constitution to take measure to meet the needs for housing, within the framework of a plan which takes into account the characteristics of cities and environmental conditions and supports mass housing projects.

6. Another article gives the State the duty to ensure the conservation of the historical, cultural and natural assets and wealth.

7. Finally, enacting the necessary legislation and taking necessary measures for the protection of forests and the extension of their areas are the responsibility of the State.

However, there are always striking differences between de facto and de jure situations and therefore provision in the Constitution may not constitute an adequate guarantee for the protection of such rights.

Although the Constitution and the laws define the general context within which planning process takes place, partisan factors and considerations usually play an important role in their actual implementations. This is largely because that planning is not a purely technical exercise, but also a political endeavor. Elected peoples at central and local levels are inherently predisposed to comply with incessant demands of the pressure groups at the expense of community interest. Mayors and council members are no less politically motivated than the politicians at higher levels in that respect. The state of political culture particularly in less developed countries and in the countries with a relatively short experience in the operation of multi-party democracy as another additional factor complicating the matter further.

Despite the fact that conflicts arising from the enforcement of planning controls are regulated by legal provisions, informal mechanisms and factors play an increasing role in the implementation stage. Several examples from Turkey's experiences may shed light into this discrepancy between de jure and de facto states.

1. One is the modifications in the approved master plan. According to the Turkish town planning legislation, changes in the plans are subject to the same procedures followed in their preparation and approval. However, in order to prevent a likely abuse by municipalities of their powers to change the plan, certain requirements are set to ensure the respect for the public interest. These are concerned with lower density development, minimum amount of open space required, widths of roads and adequate space for technical and social infrastructure in the plans.

Being so, formally, it is rarely the authorized local bodies which act as the real and ultimate power to effectuate the modifications in the plans. Rather, social and political forces in community, mostly representing the large economic interests, use all local and national political means, including the political party organizations to succeed in changing the plans.

As a result, one can often observe changing the use of a certain site, reserved by the plans, for open space to commercial zones, or from low density residential area to high-rise apartments. It is not rare to see the plans being modified to allow the construction of skyscraping hotels in the sites originally devoted to recreational purposes or green spaces. This is an example indicating the supremacy of informal forces over legally accepted norms.

2. Second is the financial dependence of cities upon central resources. There are two aspects of the question which matter legally. According to the Turkish Constitution (Art. 127), local authorities shall be provided with financial resources in proportion to their duties. A serious of legislation enacted during the last decade provided a share of the national budget ranging between 5 to 10 percent to municipalities to perform their functions, including the implementation of their development plans. These funds are under the guarantee of the Constitution and a change in political power at the center should not affect the distribution of these funds under normal conditions. This is de jure situation.

However, since the mayoral offices and the membership of city council have been filled in during the last local elections by the political parties in opposition, government attempted to impose numerous restrictions upon these municipalities. It has tried to cut down their shares at the source because of their debts to the Treasury, to the Bank of the Provinces and to the State Economic Enterprises by changing the special legislation regulating this matter by the annual Budget Law. However, this attempt was recently found unconstitutional by the Supreme Court on the grounds that cutting down the shares was only possible in case of the municipal debts to the Bank of the Provinces.

Besides, the government blocked the attempts of the municipalities to initiate financial agreements and other international contacts abroad for the realization of various municipal undertakings. Finally, it has tried to cut the amount of grants-in aid to the city governments in control of the opposition parties, in order to favor those municipalities in the hands of its own party.

As a result, large cities have been virtually deprived to the chance to implement their development plans and to realize their program of expropriation. This is another de facto situation which does not have much to do with the concept of law state and the principle of equality before the law.

3. According to the Turkish City Planning Law, the ultimate power for plan making, approval and application rests with the municipal councils. As elected local bodies, they have the power to act autonomously to work out their master plans, which are not subject to the approval of central authorities, unlike the pre-1985 period.

However, a clause of exception in the City Planning Law (No: 3194) empowers the Ministry of Public Works and Settlements to draw up master plans for municipalities in certain cases, simply by informing them. These exceptional cases are so numerous that the central government, if it wishes, can violate the local autonomy principle altogether. These cases are the followings:

a) Plan making or plan modification with the purpose of providing sites for public buildings.

b) Plan concerning the disaster areas.

c) Mass housing works.

d) Planning activities in squatter settlements.

e) Plans concerning the metropolitan regions covering the jurisdictions of more than one municipality.

f) Nodal regions at the crossroads of highways, railways and having the airport.

The powers of the central government has been expanded by Law 3394 (enacted in 1987), authorizing the Ministry of Public Works and Settlements, "temporarily", upon the approval of the Prime Minister, to use all planning power belonging to municipalities, including the master plans of metropolitan cities.

Both the Ministry of Public Works, and the Ministry of Tourism also possess vast planning powers in the regions and centers of tourism in accordance with the provision of the Law on the Encouragement of Tourism (No: 2634).

In addition, through the Bank of the Provinces, the Ministry influences the infrastructure and public service development in cities and towns. Water projects of cities of 100.000 or more inhabitants are taken care of by the State Water Works Department, and the Bank of the Provinces not only provides loans and distributes the shares of the national budget to local authorities, but also undertakes certain technical services like master plan and base map preparation, constructing sewage installations, etc. These channels are the major means to differentiate by the government among cities according to their political standing. What is being done is sometimes in line with legal norms and provisions, but sometimes in contravention of the rules of the existing legislation.

All these examples tend to indicate that legal regulations are not always final guarantee for the protection of rights and freedoms. Values, interests, struggle for power, economic, political and other concerns are, most of the time, factors determining the fate and success of planning activities, be it national, or local.

Ethical considerations therefore are of utmost importance to ensure the respect for the rights of citizens, and of future generations. The firmest guardian of the public interest as far as the cities are concerned, are ethical inclinations and social responsibility of the people. Whether this can be achieved by formal and informal educational channels or not, is one of the most difficult challenges of our time.

## Bibliography

- Alexeyev, Sergei, Socialism and Law in Society, Progress Publishers, Moscow, 1990.
- Catanese, James Anthony, The Politics of Planning and Development, Sage, Beverly Hills, 1984.
- Danielson, Michael N. and Rusen Keles, The Politics of Rapid Urbanization: Government and Growth in Modern Turkey, Holmes and Meier, New York, 1985.
- Daly, Herman E. (Ed.), Economics, Ecology and Ethics, W. H. Freeman, San Francisco, 1980.
- Firey, Walter, Law and Economy in Planning, University of Texas Press, Austin, 1965.
- Goodpaster, K. E., and K. M. Sayre (Eds.), Ethics and Problems of the 21 st Century, Notre Dame, 1979.
- Hayek, Frederick, The Constitution of Liberty, The University of Chicago Press, Chicago, 1960.
- Keles, Ruşen, Urban Poverty in the Third World, Institute of Developing Economies, Tokyo, 1988.
- Kerimov, Dzhangir, Methodology of Law, Progress Publishers, Moscow, 1989.

# Local Governance and Democracy*

## Introduction: European Institutions, Liberal Democracy and the European Standards for Local Democracy

The European standards for local democracy are embedded in the basic principles of liberal democracy. The main institutions and values of liberal democracy are representative assemblies chosen in free elections, a pluralistic party system, professional administrations accountable to the elected representatives, a free press, political, social and economic systems underpinned by law, and the existence and development of territorial democratic governments. Public protection of individual liberties, participation of various interests in the society, constitutional restraints on the power of the executive must be added to the above-mentioned principles. The existence of modern local authorities born out of the tradition of the free or chartered cities and boroughs based on an acceptance by the state of the contribution that they can make to shared wealth as free centers of trade and affluence. Local authorities have also been used in the west particularly as a tool to prevent the rise of authoritarianism by means of checks on the executive power. This objective has always been central to the progress of decentralization.[1]

---

\*    International Conference on the Relationships between Turkey and Columbia, University of Rosario, Bogota, Columbia, 2012.

1    Alan Norton, "Western European Local Government in Comparative Perspective", in Richard Batley and Gerry Stoker (eds.) *Local Government in Europe: Trends and Development,* Macmillan, London, 1991.

The development of local government in Europe is bound up in the origins of government and the state itself, and in the adaptation of government to new forces of democratization and representation. Western Europe has developed a long history of liberal democracy with a variety of local government administrative structure.[2]

Local authorities are both political institutions and contributing to the progress of democracy, conceived as the primary schools of democracy by John Stuart Mill and Alexis de Tocqueville, and also administrative agencies that are in charge of providing local public services to local communities. In addition to the professionalization of administration of local government as service delivery bodies; constitutionalism, as understood in the sense of formal electoral representation at all levels of local government, is one of the fundamental characteristics of local democracy. Combining both of these features, the commune has been, throughout the western history, as the basic unit and the fundamental building block of local democracy.

In their capacity of political institutions strengthening the foundations of representative democracy, local governments enjoy, in most of the European countries, advantages provided by the principle of the general competence, according to which, local authorities are empowered to take initiatives with respect to any matter relating to the local community in so far as the law does not explicitly provide otherwise.[3] A slightly different version of the same principle, namely, the

2    Robert J.Bennett, "European Local Government Systems", in Robert J. Bennett (ed.), *Local Governmnet in the New Europe*, Belhaven Press, London, 1993.

3    Philip Blair, "Trends in Local Autonomy and Democracy; Reflections from a European Perspective", in Richard Batley and Gerry Stoker (eds.), *op.cit.*,p.50; andA lain Delcamp, "La Charte Européenne de l'Autonomie Locale: Instrument du Développement de la Démocratie Locale dans la Grande Europe", *Les Colloques du Sénat, Les Actes, La DécentralisationFrançaise vue d'Europe,*

principle of subsidiarity, has become now the key concept in Europe used as one of the safeguards of the autonomy of local institutions.[4]

The European Union, starting from the early 1990's, began to emphasize the principle of subsidiarity as a tool to rationalize the administration.[5] The principle of subsidiarity, which is concerned with the relationships between the members of the federation and the federation itself, between the member states and the European Union, and finally, between local authorities and the central governments, has been incorporated into the Maastricht Treaty in 1992. The fundamental idea behind this principle is to ensure that the public responsibilities be carried out at the level of administration that is closest to the citizens. According to the Article 3/b (5) of the Maastricht Treaty: "In areas which do not fall within its exclusive competence, the Community shall take action, in accordance with the principle of subsidiarity, only if and in so far as the objectives of the proposed action can not be sufficiently achieved by the member states and can therefore, by reason of scale or effects of the proposed action, be better achieved by the Community".

This is a criterion for the allocation of tasks between the European Community and the member states, and not for deciding whether tasks should be assigned to a level below central government. But the basic value can not only apply as between the European Union and its member states. The

Colloque Organisé par le Sénat et le Congrés des Pouvoirs Locaux et Régionaux du Conseil de l'Europe, 26 juin 2001, pp.19-29.

4    See the Final Declaration of the International Conference on the Council of Europe Charters' of Local and Regional Self-Government: Subsidiarity in Action: Responsibilities and Finances of Local and Regional Authorities, Ancona, Italy, 14-16 October, 1999.

5    Loughlin, John, Hendriks, Frank and Lidström, Anders (eds.), *The Oxford Handbook of Local and Regional Democracy in Europe*, Oxford University Press, Oxford, 2010.

logic behind the subsidiarity principle is that within individual member states, too, public tasks should be assigned to more accessible levels of government, in preference to more remote levels, so long as they can be performed effectively and efficiently.[6]

The Amsterdam Treaty indicated at several points that member states realize they must now address themselves not just to the division of far-reaching search for ways of bringing political control nearer to Europe's citizens. It declared in its amendment to the Treaty on European Union (Lisbon Treaty) that signatory states "seek ever closer union among the peoples of Europe, in which decisions are taken as openly as and as closely as possible to the citizen." As far as the local democracy is concerned, one can safely maintain that the main principles of the European local governance include participation, closeness to the citizens, transparency, accountability, responsiveness, efficiency and autonomy.

Increasing emphasis on the principle of subsidiarity has paved the way for its recognition by the Treaty on the European Union (Maastricht) which also set up the Committee of the Regions in 1994. The Committee of the Regions, despite its advisory legal status, is establishing an important niche for itself in the institutional architecture of the European Union to represent the interests of territorial communities of Europe.

On the other hand, the Council of Europe is an intergovernmental institution which aims a) to protect human rights, pluralist democracy and the rule of law b) to promote awareness and encourage the development of Europe's cultural identity and diversity, c) to seek solutions for the problems facing

6    Nicolas Kada, *Les Collectivités Territoriales dans L'Union Européenne: Vers une Europe Décentralisée?*, Presses Universitaires de Grenoble, Grenoble, 2010.

European societies, and finally, d) to help consolidate democratic stability in the continent by supporting political, legislative and constitutional reforms. Within the framework of these general aims, fostering local and regional self-government, analyzing the administrative and legal structures and the finances of territorial authorities, promoting democratic citizenship, promoting trans frontier cooperation between local and regional authorities, and promoting regional cultural identities appear to be among the essential goals of the Council of Europe with respect to local democracy.[7]

## The Works of the Council of Europe Concerning Local Democracy

The philosophy of the Council of Europe is based on the belief that autonomous local authorities will be the foundation stones of the future united and enlarged Europe. Therefore, the Council of Europe has made a constant effort, since its establishment in the late 1940's, to strengthen and promote local autonomy, which a common and traditional democratic value all over Europe. Although the Committee of Minister had declined to accept a proposal made by the CLRAE (The Congress of Local and Regional Authorities of Europe), during the 1950's, to add the concept of "local autonomy", with a protocol, to the European Convention of Human Rights, it changed its position later on, and adopted a document that was called the Declaration on the Principles of Local Self-Government as early as 1968.

This Declaration proposed by the CLRAE in 1968 (Resolution No:64) has been supported by a Recommendation (No:15) of the Consultative Assembly in 1970. Since a non-binding "Declaration of principles" could not meet the need for the

---

7    Council of Europe, *50 Years of Local and Regional Democracy*, Series L and R, Local and Regional, Wasselone, 2007.

promotion of local democracy, the Council of Europe continued its efforts to prepare and submit to the Committee of Ministers a Draft European Charter of Local Self-Government at the beginning of the 1980's.

During the 5th (Lugano, October 1982) and 6th (Rome, November 1984) Conferences of the European Ministers Responsible for Local Government, the text of the principles was revised and adopted unanimously. The Committee of Ministers adopted the text in June 1985 and it was opened for the signature and ratification by the member states. The European Charter of Local Self-Government that is both signed and ratified by 44 out of total 47 member states by March 2013, sets out the fundamental principles of local democracy reflecting the traditional democratic values of the Europeans. It was complemented by an Additional Protocol on Participation in 2009.

It must be kept in mind that the activities of the Congress of Local and Regional Authorities of Europe are not consisted simply of the works concerning the European Charter of Local Self-Government. The Congress deals, at the same time, with all policy issues, which affect local and regional authorities, the most important among them being restructuring of local and regional self-government, rural and urban development, environmental protection, and the promotion of culture, education, public health and social services.

In addition to the analysis and monitoring of the member states' implementation of the principles of local democracy enshrined in the Charter, to assist the new democracies that are being restored in central, eastern European and Caucasian countries establish more effective local government structures, to step up trans frontier cooperation between various regions, and to promote peace, tolerance and economic growth, to bring local and regional "grassroots democracy" closer to the citizen, within the principle of sub sidiarity promoted by the Maastricht philosophy, and finally, to facilitate the integration of immigrant communities and other less privileged segments of the societies, with campaigns against racism, xenophobia and all kinds of intolerance are among the most important on which the Congress bases its major policies.

In this connection, the preparation and adoption of the European Urban Charter[8] providing towns with a practical guide for the management of such current problems as pollution, transportation, energy policy, multiculturalism and insecurity, the European Charter of Architectural Heritage, and the Outline Convention on Trans frontier Cooperation which has been in force since 1982, must be mentioned particularly [9]. Last but not the least are the European Convention on the Participation of Foreigners in Public Life at the Local Level[10], the European Charter on Regional and Minority Languages[11], and the Charter on the Participation of Young People in Municipal and Regional Affairs[12].The adoption in 1997, by the Congress, of a Draft European Charter of Regional Self-Government (Recommendation No: 34, 1997) has been for a long time on the agenda of the Committee of Ministers; but due to the objections by several member states, its title has been changed into the Reference Framework for

8   Resolution No: 234, 30 March 1992, Strasbourg; and 2008 Manifesto for a New Urbanity.

9   The Council of Europe, *Convention for he Protection of the Architectural Heritage of Europe,* ETS,No:121, Strasbourg, 1985.and The Council of Europe, *European Outline Convention on Transfrontier Cooperation Between Territorial Communities and Authorities,* ETS No:126, Strasbourg, 1982..

10  The Council of Europe, *Convention on the Participation of Foreigners in Public Life at Local Level,* ETS No: 144, Strasbourg 1992.

11  The Council of Europe, *International Conference on the European Charter for Regional and Minority Languages,* Strasbourg, 1999..

12  The Council of Europe, *The Participation of Young People,* Strasbourg, 1997.

Regional Democracy in order to avoid enacting this document as a legally binding international convention.

In this connection, I believe that the final declaration adopted at the end of the Conference of European Ministers responsible for Local and Regional Government in Valencia in 2007 possesses valuable indicators on the promotion of the principles of good democratic governance at local level. These are 1) fair conduct of elections, representation and participation, 2) responsiveness, 3) efficiency and effectiveness, 4) openness and transparency, 5) rule of law, 6) ethical conduct, 7) competence and capacity, 8) innovation and openness to change, 9) sustainability and long-term orientation, 10) sound financial management, 11) human rights, cultural diversity and social cohesion, and finally, 12) accountability. All of these principles addressing to the needs of local democracy combine both the advantages of economic and political wisdom[13]

## European Standards for Local Democracy in the Light of the European Charter of Local Self-Government

The European Charter of Local Self- Government possesses the fundamental principles of local democracy that have been developed throughout centuries. All members of the Council of Europe have been encouraged to a party to this important legal instrument and to remove all obstacles before its proper implementation. Adoption of the principles and values of the European Charter would not only help to improve the quality of local democracy, but also would contribute to the progress of democracy at national level. As mentioned

---

13   Conference of European Ministers Responsible for Local and Regional Government: Valencia Declaration: Good Local and Regional Governance-The European Challenge, 15th Session, Valencia 15-16 October 2007, MCL-15(2007)5 Final, 16 October 2007.

earlier, the basic philosophy of the Charter rests on the belief that the degree of autonomy enjoyed by local authorities may be regarded as a yardstick for a genuine democracy. The Charter aims to guarantee the political, administrative and financial autonomy of local authorities and it tends to commit the parties, which ratified the Charter, to comply with its principles in order to safeguard the rights of peoples living in local communities, as citizens of local authorities, which are the public institutions closest to citizens.

The Charter is composed of three sections. The first is the Preamble. The second deals with the details of the basic principles. Finally comes the provisions concerning the implementation of the Charter.

## The Preamble

In its preamble, the basic premises on which the principles of local autonomy are based are summarized as a) the vital contribution of local self-government to democracy, effective administration and decentralization of power, b) the important role of local authorities in the construction of the future integrate Europe, and c) the need for local authorities to be democratically constituted enjoy wider-ranging autonomy. In this section of the Charter, a direct reference is made to the existence of local authorities with real responsibilities as an administration both effective and close to the citizen. The word of subsidiarity is not used in the text.

## The Principles of Local Democracy
## The principles concerning the meaning and
## scope of local self-government

According to the Charter, the term of local government denotes the right and ability of local authorities to regulate and manage a substantial share or public affairs under their own responsibility and in the interests of the local population. Local authorities must exercise this right through the decision-making bodies (assemblies, councils), composed of the members freely elected by secret ballot, on the basis of direct, equal and universal suffrage.

The Charter does not require that executive organs be elected, but it does require that executive organs be responsible directly to the elected assemblies as councils in the Netherlands. However, the fact that a non-elected executive organ can not be dismissed by the elected council to which he or she is responsible, is now being questioned from the standpoint of the scope and nature of the concept of responsibility. Although the existence of freely elected councils is a fundamental requirement for local autonomy, this can not be regarded as sufficient. Therefore, recourse to the instruments of direct citizen participation, such as having assemblies of citizen, local referenda, etc. Has to be open to citizen.

The Charter requires that the competencies of local authorities be prescribed by the constitution or by law. But this is a minimum requirement and it could not prevent the attribution of new powers, competencies and responsibilities to local authorities.

Despite the fact that İs not mentioned literally in the Charter, the principle of subsidiarity is defined in its respective provisions (Article 4, paragraphs 2 and 3) in the following terms: "Local authorities shall have full discretion to exercise their initiative with regard to any matter which is not excluded from their competencies nor assigned to any other authority... Public responsibilities shall be exercised by those local authorities which are closest to the citizen. Allocation of responsibility to another authority will be allowed only depending upon *the extent and nature of the task and the requirements of efficiency and economy"*.

The fact that the competencies given to local authorities must be *full and exclusive,* and not be undermined or limited by another authority (central, provincial or regional), is another component of the concept of local self-government as conceptualized in the Charter. As a corollary of this provision, it is expected that local authorities be consulted in due time and in an appropriate manner, in the planning and decision-making processes for all matters which concern them directly. This requirement for consultation is particularly emphasized in connection with the protection of local authority boundaries, according to which no change in the territorial boundaries can be made without prior consent of the local communities concerned, possibly by means of referendum.

The Charter also lays down as a prerequisite for the autonomous local government, the right of local authorities to determine their own internal administrative structures in order to adopt them to local needs and to ensure effective management. In addition, the conditions of services of local government employees and local elected representatives are made subject to certain regulations in the Charter.

First of all, the working conditions of local government officials must permit the recruitment of high-quality staff on the basis of merit and competence; and training opportunities, remuneration and career prospects must be provided to them in order to promote the autonomy of local authorities. Secondly, the conditions of office for those in the category of the elected representatives must enable them to exercise their functions freely. With this aim in mind, appropriate financial compensation for expenses incurred in the exercise of their office, as well as the realistic compensation for the loss of earnings or remuneration for work done, together with corresponding social welfare protection must be provided.

## The principles regarding the administrative supervision of local authorities

The Charter defines the scope and limits of the central supervision over local authorities. In principle, any administrative supervision is permitted only in such cases and according to such procedures provided by the constitution or by law. And it must be normally aim at ensuring compliance with the law and with constitutional principles (le controle de légalité). This means a supervision with regard to expediency of the acts and decisions of local authority (le controle de l'opportunité) is not allowed in principle. Despite this fact, the latter is permitted by the Charter only in exceptional cases where the execution of certain public tasks is delegated to local authorities by the state.

As to the limits to the central control and supervision, the Charter stipulates that it must be exercised in such a way as to ensure that the intervention of the supervising authority is kept in proportion of the importance of the interests which it is intended to protect.

## The principles concerning the financial resources

So long as local authorities are deprived of financial resources commensurate with the responsibilities provided for by relevant legislation, they can not be regarded as autonomous public institutions. Therefore, the Charter underlines first the significance of this precondition and suggests that local authorities be entitled to adequate financial resources of their own, of which they may dispose freely. It is also suggested by the Charter that at least part of the financial resources of local authorities derives from local taxes and charges of which they have the power to determine he rates. It is only with flexible financial systems that these authorities could have sufficiently diversified and buoyant resources to enable them to keep pace with the real evolution of the cost of carrying out their tasks.

A particularly important aspect of the financial autonomy of local authorities is to ensure that central grants to local governments be not earmarked for financing of specific projects. To refrain from removing the basic freedom of local authorities through grants and to exercise policy discretion within their own jurisdiction are inseparable elements of local self-government. Respect for this rule would prevent partisan manipulations of the political parties in power to exercise discriminatory practices against local authorities controlled by the opposition parties.

The Charter considers, at the same time, the institution of financial equalization procedures or equivalent measures as an essential requirement for ensuring local self-government, through correcting the effects of the unequal distribution of potential sources of revenue.

Finally, once again, consultation is regarded as a necessary technique to get the opinions of local authorities on the way in which redistributed resources are to be allocated to them.

## Local authorities' right to cooperate

In order to carry out tasks of common interest, local authorities must be entitled to form consortia and have the right to belong to a national or international association for the protection and promotion of their common interests according to the Charter. This right shall entitle them at the same time to cooperate freely with their counterparts in other states.

## Right to legal protection

A final element of the concept of local autonomy is the right of recourse of local authorities to judicial remedy in order to secure free exercise of their powers and to respect for the principles of local self-government summarized above.

## Implementation of the Charter

The provisions in the last section of the Charter are concerned with the actual implementation and the obligations of the member states, which are usually included in conventions drawn up under the auspices of the Council of Europe. For example, the states are invited to consider themselves bound with a minimum number of the articles of the Charter. They have the option to specify the categories of territorial authorities to which they intend to confine the scope. Also, they have to forward to the Council of Europe all relevant information concerning legislative provisions and other measures taken for the purposes with the terms of the Charter.

## Monitoring the implementation of the Charter

The Charter does not provide for an institutionalized system and the procedures to supervise its implementation. However, monitoring is carried out by the Governance Committee of the Congress of Local and Regional Authorities of Europe. The Governance Committee has the particular task of preparing reports on the progress of local and regional democracy in Europe. The Committee which is composed of elected members is assisted by a Group of Independent Experts from the states having signed the Charter.

The Governance Committee, in cooperation with the Group of Independent Experts, exercises two separate but complementary system of supervision. The first is called *ex officio monitoring* and the second is *monitoring on request.*

For the purposes of ex officio monitoring, the Governance Committee and the Group of Independent Experts select an article or several articles of the Charter, which they consider worth investigation from the point of view of their effective implementation. The Group of Independent Experts has prepared several substantial reports during the last several years, which are the followings: 1.The Incorporation of the European Charter of Local Self-Government into the legal systems of ratifying states and possible legal remedies in the event of violation of the Charter (1994 and 1998), 2. Supervision of local authorities by central and regional government (1996), 3.Local authority finances (1999), 4. The responsibilities of local authorities and the relationship between their competencies and their financial resources (2000), 5. Institutional framework for local democracy (2002), 6. Municipal property ( 2003), 7. Executive bodies of local authorities (2004), 8. Consultation processes (2005), 9. Public participation (2005), 10. Incorporation of the European Charter of Local Self-Government with the Internal legislation of member states (2008), 11. Institutional relationships between the executive and decision-making bodies (2008), 12. Internal organization of local authorities (2009), 13. Local and regional ombudsman (2010).

Monitoring on request is based on the application made by local authorities and their representative associations. Investigation on the effective application of the Charter's provisions may only be made by authorities in those member states which have ratified the Charter.

## Reflections on Turkish local governance and democracy

All constitutions adopted since the beginning of the establishment of the Turkish Republic (1923) defined Turkey as a

politically unitary state. Basic provisions concerning territorial governments, which are actually in force, are laid down
by the Constitution of 1982. Three basic provisions concerning territorial governments may be mentioned in this respect.
According to the Article 123 of the Constitution the administration is an integrated whole, and the formation and functions of the administration will be based on two complementary principles, namely, centralization and decentralization.
The second is the Article 126 which regulates the organization of the central government and the structure of its field
organization. National territory is divided into provinces on
the basis of geographical situation, economic conditions and
public service requirements. The provinces are governed on
the basis of the principle of deconcentration. Central administrative authorities comprising more than one province may
be established in order to ensure efficiency and coordination
in the provision of public services.

The third article, namely the Article 127, is exclusively
concerned with local authorities. It requires that the duties
and powers of local authorities be regulated by law in accordance with the principle of decentralization. It is clear that
the power sharing between the State and local authorities will
not be subject to arbitrary will of the central government, but
it will be shaped in conformity with the principle of decentralization. However, the definition of the concept of decentralization can not be found in the text of the Constitution.
But, the wording of the Article 127 concerning the powers
and competencies of local authorities may be helpful in that
respect. According to the respective sentence, "Local authorities are public corporate entities established to meet *the common local needs* of the inhabitants of provinces, municipalities

and villages". The Constitution leaves to the Legislative Assembly to determine what *the local common needs* are.

Local authorities in Turkey are simply administrative entities in charge of carrying out public services conferred upon them by their respective legislation. The general system of local government in Turkey is not political decentralization, but administrative decentralization. Despite the fact the fact that recent developments in the theory and practice of local governance blurred this traditional distinction to a certain extent, no provision in the Constitution allows territorial authorities to be regarded as law-making bodies sharing the national sovereignty with the State.[14]

Legislation on various types of local authority have been renewed during the 2004-2006 period, as a part of the preconditions demanded by the European Union in the negotiation process for full membership. Historically, political and administrative system of Turkey did not recognize broad powers and extensive autonomy to territorial authorities. As a result of the unitary character of the State set by the Constitution, the central government has the power to exercise a strict control and supervision over local authorities in certain circumstances provided by the Constitution. As formulated in the Article 127 of the Constitution, central supervision is rather broad and may include the control of the expediency of the acts and decisions of local authorities, depending upon the meaning to be attributed to the concept of public interest. Because, there is no indication in the Constitution that

---

14  Ruşen Keleş, "Yerel Yönetimlerde Yeniden Yapılanma: Avrupa ve Türkiye", (Restructuring Local Governance: Europe and Turkey), Municipal Association of Turkey and Konrad Adenauer Foundation, *Uluslararası Seminer: Yerel Yönetimlerde Yeniden Yapılanma (International Seminar: Restructuring in Local Governance )*, Ankara, 1996, pp. 23-35

the administrative control and supervision of the State will be confined to legality control.

In principle, the procedures dealing with objections to the acquisition by elected organs of local authorities of their status as an organ and their loss of such status, must be resolved by the judiciary. However, one of the most problematic provisions of the Constitution is an exceptional rule to this principle that allows the Minister of the Interior to remove from office those elected organs of local authorities or their members against whom an investigation or prosecution has been initiated on the grounds of offences related to their duties, pending judgement.

The Constitution provides that local authorities will be provided with revenue sources commensurate with their duties and responsibilities. And an opportunity exists for the settlements (urban and rural) with a population exceeding 750.000 to establish a metropolitan municipality. It is expected that in such municipalities with a two-tier administrative structure, better public participation may be ensured and metropolitan wide public services can be better performed. With these expectations in mind, the number of metropolitan municipalities increased from 3 in 1984, to 16 in 1988, and to 30 in 2013.

By the new legislation, boundaries of newly established metropolitan municipalities extended to coincide with the boundaries of the provinces. The length of the provincial territory is no more than 50-70 kilometers in some municipalities, but it is as long as 250-350 kilometers in some others. The argument behind this radical change was to benefit from the scale economies, in other words to decrease the per capita expenditures for local public services. However, it was forgotten that once the optimum size is unjustifiably exceeded, not economies, but external diseconomies would begin to increase. On the other hand, increased size of the metropolitan municipalities has the disadvantage of making public participation more difficult, simply because as the size of the community concerned increases, the chance of public participation becomes less likely. This creates serious difficulties for local democracy in view of the legal obligations imposed by the European Charter of Local Self-Government.

In the light of the European experiences and the universal principles of local democracy, one can make an effort to look once again at the reform movements of Turkey to promote local democracy and governance briefly.[15]

1. Certain steps have been taken in order to reform the system beginning from the middle of the 2000's. Due regard has been given to the provisions of the European Charter of Local Self-Government. Article 4, par.3 and 4, Article 3, par.1 and 2, Article 8 and Article 10 must be particularly mentioned in this respect. However, it must be admitted that radical changes in the institutional structure of a nation which evolved over centuries can not be realized promptly.

2. As emphasized among the veto reasons of the President of the Republic several years ago regarding the changes in the legislation in force, the Constitution of Turkey does not seem suitable for regarding the central government as *secondary*, and territorial authorities as a *primary* entity. Both from the point of view of geographical scope and from a functional angle, local authorities are defined in the Constitution as legal entities with limited jurisdictions.

---

15   Ruşen Keleş, "Territorial Governance in Turkey", paper presented to the International Conference on Territorial Governance: Disintegrating States in an Integrating Europe? New and Old Challenges ", European Studies Centre, St.Antony College, University of Oxford, 28-30 November, 2006.

3. Within this framework, it is argued that the principle of subsidiarity is in contradiction of the formulation of the constitutional provision concerning local authorities. Because, the subsidiarity requires that the Constitution should enumerate the competencies of the *State* first, and then leave all residual functions to local authorities. It is also argued that the principle of subsidiarity is peculiar to federal states. I believe that is not correct. The fact that federal states to adopt and implement the principle of subsidiarity does not require that it must opportunity be regarded as a principle in the monopoly of federal states.

4. Local government reform laws lifted off the traditional system of control, auditing and inspection with a view to ensure efficiency in public administration. Weakening of the control system in public administration has the potential to encourage corruption indirectly and it can not be defended on any ground.

5. Reform laws weakened the traditional position of the provincial governors as representatives of the State. The chance of the governor for success in his office will depend now to a large extent on his close collaboration with the President of the General Council, who is actually a politician. This new regulation which might seem as a democratic arrangement at first glance, may turn out to be a source of a deep conflict resulting in unsurmountable difficulties in reconciling local interests with the general interest.

6. It has been argued justifiably that most of the reforms aimed actually at strengthening the liberal economic system in the country instead of local governance. The laws put into force recently possess provisions prohibiting even the State initiating and operating economic enterprises. This extremist position makes one think that the gap to be created as a

result of large-scale transfer of State functions to local authorities will be filled out by private firms instead of territorial authorities.

## Bibliography

- Baldersheim, Harald and Rose, Lawrence (eds.), *Territorial Choice,* Palgrave, Macmillan, London, 2010.
- Batley, Richard and Stoker, Gerry (eds.), *Local Government in Europe: Trends and Development,* Macmillan, London, 1991.
- Bennett, Robert J. (ed.), *Local Government in the New Europe,* Belhaven Press, London, 1993.
- Committee of the Regions, *Regional and Local Democracy in the European Union,* European Communities, Luxembourg, 1999.
- Committee of the Regions, *Regional and Local Democracy in the European Union: Responsibilities and Resources,* European Communities, Luxembourg, 2001.
- Conference of the European Ministers Responsible for Local and Regional Government: *Valencia Declaration: Good Local and Regional Governance - The European Challenge, 15th Session,* Valencia, 15-16, 2007, MCL-15(2007)5 Final, 16 October 2007.
- Council of Europe, *50 Years of Local and Regional Democracy,* Series L and S, Local and Regional, Wasselone, 2007
- Council of Europe, *Convention for the Protection of the Architectural Heritage of Europe,* ETS, No:121, Strasbourg, 1985.
- Council of Europe, *European Outline Convention on Transfrontier Cooperation between Territorial Communities and Authorities,* ETS No: 126, Strasbourg, 1982.
- Council of Europe, *Convention on the Participation of Foreigners in Public Life at Local Level,* ETS No: 144, Strasbourg, 1992.
- Council of Europe, *International Conference on the European Charter for Regional Minority Languages,* Strasbourg, 1999.
- Council of Europe, *The Participation of Young People,* Strasbourg, 1997.
- Council of Europe, Final Declaration of the International Conference on the Council of Europe Charters of Local and Regional

Self-Government: *Subsidiarity in Action: Responsibilities and Finances of Local and Regional Authorities*, Ancona, Italy, 14-16 October, 1999.

- Delcamp, Alain, *Les Institutions Locales en Europe*, Presses Universitaires de France, Paris, 1990.

- Delcamp, Alain, "La Charte Européenne de l'Autonomie Locale: Instrument du Développement de la Démocratie Locale dans la Grande Europe", *Les Colloques du Sénat, Les Actes, La Décentralisation Française vue d'Europe*, Colloque organisé par le Sénat et le Congrés du Pouvoir Locaux et Régionaux du Conseil de l'Europe, 26 Juin 2001, pp.19-29.

- Kada, Nicolas, *Les Collectivités Territoriales dans l'Union Européenne: Vers une Europe Décentralisée?*, Presses Universitaires de Grenoble, Grenoble, 2010.

- Keleş, Ruşen, *Yerinden Yönetim ve Siyaset*, Cem Yay., İstanbul, 2012, (8. Basın).

- Keleş, Ruşen, "European Standards for Local Democracy", Paper presented to the Conference on the Institutional Dialogue between the State and Local Authorities, Baku, Azerbaijan, 5-6 December 2001.

- Keleş, Ruşen, "Territorial Governance in Turkey: Applying the European Model", Paper presented to the International Conference on *Territorial Governance: Disintegrating States in an Integrating Europe? New and Old Challanges*, European Studies Centre, St.Antony College, University of Oxford, Oxford, 28-30 November, 2006.

- Loughlin, John, *Sub-National Democracy in the European Union: Challanges and Opportunities*, Oxford University Press, Oxford, 2001.

- Loughlin, John, Hendriks, Frank, and Lidström, Anders (eds.), *The Oxford Handbook of Local and Regional Democracy in Europe*, Oxford University Press, Oxford, 2010

- Mengi, Ayşegül, "Avrupa Birliği'ne Uyum Sürecinde Yerel Yönetimlerle İlgili Düzenlemeler" (Revisions of Local Authorities during bthe Process of Alignment), *Ruşen Keleş'e Armağan, Cilt 3, (In Honour of Ruşen Keleş)*, Volume 3, İmge Pub., Ankara, 2007.

# Territorial Governance in Turkey in the Light of the European Model*

## European Values of Local Democracy

The basic values of the European Union are mentioned in the Article 1-2 of the European Constitution as being the respect for human dignity, liberty, democracy, equality, rule of law, as well as the respect for human rights. It is also mentioned there that these values are common to all Member States in a society characterised by pluralism, non- discrimination, tolerance, justice, solidarity and gender equality. In the Article 1-5, concerning the relations between the Union and the Member States, a need is expressed "to act with respect for the national identities of the Member States… inherent in their political and fundamental structures, including local and regional autonomy"[1].

Fundamental principles to guide the exercise of the Union, such as subsidiarity and proportionality are also defined in the text (Art. 1-9) in addition to the description of functions and composition of the Committee of the Regions as an advisory organ (Article 198 Paragraphs a, b and c of the Maastricht Treaty). It is beyond any doubt that the European values

---

* Paper presented to the International Conference on Territorial Governance: Disintegrating State in an Integrating Europe? New and Old Challenges, European Studies Centre, St. Antony College, University of Oxford, United Kingdom, 28-30 November, 2006. United Kingdom.

1 Oliver Duhamel, **La Constitution européenne**, Armand Colin, Paris, 2003.

mentioned above encompass also the increasingly fashion-able concept of local and regional democracy.

The Article 5 of the Amsterdam Treaty (3/b in the Maastricht Treaty) defines the principle of subsidiarity as the following: " In areas which do not fall within its exclusive competence, the Community shall take action in accordance with the principle of subsidiarity, only if and insofar as the objectives of the proposed action cannot be sufficiently achieved by the Member States and can therefore by reason of the scale and effects of the proposed action, be better achieved by the Community". It is obvious that this principle is a criterion for the allocation of tasks between the European Union and the Member States, and therefore it can not be used, in principle, as a yardstick to decide whether tasks should be assigned to a level below the central government, namely, subnational governments.

However, the principle of subsidiarity as defined in the text of the Treaty, "makes sense only on the basis of a general preference for bringing political decision-making as near as possible to the level where citizens can directly influence it... The inescapable logic of the subsidiarity principle is that... public tasks should be assigned -so long as they can be performed effectively and efficiently- to more remote levels"[2]. This is the reason why the Committee of the Regions suggested that the concept of subsidiarity must be applied in the same way within states, as between them and the European Community. The territorial entities concerned are nothing else than local and regional authorities. Accordingly, in its Opinion on Developing a Culture of Subsidiarity (Cdr 302/98 fin. March 1999). The Committee argued that political reform in Europe should be guided by this principle, with decisions

2    Committee of the Regions, **Regional and Local Government in the Europe-an Union: Responsibilities and Resources**, Luxembourg, 2001, pp. 22-26.

being taken as close to grassroots level as possible.[3] Similarly, a declaration appended to the Treaty to Amsterdam by German. Austrian and Belgium governments asserted that "Action by the European Community in accordance with the principle of subsidiarity not only concerns the Member States but also their entities to the extent that they have their own law making powers conferred on them under their national constitutional law"[4].

On the other hand, fundamental legal and political document that serves as a guideline for the development of local democracy within the Council of Europe is they European Charter of Local Self-Government. This instrument has been put into force in l985. As rightly emphasized by Giovanni di Stasi, former President of the Congress. "The Charter has had an undeniable impact on legislative and institutional, in some cases constitutional, changes in the European countries and its role in promoting local autonomy and democracy has been unanimously acknowledged by states and local elected representatives"[5]. The Congress of Local and Regional Authorities of Europe has, among others, the mission to endure the participation of local and regional authorities in the implementation of the ideal of European Unity as well as their representation and active involvement in the Council of Europe's work. In addition, the CLRAE has the goal to ensure the establishment of genuinely autonomous local and regional administrative structures, taking into account the cultural and economic differences existing among European regions for the well-being and interests of the people. For the promotion

---

3    **Ibid**, p. 23.

4    1997 Inter-governmental Conference, Ibid., Please note that all three of these states are federal states.

5    The Congress of Local and Regional Authorities, **The European Charter of Local Self-Government 20 th Anniversary**, Proceedings, Lisbon, 8 July 2005, Council of Europe, Strasbourg, 2006, p. 73.

of local and regional democracy, the CLRAE maintains also close contact with international organizations, such as the European Union, as a part of the general external relations policy of the Council of Europe.

The basic principles of the Charter include those regarding the meaning and scope of local-sell government, the principles concerning the administrative supervision of local authorities, those concerning the financial resources of local authorities, their right to cooperate. and finally, the principles concerning the right to legal protection.[6]

Although not literally mentioned in the Charter, the principle of subsidiarity is defined enough clearly in the Article 4, Paragraphs 2 and 3 in the following terms: "Local authorities shall have full discretion to exercise their initiative with regard to any matter which is not excluded from their competences nor assigned to any other authority. Besides, public responsibilities shall be exercised by those authorities, which are closest to the citizen. Allocation of responsibility another authority will be allowed only depending upon the extent and nature of the task and the requirements of efficiency and economy".

Despite the fact that the Committee of the Region is an advisory organ of the Union, it has the function to provide an opportunity for the representatives of local and regional

---

6    Alain Delcamp, "Les Garanties de la subsidiarité et de l'autonomie régionale et locale dans les conventions du Conseil de l'Europe", Séminaire Internationale : Les Garanties en Matiere de Subsidiarité et d' Autonomie Locale et Régionale en Europe , Pérouse (Italy), 6 Octobre 2006; et Francesco Merloni, "Prospects for Strengthening the Role of the European Charter of Local Self-Government", in the Congress of Local and Regional Authorities, **The European Charter of Local Self-Government-20th Anniversary**, Local and Regional Action No:8, Strasbourg 2006, pp. 47-50.

authorities in Member States to have a say in the formulation and implementation of the Union's policies.[7]

In addition to the financial incentives provided to the Member States in the fields like environmental protection, youth, culture, health, education, scientific research, technological progress, energy and transportation, efforts are being made to reduce regional disparities between regions and the Member State. The main principles of the European local governance include the participation, closeness to the citizens, transparency, accountability, responsiveness, efficiency and autonomy. Numerous legal instruments of the Council of Europe complement the main features of the European Union's policy of local and regional democracy. The Convention on the Participation of Foreigners at Public Life and the Framework Convention on Transfrontier Cooperation may be particularly mentioned in this connection in addition to the European Charter of Local Self-Government. The latter has been ratified by Turkey in 2000 and thus lifted indirectly her abstentions put on the Paragraphs 2 and 3 of the Article 10 of the European Charter of Local Self-Government.[8]

Assuming that *the acquis communautaire* is composed of primary (rules emanating from the Treaties) and secondary (rules originating from decision of the organs of the Union) legal instruments of the European Union and is characterised fundamentally by the principles of the Charter, one can make an attempt, within the framework of this paper, to look at the system of territorial governance in Turkey briefly and

7    Ruşen Keleş, **Avrupa'nın Bütünleşmesi ve Yerel Yönetimler (European Integration and Local Authorities)**, Municipal Association of Turkey and Konrad Adenauer Foundation, Ankara, 1999, pp. 44-46.

8    Ayşegül Mengi, "Avrupa Birliği Uyum Sürecinde Yerel Yönetimlerle İlgili Düzenlemeler" (Revisions concerning Local Authorities during the Process of Adaptation into the European Union), in **Ruşen Keleş'e Armağan (Essays in Honour of Ruşen Keleş)**, (in press, Vol.3), Ankara, İmge.

to try to assess the extent to which recent reforms have contributed to the final goal of alignment. In doing this term of governance will be preferred to that of government. Because, only a system of governance with distinct patterns of institutions, actors and processes could provide a suitable framework of analysis which is wider than the institutional structures of government.[9]

## Features of Local Government System in Turkey

All constitutions adopted since the beginning of the establishment of the Turkish Republic defined Turkey as a politically unitary state. Basic provisions concerning territorial governments, which are actually in force, are laid down by the Constitution of 1982. There basic provisions of the Constitution have to be mentioned in this respect. The first is the Article 123 of the Constitution which stipulates that the administration is an integrated whole, and the formation and functions of the administration are based on two complementary principles, namely, centralization and decentralisation. The second is the Article 126 which regulates the organisation of the central government and the structure of its field organization. National territory is divided into provinces (departments) on the basis of geographical situation, economic conditions and public service requirements. There are 81 provinces at present. The provinces are further divided into lower units of administrative districts. The provinces are governed on the basis of the principle of deconcentration. Central administrative authorities comprising more than one province may be established in order to ensure efficiency and coordination in

9   John Loughlin, **Sub-National Democracy in the European Union: Challenges and Opportunities**, Oxford University Press, New York, 2001, P.20; and Peter John, Local Governance in Western Europe, Sage, London, 2001, pp. 8-14.

the provision of public services. The functions and powers of such organizations are regulated by law. For example, the Administration of Southeast Anatolian Regional Development Project comprising nine provinces had been established in 1989 as a deconcentrated legal entity, in other words, as a field organization of the central government at regional level.

The third Article, namely the Article 127, is exclusively concerned with local authorities. It requires that the duties and powers of local authorities be regulated by law in accordance with the principle of decentralization. It is clear that the power sharing between the State and local authorities will not be subject to arbitrary will of the Legislative Assembly, but it will be shaped in conformity with the principle of decentralisation. It has to be underlined that the definition of the principle of decentralisation can not be found in the text to of the Constitution. However, the wording of the Article 127 concerning the powers and competencies of local authorities might be helpful in that respect. According to the respective sentence, "local authorities are public corporate entities established to meet *the common local needs* of the inhabitants of provinces, municipalities and the villages"[10]. The Constitution left to the Legislative Assembly to determine what are *the common local needs*. In defining the concept of local public service corresponding to common local needs and in interpreting that of decentralization, the Parliament is to take into consideration such features as historical development, political and administrative needs and realities of the country, developments in the world as well as the requirements of being a candidate for the full membership of the European Union.

---

10   The provincial local governments, municipalities and the villages are three constitutionally recognised types of local authorities in Turkey. For futher details see: Ruşen Keleş, **Yerinden Yönetim ve Siyaset (Local Government and Politics)**, Cem Publishers, İstanbul, 2006 (5th ed.).

Local authorities in Turkey are simply administrative entities in charge of carrying out public services conferred upon them by their respective legislation. Because the general system of local government in Turkey is not *political* decentralization, but *administrative* decentralistion. Despite the fact that recent developments in the theory and practice of local government blurred this distinction to a certain extent, no provision in the Constitution allows territorial authorities to be regarded as law making entities sharing the national sovereignty with the State.[11] Legislations concerning the competencies of central and local governments are the laws on Provincial Local Administrations, Municipalities and Village Administrations, respectively. All these laws, except the one on the village administrations, have been renewed during the 2004-2005 period, as a part of the pre-conditions demanded by the European Union in the negotiation process.

Local councils are composed of members elected directly by people every five years, Executive bodies of local authorities do not need to be elected, whereas the mayors and the village headmen are elected directly by the residents of cities and villages, respectively. On the other hand, the governor as the executive organ of the provincial local administration, who is at the same time the representative of the State in the province, is a public servant appointed by the central government.

Historically, political and administrative system of Turkey does not recognize broad powers and extensive autonomy to territorial authorities. As a result of the unitary character of the State set by the Constitution, the central government has

11   Ruşen Keleş, "Yerel Yönetimlerde Yeniden Yapılanma: Avrupa ve Türkiye" (Restructuring in Local Governance: Europe and Turkey), Municipal Association of Turkey and Konrad Adenauer Foundation, **Uluslararası Seminer: Yerel Yönetimlerde Yeniden Yapılanma, (International Seminar: Restructuring in Local Governance)**, Ankara, 1996, pp. 23-35.

the power to exercise a strict control and supervision over local authorities in the following circumstances:

**a)** to ensure the performance of local services in conformity with the principle of the integral unity of Administration,

**b)** to secure uniformity of the public services over the national territory,

**c)** to safeguard the public interest, and

**d)** to meet the local needs in an appropriate manner.

As it is seen from these expressions in the Constitution (Art. 127), central supervision is rather broad and may also include the *expediency* of the acts and decisions of local councils, depending upon the meaning to be attributed to the concept of *public interest*. There is no indication in the Constitution that central control and supervision will be confined to *legality control.*

The Constitution allows local authorities to form unions among themselves to perform certain public services given to them by their specific legislation more efficiently. Although Turkey has reservations on the Paragraphs 2 and 3 of the Article 10 of the European Charter of Local Self-Government, concerning the right of local authorities to associate, both the Constitution and the respective legislation do not possess any obstacle to either association or cooperation. However, in order to form unions or associations, local authorities are required to get the permission of the Council of Ministers. Local authorities are entitled to be provided with financial resources commensurate with their functions. An opportunity exists for the cities with a population exceeding 750.000 to establish a metropolitan municipality, a two-tier administrative structure, which is expected to ensure a better participation and more an efficient performance of metropolitan-wide public services.

In principle, the procedures dealing with objections to the acquisition by elected organs of local authorities of their status as an organ, and their loss of such status, must be resolved by the judiciary. However, one of the most problematic provisions of the Constitution is an exceptional rule to this principle that allows the Minister of the Interior to remove from office those elected organs of local authorities or their members against whom an investigation or prosecution has been initiated on the grounds of offences related to their duties, pending judgement. A new Law on Municipalities of 2005 (No: 5393) limited the time period in which such organs will remain suspended by requiring that such decisions of the Interior Minister will be reviewed every two months (Art. 47). If continued suspension from office is not considered to be in *the public interest*, the measure shall be lifted.

## Expectations of the European Institutions

### a) Progress Reports

Expectations of the European Union from Turkey can be found under the cub-titles as the Regional Policy and the Coordination of Structural Instruments or the Reform in Public Administration. The basic documents in which such expectations are expressed can be found are the Progress Reports and the Pre-Accession Partnership Document. Since 1998, the European Commission has prepared 8 progress reports. No particular demands existed in the first three.[12] The 2000 Progress Report drew the attention to the fact that there was no considerable change in the traditional local government structure where the State had a powerful control and

---

12   Ayşegül Mengi," Avrupa Birliği'nde Uyum Sürecinde Yerel Yönetimlerle İlgili Düzenlemeler", (Revisions of Local Authorities during the Process of Alignment), **Ruşen Keleş'e Armağan (Essays in Honour of Ruşen Keleş)**, (Volume 3, in Press, İmge Publishers).

supervision over local authorities. It was also pointed out that new draft bills aiming at more decentralisation had not been enacted yet. The 2002 Progress Report emphasized the need to strengthen the governing capacity of the administration at all levels and to create new structures as appropriate. The 2003 Report reiterated the need to establish a decentralized administrative structure by drawing the attention to the fact that decentralisation was also among the priorities of the donor institutions such as the World Bank and IMF.

The Progress Report of 2004, for the first time, focused the attention on specific draft bills and the laws on local government. It referred to the fact that only the Law on Metropolitan Municipalities had been put into force, while the Laws on Basic Principles of Public Administration, Municipalities, Provincial Local Administrations had been vetoed by the President of the Republic and they were sent bant to the Parliament. The need is also stressed for the re-enactment of all these laws. According to the qualitative statements of the authors of this Progress Report, the main goal of the reform in Public Administration was to realize the transformation of a "centralized", "hierarchical" and "inflexible" administrative structure into a "decentralised", "transparent" and "responsive" one. It is argued that the success of reform efforts would also contribute to the development of administrative culture of Turkey and thus to the encouragement of Turkey's accession into the Union.

The 2005 Progress Report while praising the putting into force of the basic legislation on decentralisation argues that the efforts of reform in Public Administration were not successfully concluded. Positive contributions of the new legislation are exemplified by the formation of city councils and general (provincial) councils comprising the representatives of civil society organizations to strengthen participatory and advisory processes, in addition to such innovations as strategic planning, emergency planning, debt and borrowing limits, performance budgeting, annual performance reporting and accounting systems. Although the need to enact a law on Unions of Local Authorities was underlined in the 2005 Progress Report, that law (No:5355) was enacted at the beginning of 2006.

Finally, the 2006 Progress Report drew attention once again that "No progress has been made in adopting the Framework Law on Public Administration, which was vetoed by the President in 2004. As a result, the devolution of central government powers to local administrations was hampered. Moreover, fiscal decentralization has not been achieved. No progress has been made to establish City Councils. The Law on Associations of Local Governments was amended in January 2006. This allows villages, municipalities and budgets of the joint projects became exempt from the Court of Accounts audit. This is not in line with the principles of external audit." Attention was drawn to the need for further efforts in the area of decentralisation without mentioning the details.

### b) Accession Partnership Document

This road map is prepared to indicate the concrete steps to be taken and legislative reforms to be realised during the process from candidacy to membership. Partnership Document for Turkey was adopted in 2001 which also reflects the expectations and demands of the Union from Turkey. It possesses several goals such as privatization of public economic enterprises, furtherance of the market economy, facilitating direct foreign investment which all have the potential of affecting local authorities not directly but indirectly. Accordingly, the European Council, underlined the need to restructure the administrative machinery of the candidate countries in the medium-term with a view to put the policies of the European Union into practice. Other suggestions in the Partnership Document include lifting all obstacles before foreign investments, acquiring real estate by foreign nationals and to strengthen the administrative structure as a tool to reduce inequalities between regions. Because of its likely contribution to the economic development of frontier regions, transboundary cooperation between the candidate states is recommended.[13]

## c) European Charter of Local Self-Government

Although it is a Council of Europe convention, The Charter constitutes at the same time the basis of the policy of local democracy of the European Union. Turkey has ratified the European Charter of Local Self Government in 1991 by the Law No: 3273. The date of its entering into force is 3 October 1992. However, it has reservations put on some of the provisions of the Charter. There of these abstentions are concerned with financial issues:

(1) A sufficiently diversified and buoyant financial system to enable local authorities to keep pace as far practically possible with the real evolution of the cost of carrying out their tasks (Art. 9, Par. 4). (2) The right to be consulted on the way in which redistributed resources are to be allocated to them (Art. 9, Par. 6). (3) The principle that, grants to local authorities shall not be earmarked to the financing of specific projects as far as possible. Also the condition that provision of grants shall not remove the basic freedom of local authorities to exercise policy discretion within their own jurisdiction (Art. 9, Par. 7).

13  Ayşegül Mengi," Avrupa Birliği'nde Uyum Sürecinde Yerel Yönetimlerle İlgili Düzenlemeler", (Revisions of Local Authorities during the Process of Alignment), **Ruşen Keleş'e Armağan (Essays in Honour of Ruşen Keleş)**, op. cit.

Some other reservations of Turkey include the powers of local authorities to determine their own internal administrative structures (Art. 6, Par. 1), their right to be consulted in the planning and decision-making processes for all matters which concern them directly (Art. 4, Par. 6), functions and activities which are deemed incompatible with the holding of local elective office (Art., Par. 3), proportionality of the administrative supervision over local authorities with the importance of the interests to be protected (Art. 8, Par. 3), the right of local authorities to belong to a domestic or to an international association for the protection and promotion of their common interests (Art. 10, Par. 2), their right to cooperate with their counterparts in other countries (Art. 10, Par. 3), and finally the right to recourse to a judicial remedy for the legal protection of their rights and freedoms (Art. 11).

The European Union asks Turkey to implement the articles of the Charter which it did not have a reservation and to revise its position vis a vis the articles over which Turkey has put an abstention. It is obvious that most of the articles of the Charter on which an abstention was put may easily be subject to ratification because the rights and freedoms that they aim to provide are already extensively used at present by Turkish local governments.

In the last Recommendation of the Council of Europe (No: 176, 2005) on Local and Regional Democracy in Turkey (adopted in the Autumn Session (12) of the Congress, 8-9 November 2005), the Congress acknowledged that "there have been clear signs of a commitment to a substantial institutional Change showed by the Turkish Government as regards modernisation of local as well as provincial government and that the Turkish Government has embarked upon substantial reforming programme of legislative change. However, the programme is still in the course of implementation and a full assessment of its effect cannot yet be made. It should also be noted that devolution reform is not unanimously received in all political circles in Turkey. Some argue that devolution may have the potential of distorting the unity and the integrity of the State as well as consistency and complementarity of public services". The basic criticisms centered around "the continuing dominance of the Provincial Governors, the restricted functions of smaller municipalities and the weaknesses of village administrations". One general observation of the Congress was that "many functions which might reasonably be expected to be exercisable by local authorities are, in practice, being privatized". Therefore, it recommended that "those services which might reasonably be expected to be delivered by local authorities, should be delivered by them".

Easing the system of State tutelage over local authorities and accelerating the process of putting a new law on local finance that might put an end to the heavy dependence of subnational units on the State are among the recommendations of the Congress. Another significant point underlined by the Congress recommendation No: 176 has something to do with the status of provinces. It recommended that "further thinking should be given to greater decentralisation at provincial level, including *gradual establishment of politically significant provinces* able to manage a substantial share of public affairs with their own capacities". This final statement ignores the fact that local authorities in Turkey, including the provincial local administrations, are merely sub-national entities functioning in accordance with the principle of administrative decentralisation. As such they are *politically significant only* in that sense and therefore entitled to enjoy only a certain degree of autonomy recognised to them by the European Charter of Local Self-Government.

## d) Five-Year Development Plans

7th Five Year Development Plan covers a period (1996-2000) where the efforts of alignment with the European Union's acquis were intensified mostly. That is the reason why this Plan recommended a revision of the sharing of competencies between the State and local authorities in parallel to the increasing popularity of the principle of subsidiarity among the policies of the Union. Thus, a recommendation was made in order to prepare a framework law for a redivision of public responsibilities and financial resources between different levels of authority. The main laws to be amended or renewed in the direction of forming an administratively and financially autonomous local government are the followings: The Village Law (442), The Law on Municipalities (1580), The Law on Metropolitan Municipalities (3030), The Law on Provincial Local Administrations (3360), The Law on Local Elections (2972), The Law on Local Finance (2464), The Law on Local Shares from the National Budget (2380), The Law on Real Estate Tax (1319), The Law on Provincial Administration (5442), The Law on Urban Development (3104) and The Law on the Bank of Local Authorities (4759).

There are other recommendations in the 7th Plan such as the creation of a new Ministry to be in charge of coordinating administrative, financial and legal initiatives of local authorities in the fields of such public services as planning, infrastructure, transportation, housing. Easing the financial dependence of local governments on central government, leaving local resources to local authorities, and ensuring that they can function with their own resources are the other suggestions laid down in the Plan.

The 8th Five Year Development Plan (2001-2005) draws the attention to the impact of globalization on decentralisation and stresses the need to strengthen their institutional set up, administrative powers and financial resources. An emphasis is also put on developing local authorities in such a way as to strike a balance between their interests and the national interests. Recommendations in the previous Plan are repeated in the 8th Development Plan together with the need for a new legislation for taxing incremental values deriving from real properties and encouraging the participation of people in decision-making at sub-national levels.[14]

In the 9th Development Plan (2007-2013), almost the same themes as discussed in the previous Plan are dealt with such as the modernization of power sharing between different tiers of authority, subsidiarity, control and supervision of local authorities by the State, encouragement of new participatory techniques and the emphasis on the legality control instead of expediency control.

### e) National Programme

A National Programme laying down the priorities of accession partnership with the European Union has been prepared, adopted by the Council of Ministers and submitted to the European Commission in March 2001. The revised Accession Partnership Document has been published by the Commission in March 25, 2003 taking into consideration the detailed priorities of the National Programme. Not a separate sub-title exists in the latter, but under the title of "Strengthening Governance in the Public Sector" issues of local democracy with high priority are assessed together with the Framework Law on Public Administration in the revised National Programme. The need for a radical restructuring in the public sector, in bureaucracy and in understanding of the administration is underlined. The revised National Programme described the basic goal of the public administration reform as

14   Ayşegül Mengi, op. cit.

the increase of efficiency and further democratization. Provision of the public services in a manner which is both efficient, transparent and participatory is among the fundamental objectives of the reform. Acceleration of the privatization process, easing and encouragement of direct foreign investments and lifting all administrative and bureaucratic obstacles before such goals are also among the preferences of the National Programme.

The National Programme suggests that instead of enumerating the powers and responsibilities of local authorities one by one, a better method is to adopt the principle of *"general competence"* by which the competencies of the central government can be determined and all the remaining functions and services may be left to local authorities. It is essential that local authorities, in accordance with the principles and standards set by the State and with the regional plans, have to take their own decisions, create their own resources, carry out their own projects and become modern and accountable administrative entities.

## Reforms of Local Government

The Parliament enacted a number of laws during the last several years, especially between 2003 and 2005.

(a) The first law (No: 5227, dated 15 July 2004) laid down the basic principles to restructure public administration in general. According to these principles, administration must function in conformity with such rules as participation, transparency, accountability, and be respectful for human rights and liberties. The principle of *subsidiarity* in the performance of public services has also been incorporated in the law, in such a way that powers, competencies and duties be performed by those administrative authorities that are closest to the citizens. The powers and competencies of the central government have been specifically enumerated such as justice, defence, security, information, foreign affairs, public finance, foreign trade, treasury, customs, national economic, social and physical planning, national education, religious public services, social security, land registry, population, pious foundations, civil defence and disaster management and the public services which need to be carried out on a regional basis. On the other hand, all other *(residual)* public services of local nature, and powers and duties concerning them are left to local authorities.

Local authorities are required to carry out their duties in accordance with the principles of the integral unity of administration, of legal procedures set by laws, the targets and principles of economic and social development plans and the objective performance criteria. Central government is *prohibited* from setting up organisations, and making expenses for those duties and competencies falling within the sphere of responsibilities of local authorities. Local authorities are to be provided with financial resources commensurate with their competencies. They have the option to demand these public services be performed by the central government agencies, the private sector, the unions of local authorities, and the universities.

Although the law allows the formation of regional offices of the ministries in accordance with the principle of deconcentration, ministries which are organised on the basis of the provinces, an ombudsman will also be elected by the qualified majority of the members of the General Council. This law abolish the former system of control and inspection in public administration, and replaced it by a new system, a more flexible one, which will exercise both internal and external auditing powers, the latter to be used by the Higher Court of Accounts.

This law has been vetoed by the President in August 2004. The President argued that the unitary state system requires a centralised legal structure, and allows the organization and functioning of local authorities only under the control and supervision of the State. According to his view, decentralisation may have the potential to distort the integral unity of the State and he consistency and complementarity of public services. The Article 127 of the Constitution allows both the principles of legality and expediency control over local authorities by the State.

The President maintained that what this law did was to regard local authorities as *principal* organisations and the central government as *secondary (subsidiary)*. This was unacceptable.[15] Such an understanding according to him, would cause weakening of the State itself, and would potentially replace the unitary state system by rendering the traditional and constitutional tutelage function of the central government over the territorial authorities ineffective. Local authorities are organised on the basis of a geographically limited area, and also within limited functional jurisdictions, contrarily to what has been actually enacted by the Parliament.

There were other arguments used in the veto reasons. But the Parliament did not take action so far on its original text.

**(b)** The second law (No: 5215, dated 9 July 2004) is the Law on Municipalities which passed during July 2004. It replaced the former law dated back to 1930. The new law

---

15    Gerard Marcou did not see the principle of subsidiarity neither pertinent nor compatible with the French legal tradition : "Prencipe de Subsidiarité, Constitution Française et Décentralisation", Jean-Claude Nemery et Serge Wachter, **Entre l' Europe et La Décentralisation**, DATAR, Ed. de l'Aube, Paris, 1993, p. 88. However one could assume that this objection is no longer valid since the amandement realised in the Constitution of France during 2003; Jean-Luc Boueuf, **Decentralisation et experimentations locales**, La Documentation Francaise, No: 895, Paris, Decembre 2003.

raised the minimum level of population required of a settlement which intends to acquire the status of a municipality from 2.000 to 5. 000. Basic principles of public administration defined in the above-mentioned law, as they affect the sharing of competencies between the central government and local authorities, are repeated in the Law on Municipalities. The municipal council is composed of members elected by the inhabitants of the community for a four-year term as before. The standing committee will be composed of both elected and appointed members, but the number of the appointed members of the standing committee will be equal to the number of elected ones. The new law introduced new concepts such as the strategic and performance plans. The decision to suspend the mayors in case of an offence relating to the performance of their duties will be reconsidered every two months, and it will be lifted if it can not be justified on the ground of public interest. Municipalities will be free to organise their internal administrative structures in accordance with the norms established by the Council of Ministers. In each municipality there will be standardized units of service, such as secretarial services, financial affairs, public works and the municipal police. The creation of other needed administrative units will be subject to the decision of municipal council.

This law was vetoed by the President in July 2004 on the grounds that the transfer of so many powers by the State to municipalities was incompatible with the Constitution. He insisted that the Constitution visualizes local authorities *as secondary legal entities with limited functions, functioning within a limited territorial jurisdiction,* while the central government is regarded as the *primary legal authority.* Within this context, he argued that public services to be carried out by local authorities should have been clearly mentioned one by one in the law. Yet, the fact that in present formulation, they are described in *general, abstract and ambiguous manners,* would cause imbalances in the performance of these services at local and regional levels. The same law was passed without any change by the Parliament in July 2005 (Law No: 5393). It has been taken to the Constitutional Court by the President on the ground that its provision regarding the allocation of all competencies that are not left to the central government will be carried out by municipalities is unconstitutional.

(c) The third is the Law on the Provincial Local Administration (Law 5197; dated June 24 2004) The most important change realised by this law is to put an end to the capacity of the centrally appointed governor to serve as the president of the General Council, the deliberative organ of the Provincial Local Administration. From now on, the General Council will be presided by its own president to be elected by itself from among its own members. As different from the previous legislation, the new law changed the composition of the Provincial Standing Committee in such a way that an additional two members, who are appointed civil servants, will also be serving in the Committee.

This law was also vetoed by the President on both general and technical grounds as expressed with respect to the veto reasons concerning the Framework Law on the General Principles of Public Administration and the Law on Municipalities. He argued that the new General Councils will almost be independent rather than autonomous institutions, and thus they would contribute to further weakening of the State. This was a potential threat to the unitary character of the State. Even if it is not seen clearly in the text of the new laws, he believed that such radical changes in administration might facilitate the steps towards a state model which will be no longer a unitary state. The weakening of the position of the governor as the representative of the State in the province is one of its indicators. In addition, referring to the Article 14, Par. 2 of the law, the President stressed that national education can not be left to Provincial Local Administrations. Such a formulation would be in contradiction with the principle of uniformity in national education, integral unity of the nation, democracy, secularism, etc.

Upon insistence of the Parliament in its original text with some minor changes, a new law was enacted in 2004 (No: 5203). Several provisions of the new law have been taken to the Constitutional Court by the President.

(d) The fourth law is the Law on Metropolitan Municipalities (Law No: 5216, dated 10 July 2004). This is the only law that was not vetoed by the President. This law replaced the former one of 1984 (Law No: 3030) and realised several changes needed to overcome the implementation problems faced by the practitioners. In order to establish a metropolitan municipality, at least three district municipalities should exist within the boundaries of metropolitan area. And the total population should not be less than 750.000. Surrounding smaller municipalities and villages may be annexed to the metropolitan municipality in order to increase efficiency in the performance of public services by the decision of the Council of Ministers. No referendum is provided in such cases. There is not much change in the competencies of metropolitan municipalities as compared with the previous law except in master planning where the final authority will lie with the upper-level municipality instead of district municipalities. In other words, decisions of the upper-level municipality will be binding for district municipalities for a uniform and effective implementation of city master plans.

The composition of the Standing Committee was changed in such a way that the number of civil servants was reduced to five, which is equal to the number of the councilors to be elected by the city council from among its own members. The new law prohibits the mayors of metropolitan municipalities from active work in the political parties to which they belong.

As different from other new laws on reforming local authorities which do not possess any provision with respect to financial resources, the Law on Metropolitan Municipalities has a section on the matter. The shares out of the national budget and a special annual share out of all taxes collected within the municipal boundaries will be the main financial resources in addition to their own resources. There will be no longer an approval power of the governor over the budgets of metropolitan municipalities.

(e) The Parliament passed a Law on the Unions of Local Authorities (No: 5355, dated May 2005), allowing territorial governments to co-operate in order to realise projects of common interest. Another important bill regarding local revenues is in the Parliamentary committees.

## Brief Assessment

The western European countries which started the competition for the democratization goal much earlier than Turkey have realised outstanding achievements in local democracy. The nations joined that competition much later have a change to examine the successes and the factors underlying their successes and not to repeat their mistakes. There are of course important lessons to be taken from the experiences witnessed by the western European countries in the field of local democracy. The basic principles of local democracy developed during the last several decades within the Council of Europe and the European Union seem to be extremely important in this respect. The European Charter of Local Self-Government possesses the fundamental guide-lines. In addition, following observations may serve as useful experiments:[16]

1) An increasing number of states are determined to reduce the number of their local authorities. They try to encourage smaller communes to unite among themselves and form larger units.

2) The principle of subsidiarity is being largely accepted and put into practice. As a result, central authorities are becoming more relaxed as they transfer some of their competencies and responsibilities to lower-level units.

3) Although there are shortcomings in providing local authorities financial resources commensurate with their functions, the number of taxes which local authorities can use independently and fix their rate themselves increase gradually. To have independent revenue sources can be regarded as a symbol of genuine local autonomy.

4) Central government is gradually abandoning its functions as a higher-level authority exercising control and supervision over local authorities, but it is becoming a cooperating institution guiding and encouraging them.

5) Supervisory powers of the central authorities are being transformed to a kind of control which consists of checking the conformity of the action or decision with the law and the Constitution. Expediency control is being gradually abandoned. Similarly *ex post* supervision is gradually replacing *ex ante* control and supervision. All kinds of supervisory action is becoming subject to judicial control.

6) In some countries with similar administrative organisation as in Turkey, provincial governors are no longer the chief executive of the provincial local administration. This

---

16   Ruşen Keleş, "Globalization and Local Autonomy", **Journal of Behavioral and Social Sciences,** 1997 No: 2, pp. 129-144, Research Institute of the Social Sciences, Tokai University.

position is held by the president of the general council, elected from among its own members. However, it should not be forgotten that particular conditions, historical features and political realities of each country have to be taken in consideration in deciding such matters.[17]

7) In order to prevent the local autonomy being transformed into a kind of irresponsibility and corruption, necessary safeguards, including self-control, responsiveness, accountability and transparency are being taken into effect in an effective and democratic way.

8) New status are being given to some geographical regions, varying between administrative decentralisation and political decentralisation, taking into account the characteristics of socio-cultural and economic structures and on the condition of providing some sort of guarantee by the constitutions for national unity and territorial integrity. However, one should also keep in mind that such goodwill initiatives may face disappointments if and when "the parties seeking the independence of their territories from the nation-state use the European project to advance their cause", as rightly pointed out by Peter John.[18]

9) In order to make the local people benefit fully from the public services, administrative mechanisms aimed at coordinating the services of the State at local and regional levels, are being developed.

10) Participation channels are being kept wide-open in order to enable the people to take part more effectively and more intensively in decision-making at the local level.

---

17  Antony Kuklinski, "Towards a New Spatial Order in Europe", **European Spatial Research Policy**, 1/1, 1994, pp. 73-75; and Ruşen Keleş, **Fransa'da ve İspanya'da Yerinden Yönetim (Decentralisation in France and Spain)**, Municipal Association of Turkey and Konrad Adenauer Foundation, Ankara, 1994.

18  Peter John, Local Governance in Western Europe, Sage, London, 2001, p. 115.

In the light of the European experiences and the universal principles of local democracy, we can make an effort to look once again at the reform movements of Turkey to promote local democracy.

1) It is obvious that in the preparation of the reform legislation due regard has been given to the provisions of the European Charter of Local Self-Government. Article 4, Par.3, Article 3, Par. I and 2, Article 4, Par.4, Article 8, and Article 10 must be particularly mentioned in this respect. However, it must be admitted that a radical change in the institutional structure of a nation which evolved over centuries can not be realized promptly.

2) As emphasised among the veto reasons of the President of the Republic, The Constitution of Turkey does not seem suitable for regarding the central government as secondary, and territorial authorities as primary. Both from the point of view of geographical scope and from a functional angle, local authorities are defined in the Constitution as legal entities with limited jurisdictions.

3) Within this framework, it is argued that the principle of subsidiarity is in contradiction with the formulation in the Article 127 of the Constitution. Because, the subsidiarity requires the enumeration of the competencies of the state first, and then leaves all residual functions to local authorities. The President of the Republic did not take the provision regarding the principle of subsidiarity to the Constitutional Court, because no judicial control by the Constitutional Court of the international conventions ratified in an appropriate manner is possible. On the other hand, the government did not put an abstention on this principle in ratifying the Charter.

4) It is argued that the principle of subsidiarity is peculiar to federal states. I believe that this is not correct. The fact that federal states to adopt and implement the principle

of subsidiarity does not require that it must be regarded as a principle in the monopoly of federal states. 42 out of 46 member states of the Council of Europe have unitary state systems and a great majority of them did not hesitate to ratify this principle of the Charter. We must remember that the number of the federal states among 25 members of the European Union is no more than 3.

5) Another argument advanced in the veto reasons of the reform laws by the Presidency is that through these laws government paves the way to a transition from the unitary state system to federalism consciously or unconsciously. Fears have also been expressed in the press that the state was going to be fragmented or disintegrated through taking steps in this direction. I believe that unless the legislative power of the nation state is shared with regional or other sub-national decision-making bodies with legislative mandate, it would be meaningless to talk about a full transition to the federal system.[19] The Turkish Constitution regulates local authorities as public corporations as a part of the Administration carrying out certain executive functions concerning public services of local nature. Furthermore, neither the legislation of the European Union nor the European Charter of Local Self-Government possess any provision that aims to dictate a requirement to the member states to change their state system as a precondition for the membership. The latter leaves a certain flexibility to the member states of the Council of Europe in most of its provisions as in the cases of such expressions as "preferably", "where practicable", "generally ", "within the limits of law", "as practically possible", "as are enshrined in the constitution or domestic legislation".

19   François Saint-Ouen, **Le Fédéralisme**, Infolio, Gollion, 2005; François Vergniolle de Chantal, **Federalisme et Antifederalisme,** Presses Universitaires de France, Paris 2005.

6) Local government reform laws lifted off the traditional system of control, auditing and inspection with a view to ensure efficiency in public administration. Weakening of the control system in public administration has the potential to encourage corruption indirectly, and it can not be defended on any ground.

7) Reform laws weakened also the position of the provincial governors as representatives of the State. The chance of the governor for success in his office will depend to a large extent on his close collaboration with the president of the general council, who is actually a politician. This regulation which might seem as a democratic arrangement at first glance may turn out to be a source of a deep conflict resulting in unsurmountable difficulties in reconciling local interests with the general interest.

8) The transfer of great many competencies to local authorities may result in leaving most of these newly transferred public services unmet. Because very few of the 3300 municipalities are equipped to be able to receive and carry out these services satisfactorily.

9) It has been argued justifiably that these reforms aimed at strengthening the liberal system in the country instead of local authorities. As mentioned earlier, the laws possess provisions prohibiting even the State from initiating and operating economic enterprises. This extremist position makes one think that the gap to be created as a result of the large scale transfer of State functions to local authorities will be filled out by private firms instead of territorial authorities themselves.

10) Attempts to reform local democratic institutions have also been met with reaction by those who do not really trust in the value of local democracy at all. They believe that local authorities do not have much to contribute to the progress of democracy. Instead, they are used as instruments to share

the profits they create with the followers of political parties controlling them. They forget that in that respect there is not much difference between them and central authorities, because all of them are kept in power by almost the same social and political forces.

11) A final point with regard to the assessment of the reforms in local democracy is that there are two different movements in Turkey whose interests coincide in supporting externally backed democratization at local level or the promotion of local autonomy. They find it in their favor to enjoy the tolerance for local autonomy which is historically a common value in western Europe and highly respected within the European institutions. The first group includes the representatives of separatist groups whose basic aims are far from supporting democratic institutions in the country. They are striving for the establishment of a separate state in the Southeast of Turkey or the replacement of the unitary Republic by a federal state. On the other hand, a second group finds it in its favor to back the progress of local democracy simply to challenge the secular character of the Republic and other constitutional features of the State more easily. It seems obvious that systematic weaking of the position of governors as the representatives of the State in the field and an exaggerated transfer of powers to sub-national territories have increased these justified fears for the future.

## Short Bibliograph

- BOEUF, Jean-Luc, **Decentralisation et experimentations locales**, La Documentation Francaise, No: 895, Paris, Decembre 2003.
- CLRAE, **The European Charter of Local Self-Government: 20 th Anniversary, Proceedings**, Lisbon, 8 July 2005.
- Committee of the Regions, **Regional and Local Government in the European Union: Responsibilities and Resources**, Luxembourg, 2001.

- De CHANTAL, Françoiş Verniolle, **Fédéralisme et Antifédéralisme**, Presses Universitaires de Franca, Paris, 2005.

- DELCAMP, Alain, (Dir.), **Les collectives décentralisées de l'Union européenne**, La Documentation Française, Paris, 1994.

- DELCAMP, Alain, "Les garanties de la subsidiarites et de l'autonomie regionale et locale dans les conventions du Conseil de l'Europe", Seminaire Internationale: Les garanties en matière de subsidiarité et de l'autonomie locale et régionale en Europe, Pérouse (Italy), 6 Octobre 2006.

- DUHAMEL, Olivier, **La Constitution européenne**, Armand Colin, Paris, 2003.

- JOHN, Peter, **Local Governance in Western Europe**, Sage, London, 2001.

- KELEŞ, Ruşen, **Yerinden Yönetim ve Siyaset (Local Government and Politics)**, Cem Publishers, İstanbul, 2006 (5th ed.).

- KELEŞ, Ruşen, **Avrupa'nın Bütünleşmesi ve Yerel Yönetimler (European Integration and Local Authorities)**, Municipal Association of Turkey and Konrad Adenauer Foundation, Ankara, 1999.

- KELEŞ, Ruşen, **Fransa'da ve İspanya'da Yerinden Yönetim (Decentralisation in France and Spain)**, Municipal Association of Turkey and Konrad Adenauer Foundation, Ankara, 1994.

- KELEŞ, Ruşen, "Yerel Yönetimlerde Yeniden Yapılanma: Avrupa ve Türkiye" (Restructuring in Local Governance: Europe and Turkey), in **Yerel Yönetimlerde Yeniden Yapılanma : Avrupa ve Türkiye (International Seminar on Restructuring of Local Authorities)**, Municipal Association of Turkey and Konrad Adenauer Foundation, Ankara, 1996, pp. 23-35.

- KELEŞ, Ruşen, "Globalization and Local Autonomy", **Journal of Behavioral and Social Sciences**, 1997 No: 2, pp. 129-144, Research Institute of the Social Sciences, Tokai University, Japan.

- KELEŞ, Ruşen, "Avrupa Birliği Ülkelerinde Yerel Yönetimlerin Görevleri ve Yetkileri" (Duties and Competencies of Local Authorities in the Member States of the European Union), Konrad Adenauer Stiftung, **Avrupa Birliği ve Yerel Yönetimler (European Union and Local Authorities)**, Ankara, 2006, pp. 27-44.

- KUKLİNSKİ, Antony, "Towards a New Spatial Order in Europe", **European Spatial Research Policy**, 1/1, 1994, pp.

- LOUGHLİN, John, **Sub-National Democracy in the European Union: Challenges and Opportunities**, Oxford University Press, New York, 2001.

- MARCOU, Gerard, "Prencipe de Subsidiarité, Constitution Française et décentralisation", Jean-Claude Nemery et Serge Wachter (dir.), **Entre l' Europe et La Décentralisation**, DATAR, Ed. de l'Aube, Paris, 1993, pp. 85-92.

- MENGI, Ayşegül, "Avrupa Birliği Uyum Sürecinde Yerel Yönetimlerle İlgili Düzenlemeler" (Revisions concerning Local Authorities during the Process of Adaptation into the European Union), in **Ruşen Keleş'e Armağan (C. 3) (Essays in Honour of Ruşen Keleş), (Vol.3)**, (in press), Ankara, İmge.

- MERLONI, Francesco, "Prospects for Strengthening the Role of the European Charter of Local Self-Government", The Congress of Local and Regional Authorities, **The European Charter of Local Self-Government : 20th Anniversary**, Local and Regional ACTION No:8, 6 September 2006, Peugia, Italy.

- RUPNİK, Jacgues, Le dechirement des nation, Ed. Seuil, Paris, 1995.

- SAINT-OUEN, François **Le Fédéralisme**, Infolio, Gollion, 2005.

# Legal Opinion Regarding the Case of Mr. Philippe Mettens, The Mayor of Flobecq, And The President of The Federal Public Service in Charge of The Scientific Policy

## I. The Facts

1. Mr. Philippe Mettens is elected Mayor (Bourgmester) of Flobecq, a town of nearly 3.500 inhabitants, situated in the Wallon Region of the Federal State of Belgium. He serves as the mayor of the town for the last 12 years (since 2001). His last reelection to the same post has taken place in 2011.

2. Mr. Mettens holds, at the same time, an appointed post at the federal level which he executes since 2003. He is the President of a federal committee which is in charge of programming the scientific policy of the federal government. This position was renewed, in 2009, for another 6 years, and it is expected to end by 2015. Both of the posts that Mr. Philippe Mettens holds are paid functions, no matter how large is the amount of the salary he receives.

3. Belgium is a federal state which is composed of 3 Regions, 3 Communities and the Region of Brussels. The town of Flobecq is a local authority (commune), located within the Heinaut Province of the Wallon Region. As in all other federal states, the status, functions, revenues and the personnel of the communes are regulated by the federated units in which they are located, in accordance with the principles laid down by the Federal Constitution. It is generally believed

that the efforts devoted to the regionalization process in Belgium have not been to the benefit of local governments (Ellen Waynberg, Filip de Rynck, Kristof Steyvers, Jean-Benoit Pilet, "Belgium: A Tale of Regional Divergence", in John Loughlin, Frank Hendriks and Anders lidström (eds.), *The Oxford Handbook of Local and Regional* Democracy in Europe, Oxford University Press, Oxford, 2011, pp. *71-95*).

4. The Legislative Assembly of the Wallon Region, using its constitutional authority, issued a Decree with Force of Law in November 2010, that was put into force in January 2013, regarding the prohibition of "cumul de mandats" (holding more than one posts simultaneously), for certain categories of public functionaries holding elected positions. According to this new rule (Livre 1 er, Titre II, Chapitre V, Articles regarding the incompatibilities and conflicts of interets), bringing about a radical change in the Law of Local Democracy and Decentralization, allowing no longer the simultaneous holding of more than one functions.

5. In accordance with the new rule of the revised legislation on Local Democracy and Decentralization, it is argued that Mr. Philippe Mettens can no longer continue to hold both of his positions simultaneously. This viewpoint is also openly expressed by Mr. Paul Furland, the Minister of Local Authorities, Cities and Tourism of the Federal State, as the supervisory agent of the State, who asked the mayor to make a choice between the two posts and resign from one of them.

6. In the note prepared by the lawyers of Mr. Philippe Mettens, namely by Mr.Philippe Levert and Mr.Mathieu Veighe, in defense of the mayor, (Mons, 23 April 2013), there is a reference to a decision taken by the Constitutional Court (dated 27/2012, 1 March 2012), refusing the application of Mr.Mettens, maintaining that the new law did not restrict the right of the mayor for eligibility, but rather its purpose

was simply to avoid an incompatibility situation in the exercise of a non-elective post, such as a federal, regional, or communal public service or another public organization, and an elected function in the communal college (Art.L1123-4).

7. In view of the legal rules regulating the case, the following factors should be taken into consideration:

a) The respective legislation concerning the incompatibility between an elected position and a function as a civil servant does not make any differentiation depending upon the size of the communes concerned. Therefore, the argument of Mr. Philippe Mettens in his letter of 22 April 2013, emphasizing that he is the mayor of a small municipality does not seem to be a valid argument that can be used in favor of the continuation of simultaneous performance of his two posts. Since the concerned rule does not make any difference according to the size of the commune the prohibitive rule is valid for the case under discussion.

b) Secondly, no relationship is sought by the legislator between the nature of the elected position and the kind of appointed function carried out at the federal level. In other words, the legislation does not take into account the specific nature of the function concerned, whether it is important, strategic, time consuming etc., as factors to be used to remove the incompatibility argument.

c) Thirdly, there is no reference to the amount of the salary received from both of the functions, as a factor to be taken into account in the process of judging the existence of incompatibility.

d) Finally, the fact that the investigation carried out either by the respective authorities of the Wallon Government or by the federal government, does not invalidate the procedure for the incompatibility no matter how the investigation ends; in another words, whether a disciplinary sanction or in resignation.

## II. The European Charter of Local Self-Government

a) Belgium is a member state of the Council of Europe. It signed (1985) and ratified (2004) the European Charter of Local Self-Government. So long as it has no abstention on any of its principles (to be verified), all articles of the Charter must be regarded as legally binding for Belgian Government. Belgium does not have any abstention (to be verified) on the Article 7, Paragraph 3 of the Charter, which specifically is concerned with the incompatibility cases.

The said paragraph reads as the following: "Any functions and activities deemed incompatible with the holding of local elective office shall be determined by statute or fundamental legal principles". In the explanatory note of the Charter's principles, it is stated that "disqualification from the holding a local elected office should only be based on objective legal criteria and not on ad hoc decisions. Normally, this means that the case of incompatibility will be laid down by statute". It is quite clear that the Charter leaves it to the member states to regulate the cases of incompatibility by their own acts of parliament in an objective manner.

b)   On the other hand, the Article 11 of the European Code of Conduct for Local and Regional Elected Representatives (ISBN 978-92-831-6856-6), not as a binding legal rule, but as a guiding moral principle, deals with the limits on concurrent holding of two or more appointments. According to this rule, "Elected representatives shall comply with any regulations in force aimed at limiting the concurrent holding of two or more political appointments. Elected representatives shall not hold other political appointments where this prevents them from performing their functions as an elected representative. Nor shall they have or hold functions, elective mandates, occupations or official appointments which entail supervision of their own functions as an elected representative or which they themselves are supposed to supervise in their capacity as an elected representative". Mr. Philippe Mettens and his lawyers, in their letters to regional and federal authorities, mentioned that his federal post does not have any relation of supervision with his elected post of bourgmestre. But, this conflict does not stem from the characteristics of the posts he holds, but from the legal norms themselves.

## III. Conclusion

I have the impression that the case is clear enough and no reason exists to be able to defend the position of Mr. Philippe Mettens who holds a federal mission in addition to his elected post as bourgmestre. The respective principle of the European Charter of Local Self-Government (Art.7, Par.3) leaves it to the member states to solve the issues of incompatibility in accordance with their own legislation. Therefore, the tendency of the Belgian authorities to invite Mr. Philippe Mettens to resign from one his posts seems to be well justified from a legal point of view.

Kind regards,

Prof.Dr.Ruşen            KELEŞ 20 May 2013, Ankara
Ankara University

# Administrative Culture in Turkey*

## (I)

According to a French definition, culture is something that is remained when everything else is forgotten (La culture consiste a ce qui reste quand on a tous oublie). The main idea behind this definition is to underline the fact that culture represents an accumulation or a combination of values, norms, orientations and attitudes which become gradually enduring in society. This understanding has close similarities with the definition made by Kommunalwissenschaftliches Institute der Universitaet Potsdam which emphasizes that administrative culture is composed of patterns, which have developed during a long period. Therefore, within the context of this Conference it would be appropriate to rely on this definition of culture which would help clarify developmental features of administrative culture which evolves over a considerably long period of time under the impact of numerous political, economic and socio-cultural factors.

The Republic of Turkey inherited an administrative bureaucracy from the Ottoman Empire that was shaped over several centuries. The most important image associated with that system was undoubtedly that of the Sultan, in other words, the Emperor, who was representing in the world not only the whole nation, but also the Prophet. His immense

---

\*     Draft Paper to be presented to the Conference on Administrative Cultures in Europe, 12-13 October 2006, Council of Europe, Strasbourg.

aristocratic powers were reflected in his rescripts (fermans) which had the force of statutes.

However, as a result of the impact of western intellectual developments following the adoption of the Universal Declarations of Fundamental Rights and Freedoms of Citizens in the West during the 17 th and 18 th centuries, the Ottoman system of politics and administration has undergone considerable changes. As a consequence of this development, a need was felt to restrict almost limitless powers of the ruler, and to introduce certain legal guarantees for citizens. These reforms, namely Tanzimat (1839) and Islahat 1856) have been realized during the 19 th Century. They are usually considered as the beginnings of the constitutionalist movement in the Empire. The rescripts concerning the reforms were no more than a unilateral declaration and recognition by the Sultan of certain basic human rights, including security of life, honour, and property, fair and public trial of persons accused of crimes, and equality of all subjects irrespective of religion. These documents signified the first important break with the autocratic and absolutist political traditions of the Empire.[1] Towards the end of the 19 th Century, efforts to reform the administrative structure continued and the French administrative model which concentrated all major political and administrative powers at the central government was adopted. The Ottoman Constitution of 1876 attempted to create a workable balance between the powers of the Sultan and the legislative assembly. This constitution was substantially amanded in 1909 to increase the powers of the legislature and to restrict those of the Sultan. This was more or less similar to the parliamentary monarchies of Western Europe.[2]

---

1    Ergun Özbudun, "Constitutional Law", Tugrul Ansay and Don Wallace (eds.), Introduction to Turkish Law (2nd ed.), Oceana Publications, Inc., New York, 1978, pp. 23-25

2    Ibid, p.24

**(II)**

Kemalist Revolution that took place during 1918-1923 has turned down the several-century old Ottoman rule, with its political and administrative culture institutions and traditions, and ended up with the establishment of a secular Turkish Republic in October 1923. The main philosophy on which the new Republic is founded was reflected in the basic principles of 1924 Constitution followed by 1961 and 1982 Constitutions. Within the legal framewok designed by these Constitutions, the supreme power was vested in the people itself, as represented by the Parliament. The principle of the separation of legislative, executive and judicial powers of the State, a system of checks and balances between them, the rule of law, as institutionalized in the independent courts and autonomously acting judges, guarantees of fundamental human rights and civil liberties for all citizens, and complete separation of the State institutions from religious affairs, free election of the members of Parliament, were the main political values in the Constitution, reflecting the world view of the creators of the New Republic.

Undoubtedly, there were nuances between the perceptions of all these values by different citizen groups, civil servants, public authorities, local governments, politicians and the political parties. The adoption of the multi-party system at the end of the Second World War helped considerably strengthening of these values and narrowing down of the differences between such attitudes.

For centuries, the Ottoman Empire was ruled on a more or less decentralized model of administration. In fact, vast territories expanding to more than one continent could not be governed from a single center. However, beginning from the 19th Century, the adoption of the Napoleonic system of centralized administration contributed to the establishment of an excessive centralization in which sub-national territorial units were no more than simple branches of the central government This pattern was also needed by the newly established Republic which had to establish the supremacy of the State over its territory. As a result, two complementary principles of administration, namely centralization and decentralization were put in the Constitutions side by side, to function within the framework of the principle of the integral unity of administration. The Constitution visualized decentralized institutions, in other words, local authorities, as self-governing or autonomous bodies, but not as institutions independent of the State. Therefore, they have been put under the administrative control and supervision of the State. This control and supervision has been implemented both from expediency and legality points of view.

The representative of the State, the Governor, was given the power to act as an intermediate authority who was in charge of striking a balance between the interests of the nation on one hand and those of local communities on the other. More reliance was put legally, (de jure) and practically (de facto) on the constitutional principle of deconcentration than decentralization Decentralization was understood as a system of governance which was no more than administrative decentralization. Political decentralization was not acceptable to the founders of the Republic. This design was necessitated by the concerns of national unity and territorial integrity of the State as exemplified in the French Constitutions. These fundamental principles continued to exist in 1961 and 1982 Turkish Constitutions.

The great majority of the governors, who are centrally appointed public servants, believe that local authorities need to be under strict control of the State for administrative, financial and political reasons. Even the political parties, the media and the academicians still differ in their views concerning the extent of autonomy to be enjoyed by local authorities. There is no doubt that bureaucracy has its own rules and traditions everywhere, and administrative culture is nothing else than a different facet of the culture of democracy in general.

Until the beginning of the World War II, absolute reliance upon the guidance of the State in economic and socio-cultural development was particularly striking. Because, the State itself had the mission to reduce regional inequalities, to redress uneven income distribution and to encourage industrial development, in the absence of a powerful private sector to lead development. The single-party political system did not allow to develop democratic values to be reflected in administrative practices legally and practically. Inferior civil servants had simply to implement the orders of their superiors without any objection. A different conduct might result in putting an end to their terms of office. The only exception is the right recognized to civil servants to decline by a written petition from implementing the order of the superior, which they consider to constitute a crime.[3]

One important feature of the administrative culture during the first four or five decades of the Republic was a clear and conscious distinction between the rules governing public administration and business administration. The maximization of the public interest, but not the consumer satisfaction, was the guiding principle orienting the goals of administrative culture in this period, despite the fact that the concept of public interest was far from being clearly defined. The citizen was valued as a member of local community or the nation with

---

3   Cahit Emre, "Kaltürel Değerler. Ahlak ve Türkive'de Kamu Yönetimi". (Cultural Values. Morality and Public Administration in Turkey), in Cahit Emre, Yönetim Bilimi Yazıları (Papers on Administrative Science), Imaj, Ankara, 2003, p.466.

its own rights and freedoms, but not regarded on the basis of the value of his purchasing power in the market. According to the prevailing concept of public service, the latter had to be performed exclusively by public authorities, and in accordance with the provisions of the Public Law.

The scope of the administrative discretion of superiors was considerably broad. It was depended upon the personal qualifications of the superior to allow his inferior to express his personal opinions in various matters, tolerate their mistakes. Following the adoption of the multi-party parliamentary regime in 1946 de facto political orientations of the civil servants played an increasing role in the relationships between them and their superiors. As a result, following every parliamentary elections, particularly the public servants occupying higher-level administrative posts have faced the threat to lose their jobs.

According to a prominent scholar specialized in Public Administration, some of the basic moral values characterizing Turkish public administration are such values as loyalty, impartiality (neutrality), interests of the State, equality, care for not accepting gifts and benefits, directly or indirectly from the people with whom they have official relations.[4] Most of these values have become legal provisions during the Republican period guiding the conduct of the public personnel.

## (III)

The evolution of administrative culture and its value components have undergone a tremendous change beginning from the early 1980's, where the liberal-minded Ozal government has taken the power. This is the period in which all aspects

---

4    Cahit Emre. "Cultural Values, Morality and Public Administration in Turkey", in Yasushi Hazama (ed.), Emerging Changes in Turkish Politics and Society, Tokyo, IDE, 2000, pp.30-47.

of societal life have been consciously exposed to the effects of world-wide globalization increasingly. Liberalization, privatization and deregulation have become the main targets of this transformation. Within this context, particular emphasis was put on the assertion that the distinction previously made between public administration and business administration was not meaningful, and therefore no longer necessary to make and the same traits of administrative culture may well apply to both. All values and institutions were subject to tremendous changes necessitated by the requirements of globalization. Because, as noted by Raymond Williams, "Culture is a description of a particular way of life, which expresses certain meanings and values not only in art and learning, but also in institutions and ordinary behaviour. The analysis of culture is the clarification of the meanings and values implicit and explicit in a particular way of life, a particular culture."5 In our days, the administrative culture does not fail to receive its share out of these changes.

As different from the prevailing approaches during the 1960's and 1970's, it appears to be a more commonly accepted view that there is no substantial difference between public administration and business administration. It is argued that both use the same techniques for analysis, serve the same purposes of which the most important is the maximization of consumer satisfaction. In order to achieve the ultimate goal, such rules of conduct as transparency accountability, openness to innovation, consultation, participation, negotiation, maximization of consumer satisfaction have become more frequently pronounced concepts at present. The term of Governance where an increasing role is attributed to all stakeholders involved in the decision-making process, including the public and private actors, and the representatives

5    Raymond Williams, The Long Revolution, Harper, New York, 1961, p.41

of civil society organizations, replaced the concepts of government or administration.

Since the relationships between the government and the citizens turned out to be one between the producer and the consumer, or the seller and the buyer, the price mechanism has become the main yardstick to enable the consumer to have access to certain goods and services, including basic public goods, which were formerly provided with exclusive concern for the public interest. It seems that in the new administrative culture required by the New Public Administration Movement the concept of public interest is becoming gradually an old-fashion goal. In other words, a new understanding of public interest in the sense of the sum of the interests of the private individuals, which in fact reflecting the philosophy of the 18th century, is emerging.

The effects of two phenomena have to be touched upon briefly in this connection. The first is the new terms and concepts introduced by the Habitat II Conference of the UN that took place in İstanbul in 1996. Governance enabling strategies, civic engagement, etc. are a few of these terms reflecting some values underlying the emergence of a new administrative culture at the local level. The second factor has something to do with the requirements of the candidacy of Turkey for full EU membership which has a particular significance for the realization of certain reforms in Public Administration. The new approaches and values touched upon above briefly, such as the governance transparency accountability, consultation, negotiation, subsidiarity, participation, responsiveness, total quality management, cost recovery are some of the new administrative concepts that attract increasing attention. It is expected that each of them could usefully contribute to making administration more efficient, more democratic and more responsive to the needs of the citizens.

Reform laws in local authorities have been designed and put into effect during 2003-2006 with these new values of governance in mind.

Particularly, the principle of subsidiarity, which requires carrying out of the public services by the public authorities as close as possible to citizens is debatable from legal, administrative and political points of view. As conceived in the Article 4, Par.3 of the European Charter of Local Self- Government and the Aticle 5 of the Amsterdam Treaty, the principle of subsidiaity can provide a unique opportunity to foster public participation and to bring administration closer to the people. Yet, there are fears that present Constitution (Art. 127) does not allow regarding local authorities, but not the central government, as principal public authorities. In other words, from a legal point of view, local government can not be given a status which is more than secondary to the State. The Constitution stipulates that all public affairs must be performed within a spirit of cooperation between the central government and local authorities in accordance with the principle of the "integral unity of administration".

A related consideration which could have a political consequence was the one expressed recently by the President of the Republic in connection to the debates concerning the constitutionality of the subsidiarity principle seems to be significant. According to him, the adoption of this principle could render questionable the very nature of the unitary state system which must be based soley on the supremacy of the State. In other words, it would imperil the constitutional principle of national unity and territorial integrity. In this connection, I have to note that Turkey as a State that has become a party to the European Charter of Local-Self-Government did not have any abstention on the provision concerning the principle of subsidiarity.

Although policy-oriented research findings are not available, everyday observations reveal that good results in administration (as defined by laws) are acknowledged, increased carrier prospects are more and more provided to younger civil servants and new technologies are used increasingly more frequently in all aspects of public life. In the absence of reliable research findings, it is not easy to undertake comparative studies on administrative culture. In a small-size scientific meeting held at the Middle East Technical University during March 18-19 2001, it was found out that always a traditional-vertical type of culture nourished organizational relationships, but it turned out to be a prestige-focused, vertical and individualistic sub-culture in the early 1980's. The last stage in administrative cultural developments that began in the 1990's was identified as being horizontal, innovative and more individualistic. The leadership patterns used more frequently were hierarchical, paternalistic and liberal.[6]

A comparative study of institutional culture encompassing 61 states came out with the results that although the features of these cultures differ greatly from one country to another, it is possible to group them on the basis of their geographical proximity, ethnical, religious and language characteristics and the levels of socio-economic development. After having added such factors as attitudes, values, working conditions, and leadership characteristics, 10 different groups of organizational culture have been identified and Turkey has been put into the group that is called Turkey-Arab Countries (together with Quatar Morocco Egypt and Kuveyt). This Middle-Eastern institutional culture stands between the most and the least developed cultural patterns. Mainly based on the cultural traits observed in business firms in the private sector, it

---

6    Middle East Technical University, Management Club, Administrative Culture in Turkey, 2001

tends to rely to a certain extent, on traditions and moral principles in order to reduce uncertainties .The degree to which
future-oriented planning, investment encouragement for increasing the performance of the manpower is rather limited.
And gender inequality works in favor of males.[7]

## (IV)

Administrative culture in Turkey is not a subject that is studied extensively by scholars. The number of the studies related
to the subject-matter are few. No applied and policy-oriented
research findings are available to make cross-cultural com-
parisons feasible. Therefore, main traits of the administrative
culture in Turkey has been summarized in this paper generally. Attention was drawn to the macro characteristics of
the administrative and political system as well as some mi-
cro-principles that are supposed to guide the conduct of public servants. Because I believe that basic moral guidelines for
civil servants are shaped and developed depending upon the
general cultural development of the nations.[8] These principles can be found in the Constitutions and they may be reflected in other legal sources. That is the reason why a brief
historical development of democracy was regarded as a per-
condition to review administrative culture in Turkey.

---

7   Muzaffer Bodur and Hayat Kabasakal, "Türkiye-Arap Kümesinde Kurumsal
    Kültür (Instititutional Culture in Turkish Arab Group): GLOBE Araştırması
    (GLOBE Research) (Global Culture and Organizational Behaviour), Yöne-
    tim Araştırmaları Dergisi (Journal on Administrative Research), 2002, Vol.2,
    No:1, pp.5-22

8   Ömer Bozkurt (ed.), Yönetim Sosyolojisi (Sociology of Administration), Ins-
    titute of Public Administration for Turkey and Middle East, Ankara, 1977